LARGE
PRINT

THE CHURCH AWAKENING

AN URGENT CALL FOR RENEWAL

Charles R. Swindoll

FaithWords
Hachette Book Group
237 Park Avenue
New York, NY 10017
www.faithwords.com

The Author is represented by Yates & Yates, Attorneys & Literary Agents.

Unless otherwise noted, Scripture quotations are from the New American Standard Bible®. Copyright © 1960, 1962, 1963, 1968, 1971, 1972, 1973, 1975, 1977, 1995 by The Lockman Foundation. Used by permission.

Quotations designated KJV are from the King James Version. Quotations designated MSG are from *The Message,* copyright © by Eugene H. Peterson, 1993, 1994, 1995, 1996. Used by permission of NavPress Publishing Group. Quotations designated NIV are from The Holy Bible, New International Version. Copyright © 1973, 1978, 1984, International Bible Society. Used by permission of Zondervan Bible Publishers. Quotations designated NRSV are from the New Revised Standard Version Bible, copyright © 1989, by the Division of Christian Education of the National Council of the Churches of Christ in the United States of America.

Other quotations, as noted in the text, are from the following sources: J. B. Phillips: The New Testament in Modern English, Revised Edition. Copyright © J. B. Phillips 1958, 1960, 1972. Used by permission of Macmillan Publishing Co., Inc.; *The Living Bible,* copyright © 1971. Used by permission of Tyndale House Publishers, Wheaton, Illinois 60189. All rights reserved; *Holy Bible,* New Living Translation, copyright © 1996. Used by permission of Tyndale House Publishers, Inc., Wheaton, Illinois 60189. All rights reserved.

Printed in the United States of America

First Large Print Edition: February 2012
10 9 8 7 6 5 4 3 2 1

FaithWords is a division of Hachette Book Group, Inc.
The FaithWords name and logo are trademarks of Hachette Book Group, Inc.

The Hachette Speakers Bureau provides a wide range of authors for speaking events. To find out more, go to www.hachettespeakersbureau.com or call (866) 376-6591.

The publisher is not responsible for websites (or their content) that are not owned by the publisher.

Library of Congress Cataloging-in-Publication Data

Swindoll, Charles R.
    The church awakening : an urgent call for renewal / Charles R. Swindoll.—1st ed.
       p. cm.
    ISBN 978-0-446-55653-8
    1. Church renewal.   I. Title.
    BV600.3.S95 2010
    262'.7—dc22
                                                                    2010004792

ISBN 978-1-4555-0738-2 (pbk.)

*It is with heartfelt gratitude for his life and
ministry that I dedicate this book to
Dr. Stanley D. Toussaint
whom I have learned from as an
outstanding professor, always admired as
a biblical expositor, greatly respected
as a wise mentor, and now serve
with as a fellow elder at
Stonebriar Community Church*

*When the Church is absolutely
different from the world, she
invariably attracts it.*

*It is then that the world is made
to listen to her message, though
it may hate it at first.*

—D. Martyn Lloyd-Jones

Contents

Contents

Introduction

Here is the great evangelical disaster—the failure of the evangelical world to stand for truth as truth. There is only one word for this—namely, accommodation: *the evangelical church has accommodated to the world spirit of the age.*

—Francis Schaeffer

Introduction

While we weren't paying attention, everything became unhinged. Our world is no longer the world of our grandparents...or of our parents for that matter. While we weren't noticing, things were changing—or perhaps I should say, they were *eroding*. We slipped from what we used to call a "modern world" into a "postmodern world" without even realizing it. We've drifted from a "Christian era" into a "post-Christian era." That's why we find ourselves in a world that is less friendly to the church and more than ever disconnected from the Bible. So it's no surprise that today's citizen is more biblically ignorant than people of virtually any other time since the Dark Ages.

All of us remember watching *The Tonight Show* with Jay Leno. Much of what Leno did was tasteless and over the top, but that's how he kept his ratings up. One night Leno was engaged in one of his on-the-street interviews. It was hilarious and tragic at the same time. He went out to the streets and asked unsuspecting people about the Bible. The questions weren't hard or tricky. In fact, they were designed to be easy. That's what made it so funny.

Leno asked one person, "Did Adam and Eve have any children?"

A woman, after a few seconds of deep thought, said, "No, no, they never had any kids."

"Name the two brothers, Cain and _____."

Absolute blank stare. Had no idea. They probably were thinking, *Cain and Hurricane*, or something like that. No...she had no answer.

"Okay...what happened to Lot's wife?"

Zero response. And then one of the bystanders blurted out, "Who was Lot?"

Little hint: "She turned into _____."

The person said, "An angel."

Leno turned to someone else. "Can you name one of the apostles?"

No reply. He continued, "Okay, then, name the four Beatles."

Immediate response: "John, Paul, George, and Ringo." The crowd cheered.

"How many commandments are there?"

One guy boldly announced, "Three. There are three commandments."

Another person said, "No, there are twenty. Twenty commandments."

Another one said, "No, it's like the disciples—there were twelve."

"Can you name four of them?" asked Leno.

Nobody could name four.

"Can you name one of them?"

And one fellow said, "Something about not coveting your neighbor's wife." (Interesting he remembered that one.)

Jay said, "You mean, if she's pretty."

And he said, "Yeah, I . . . I think that's it."

Jay said, "Is your neighbor's wife pretty?"

The man said, "No, she's not pretty." I thought, *I wonder if the neighbor's wife is watching?*

"Who was swallowed by a whale?"

"A whale?" was asked. "This some kind of trick question?"

"No, let me give you a hint: Jo_____."

"Joan of Arc," was the quick response.

"No, Jo_____."

"Joe DiMaggio."

"No."

"Pinocchio."

Jay pressed on. "Which two cities were destroyed, according to the book of Genesis? Let me give you a hint: Sodom _____."

After a brief pause, the person on the street guessed, "Saddam Hussein?"

Our world is not only ignorant of the basic facts of the Bible, most now are skeptical, convinced there is no such thing as *absolute truth*. The deception is so subtle we can be led to believe that what is wrong is right, and what is bad is, in fact, good. And, tragically, most people don't realize either until it is too late.

Ours is a whole new world, and nothing has been more adversely affected by postmodernism than the church and its relationship to God's Word—the Holy Scriptures. When the Bible loses its central place in the church's worship—even if good things replace it—the fallout is biblical ignorance. The longer substitutes replace the preaching of the Word as the centerpiece of Christian worship, the more we will witness the drift into ignorance intensifying. The more postmodern thinking dominates the church, the weaker and less important the church becomes in the eyes of the world. Over time, a congregation that is distant from the

Word of God seeks more entertainment and less biblical truth.

One astute observer notes, "When the church becomes an entertainment center, Bible literacy is usually an early casualty. People go away from the event with a smile on their face but a void in their life."[1] Decades ago, the theologian Francis Schaeffer wrote, "Here is the great evangelical disaster—the failure of the evangelical world to stand for truth as truth. There is only one word for this—namely, *accommodation*: the evangelical church has accommodated to the world spirit of the age."[2]

The good news? It can change. *The Church Awakening* is a call for the church to become aware of how far we have drifted. The time has come to wake up and renew our passion for what Jesus is building. This new volume stems from my firm belief that we can stop the church's drift only when God's people commit to following the inspired blueprint set forth in God's timeless and ever-relevant Book.

I have written *The Church Awakening* primarily to two groups of people. First, to serious-thinking churchgoers who know there is a better way. In the Bible there was a group of clear-thinking, tough-minded men called the "sons of Issachar"

(1 Chron. 12:32). They were those who "understood the times [and knew] what Israel should do" (v. 32). We need that same clearheaded discernment today in the church. And along with discernment, we need an equal supply of courage. My aim is to ignite that passion within those who are willing to think seriously.

I am also writing to pastors, especially to those who are on the fence, who need a voice of *permission* to buck the tide and to put the preaching of the Word of God back in its central place of the church's worship.

I'm concerned about the intensifying embrace of postmodernism. The result of this is that we have eroded from a Christian era to a post-Christian era. I remember when we used to say that about Great Britain. I now say it about the United States of America, the land I love, a land I have served to help protect. But over the past thirty years we have slid into the murky waters of a post-Christian swamp.

Instead of life being interpreted honestly, it is now interpreted emotionally. Instead of real being real, virtual reality has taken charge. And since the reality is now distorted and viewed as distasteful, the younger generation prefers virtual reality.

Reality bores them. We have changed our thinking based on objective instruction from the truth of Holy Scripture to the subjective, secular thinking based squarely on a horizontal, humanistic perception, where self is always predominant.

Need a good definition of *postmodernism*? Let's see if I can hammer one out for you. A description might be more helpful than a definition. Postmodernism thrives on chaos. It desires to destroy all *moral* criteria and replace it with *no* criteria. It seeks a world in which everything is relative, where there is no truth, and perception alone is reality. Since God's eternal truth has no place in such a world, with the rise of postmodernism we witness a commensurate decline in biblical knowledge.

The way this has evolved is interesting. Postmodernism began in the rarefied atmosphere of the academic literary community. It soon began to ooze from the erudite eggheads in academia to virtually everyone in any position of leadership. It has morphed from the halls of academia to the halls of Congress, to the halls of public schools, and finally into our private homes. We're now submerged in this philosophy of thinking, a form of thinking that is both insidious and subtle. No big-time public announcement will ever be made: "We are now embracing postmodernism!" It doesn't come in like that. It comes "like a thief in the night" (1 Thess. 5:2).

The greatest tragedy of all is that the evangelical church of the twenty-first century has capitulated. The slumbering evangelical church has now bought into this way of thinking. I hope to explain why and how in this book. But let me add that I am not writing this book just to point out all that's wrong. That is not my intention. My writing has always had an emphasis on grace, which is God's emphasis in the Bible. I intend each chapter to address solutions, not just expose problems—and to point to the hope that God offers in His Word.

In my almost fifty years in ministry, I have never been more passionate, or hopeful, for *The Church Awakening*—that is, for the church to wake up, to see how far it has drifted, to begin walking with God, and to engage the culture for Jesus Christ. It is my hope that God will use this new volume in a powerful way to contribute to the master plan Jesus is building. He was the One who promised: "I will build My church; and the gates of Hades will not overpower it" (Matt. 16:18).

Finally, I want to thank my longtime friends Rolf Zettersten and Joey Paul of FaithWords.

Their enthusiastic and tireless commitment to getting this book into as many hands as possible has greatly encouraged me. And I must add my heartfelt appreciation to my gifted and capable editor, Wayne Stiles. I sincerely appreciate the time and effort he invested. Knowing that Wayne was just as passionate about the message of this book as I am helped spur me on. I've dreamed of writing these things for well over a decade, but I needed an enthusiastic publisher and a competent editor. Having both in place has turned the dream into reality...and my gratitude knows no bounds.

—Chuck Swindoll
Frisco, Texas

THE CHURCH AWAKENING

CHAPTER 1

The Church: Let's Start Here

*The world is waiting to hear an
authentic voice, a voice from God—
not an echo of what others are doing
and saying, but an authentic voice.*

—A. W. Tozer

The Church:
Let's Start Here

My fondest memories as a boy go back to the summer vacations and family reunions at my maternal grandfather's cottage in south Texas. The small, four-room cabin named Bide-a-wee overlooked Carancahua Bay, near Palacios, Texas, on the edge of Matagorda Bay, leading into the Gulf of Mexico. It was a sleepy little spot where the air smelled like salt and shrimp 24/7.

The cottage sat back about a hundred yards from a small cliff that dropped off toward the muddy bay waters. My grandfather had carved out a narrow path that wormed its way down to a boathouse where he kept a small motorboat. I am confident he had no idea how much his towheaded grandson named Charles loved to drive the ten-horsepower Johnson all over Carancahua Bay. We would swim in the bay, seine for shrimp early in the morning, go out fishing for speckled trout and redfish during the day, and wade the shoreline in old sneakers floundering at night. Wonderful memories, all!

I remember one day when I was about ten years old. My grandfather took me outside and said, "Every year this cliff drops off a little and wears away; I want to show you." He used a big word I had never heard before: *erosion*. We walked some distance from the edge, and he measured the space from that point to where the cliff dropped off down to the water. He drove a stake into the ground to mark the spot. "You're going to be here next summer," he told me, "and we'll measure this again then."

When I came back the next summer, there had been two powerful Gulf Coast hurricanes, several superhigh tides, and rough waters the previous year. I ran to the cliff and measured back to our stake. Eight inches were gone. All that dirt and grass had disappeared! I would *never* have noticed it if we had not secured a stake in the ground and measured it. The next year he wrote to me and said, "Twelve more inches eroded this year." I would love to go back and see the old place today. It's possible that by now the cottage itself has washed away.

Webster defines *erode* in simple terms: "To diminish or destroy by degrees.... To eat into or away by slow destruction of substance.... To cause to deteriorate or disappear."[1] Over the years, I have discovered three simple truths about erosion, all of which parallel Webster's description. Rather than occurring rapidly, erosion is *always slow*. Instead of drawing attention to itself, erosion is *always silent*. And in place of being obvious, erosion is *always subtle*.

The slow, silent, and subtle effects of erosion are not only a concern to us physically, they are an even greater concern spiritually. F. B. Meyer, British pastor of yesteryear, put it this way: "No man suddenly becomes base." Spiritual erosion occurs, instead, "by degrees... by slow destruction." It can happen in individuals... and it can certainly happen in a church.

A close friend recently visited a local church that stemmed from a denomination with deep, centuries-old roots in conservative theology. Those who originated the denomination loved the Scriptures, proclaimed the Word of God, and aligned their lives with its truths. In fact, their peers laughed at them for being so "narrow-minded." These individuals never planned to start a denomination, and yet their lives sparked a movement that swept the land of England and eventually made its way across the Atlantic into America. However, as my friend and his wife sat in the church that morning with several hundred other people, they noticed that only the two of them and one other person had brought a Bible. Erosion was taking its toll. The denomination's drift from its sturdy theological roots did not occur in two months, or two years, or even two decades. Instead, it was on a slow, silent, and subtle slide. Given enough time, the denomination will hardly resemble or even remember its original convictions.

C. S. Lewis, in his cleverly written work *The Screwtape Letters,* wrote, "Indeed the safest road to Hell is the gradual one—the gentle slope, soft underfoot, without sudden turnings, without milestones, without signposts."[2]

Two words from Lewis's pen stand out: *without milestones.* For the church to awaken from its long drift, we *need* milestones. A milestone reveals one of two things: it can reveal how far we've come in accomplishment—and give cause for celebration— or it can expose how far we've drifted—and urge us to turn around. Like that stake my grandfather drove into the ground, a milestone represents a point where we take an objective measurement. We stop, look back, and recall why we began the journey in the first place. We need to remember and restate our original objectives, then ask, "Are those goals still ours? Are we on target?"

We need places in our journey where we force ourselves to pause and evaluate whether or not a drift is taking place. Why? Because a church *without milestones* will drift. And like erosion, we will not see it occurring if we don't look for it.

Milestones: Looking at a Church . . . and Remembering

In marriage, anniversaries are great occasions for reflection and evaluation. They are like cyclical milestones that give a husband and wife an opportunity to look back where they've been, to look within to see where they are, and then to look ahead to determine where they're going—all examined and evaluated against the vows stated at the altar. The passing of time neither changes nor erases the vows. The years bring challenges and introduce struggles, but those vows stand firm. They are like marital milestones.

I've been thinking a lot about church milestones lately. The church where I currently serve as senior pastor, Stonebriar Community Church, celebrated its tenth anniversary in October 2008. As churches go, we're not an old church. If you tell someone in Europe that your church is ten years old, you'll see a smile. Why? Most of the European churches are *so* old they're celebrating their two-hundredth anniversaries. In fact, some date back to the Middle Ages! Our church is young, but you can't tell by looking. In the last ten years we have had tremendous growth…and that's great! All of us are grateful for the rapid growth, where people of all ages and stages in life have joined ranks with us. But something else has occurred in the last decade: *erosion.* Let me explain.

Back in the mid-1990s, the Lord clearly guided me to Dallas Theological Seminary to be a part of its leadership team. I had never led a seminary, and I had difficulty seeing myself as a president. I simply came as what I was—a leader, a pastor, and a shepherd. (I had been with sheep so long I even smelled like sheep!) And so, naturally, I planned to return to pastor a church at some future date. The chairman of the board asked me, "Would you be willing to give us your full attention at least these first two or three years, without starting a church?" I promised them I would—in fact, I served in that role seven full years. But during those years I continued to have a burning desire to be preaching and teaching the Word of God as a local pastor. I just didn't know where or how the Lord would bring it about.

Let me assure you, as God began to open that door, I didn't hear a voice from heaven. I didn't see skywriting or have night visions, nor did I see Jesus' face in a taco. I just sensed deep within that God was leading me to begin preaching on a regular basis... and to trust Him to lead. So one day I said to my wife, Cynthia, "Let's start a Bible class—just a small gathering of people. I really have a passion to be preaching again." She said, "That's great. I'm for it!"

Word got out regarding this class through our radio ministry, *Insight for Living*, and at the first meeting we held at a local country club, to my shock, three hundred people showed up! The next week we doubled in size and had to open all the accordion doors to the room where we met.

I remember asking one guy, "Do we know what we're doing?"

He said, "I have no idea, but you're here, so let's go!" (What he didn't realize was I didn't know either!)

After the third week, the country club told us we could not keep meeting there if we kept expanding. I'm told that ours was the fastest-growing church in

America. I didn't know that at the time, and if I had known it, I wouldn't have believed it. This idea was already growing faster and going far beyond what I expected. We didn't have a church start-up in mind to begin with, just a Bible class. But God had different plans. Big surprise, huh? God had a plan that outstretched anything I would have ever dreamed possible. What else is new?

During this time our radio ministry was still located in Southern California. Cynthia and I would commute back and forth to Dallas, where I led the seminary during the week, including several significant changes and accomplishing a major fund-raising campaign. I also preached on Sundays at our growing body of believers, which by then had officially become a church. By now the congregation was meeting at a community college and numbered a little over a thousand people. I also continued my writing ministry. I mention all of this to help you get the picture. While my heart was full, and while I loved all I was doing, my plate was also full. *Very full. Too full.* And all the while, our "little church" kept growing... and growing... *and growing!*

Let me illustrate what it felt like as our church approached its tenth anniversary. It was like a young couple who have been married for ten years, but they have fifteen children! How could that be possible? A year after marriage they have a set of twins, and two years later, triplets. The following year, out of compassion, they adopt four children from other countries. That totals nine kids. Two weeks later she discovers she's pregnant again—with triplets! So she locks him out of the bedroom, telling him not to come back in until he gets a vasectomy. He gets the surgery, but it fails, and she's now expecting triplets once again. If I figure correctly, that totals fifteen. I should also mention she's homeschooling the kids, and they are still living in the same house as when they first got married. That was Stonebriar Community Church!

Let me take this illustration a step further. As would be true of any couple in that situation, there wouldn't be time to effectively meet each child's need. There wouldn't have been adequate attention or training provided. In a brief, ten-year period, some things would erode. Of course, neither parent would *want* the family to erode; it just would happen as a result of unexpected, rapid growth and not enough time to be available and meet needs and give some essential direction in critical decisions.

Admittedly, like a mother with too many kids,

I was a pastor with too many people. I could not keep up with the details of our expansion, so I delegated too many of the responsibilities to others. They were good individuals, but I discovered some of them did not share my heart or vision for ministry. I realized I had delegated without mentoring, training, or shaping the thinking of those leaders. Staff had been hired who never should have been hired. Some elders were appointed who, frankly, weren't qualified (according to biblical standards). And when I finally realized all of this, the erosion was well under way. I should also mention that we had just begun another aggressive building campaign! I'll be honest: that's a tough place to find yourself. I felt like the lookout atop the *Titanic* the moment he saw that massive iceberg in the distance. I prayed fervently that we could turn our large ship in time to save it.

It was not easy. In fact, those were the most difficult months of my five decades in ministry. *Very* challenging. *Very* stressful. *Very* painful. Stopping the erosion and getting back on target meant moving in a direction we had not been going. It meant certain staff did not remain. It meant some elders could not stay. There were difficult times that included tears, hurt feelings, tough decisions, sleepless nights, hard moments, and misunderstandings. I'm grateful that we never lost our financial integrity. We never had fistfights in the back room. There were no lawsuits or ugly public temper flare-ups. I simply realized how far we had drifted from God's plan for us, and I resolved to stop the erosion wherever it was, regardless of the cost, and in spite of others' reactions. I determined to pay no attention to harsh letters or lengthy e-mail messages or the wagging tongues of some who participated in gossip. Thankfully, God was merciful.

Why do I share all of this with you? Because erosion can happen to anyone and in any church; it happened in our church...and it can occur in yours. Maybe it already has. I also share it to assure you it can be stopped. But it won't be easy!

Our church's tenth anniversary was a good time for evaluation and course correction. The events of those difficult months have convinced me how essential it is for every church to have cyclical milestones—deliberate times to *look back* at the church's initial vision, to *look within* and evaluate the current situation, and then to *look ahead* to determine where the Scriptures say the church should be going. All the while there must be a strong commitment to doing what the Bible says, not doing what people want, not doing what other churches do.

I can say from experience, when that process is carried out correctly, the result is *a church awakening.*

Looking into the Scriptures . . . and Discovering Church

Let's enter an imaginary time tunnel and journey back about twenty centuries. As we do, remember that in the place we find ourselves there is no United States of America. The modern civilizations of Europe, Australia, and Canada—as well as other contemporary cultures—do not exist. Even the nation of Israel looks completely different. In the first century, there are no Christian traditions, and we certainly find no denominations or churches. Where we're imagining ourselves standing, no one has even heard the word *church* before. And the Jewish culture of the day exists in the context of a pagan Roman government that dominates the land of Israel. On top of all that, the official religious leaders of the day are proud, self-serving, and corrupt. It was in such an environment that "the church" began.

Whenever we want to understand a topic or term, such as *church*, we should begin at the passage of primary reference. It helps to ask, where did the word first appear, and in what context was it used? Surprisingly, the first mention in the New Testament of the word *church* wasn't from the pen of the apostle Paul. Peter didn't coin the term, nor did any of the other apostles. It was Jesus.

Matthew describes the scene for us. He writes of the time Jesus took His disciples up north into the Gentile area of Caesarea Philippi. While there, the Lord asks His men what the public is saying about His identity:

"Who do people say that the Son of Man is?" And they said, "Some say John the Baptist; and others, Elijah; but still others, Jeremiah, or one of the prophets." He said to them, "But who do you say that I am?" Simon Peter answered, "You are the Christ, the Son of the living God." (Matthew 16:13–16)

The culture around Jesus viewed Him as nothing more than a great man. But Peter voiced a different opinion. Speaking for the disciples as a whole, Peter was never more accurate: "You are *the* Christ, *the* Messiah, *the* Anointed One…*the* Son of the living God." Peter nailed it! At that point in the discussion, Jesus changed the dialogue to a monologue and commended Peter for his statement:

Blessed are you, Simon Barjona, because flesh and blood did not reveal this to you, but My Father who is in heaven. I also say to you that you are Peter, and upon this rock I will build My church; and the gates of Hades will not overpower it. (Matthew 16:17–18)

In commending Simon Peter for his spiritual insight about *who Jesus was*, the Lord unveiled even more truth about *what He would do*. In essence, Jesus told Peter, "Your words about Me are true. In fact, they are a foundational statement—like a rock. And on this rocklike declaration *I will build My church*." He also promised that the gates of Hades would not erode it or erase it. The *church* would have staying power. Against all odds, it would prevail. Not even the adversary would overpower it. *I will build My church*. Let's examine the implications of those five monosyllabic words in this primary reference.

First, *I*—Jesus made it clear from the beginning

that the church as God intended it would have Christ as its Architect. Make no mistake about it—*He* is the Originator of the church. It was *His* idea. He protects it. He leads it. He alone is its Head.

Second, the word *will* looks to the future. Jesus didn't say, "I have built," or even "I am building," but "I *will* build." The church had yet to begin when Jesus made this statement; it was a promise for the future—for the very near future. But at the time He spoke these words, Peter and the other disciples had no clue what *church* meant.

Third, the term *build* suggests not only a beginning, but also an ongoing process. If you read music, think of a crescendo mark over Jesus' statement. Try to imagine the excitement and energy in the Master's voice as He communicated the future to these disciples. The church would begin at a certain point (we'll look at that next), and then it would grow and grow...and keep on growing. Why? Because Christ will construct it. He will enlarge it and shape it as He pleases.

Fourth, the word *My* affirms ownership and authority. Not only is Christ the Originator of the church and the Builder of it, as I mentioned, He is also its Head (see Col. 1:15–18). It's essential to keep asking ourselves, as I try to do, *Is Christ the Head of our local church? Does He have first place in our ministry? Is what we do all about Jesus, or have we drifted from that singular focus?* To guard against erosion, we must keep Jesus as the Head of the church. It is *His* church. Never forget that.

When Matthew recorded Jesus' word for "church"—the first mention of that term in the Bible—he chose the Greek word *ekklesia*. It's a compound word, from *ek*, meaning "out, from," and *kaleo*, meaning "to call."[3] It refers to those who have been "called out" from among others. The term more accurately reflects an assembly of people defined by a distinct purpose. The word was in use hundreds of years before Jesus was born, but by adding the word *My* to the term, Jesus revealed that He would build His own *ekklesia*— a people defined by faith in the truth that Peter had just revealed: "You are the Christ, the Son of the living God." We now call this unique assembly over which Jesus serves as Head "the church." How valuable it is to return to the origin of this term and make a serious examination of its purpose!

Why study the origin of *church*? Because it's there we see God's intention. Our understanding and application of what church should be will erode if we don't examine and keep in mind its Founder and its foundation.

The church is a body of people called out from among the world for the distinct and unique purpose of glorifying their Savior and Lord, Jesus Christ. Jesus was referring to the *universal* church, not to the church on the corner. He was not referring to a building on real estate but to a body of individuals who love Christ supremely. This body is without political roots or cultural boundaries; it is devoid of linguistic or racial barriers. It has no denominational or political ties. The church of Jesus Christ is not a corporation—I urge you to remember that! A local church, therefore, is not a business establishment with a cross stuck on top. Rather, the church Jesus promised to build was a *spiritual* entity, and He alone would be the Head. So what did the church look like when Christ began to build it?

Looking in on the Early Church... and Learning

Journey forward in our time tunnel to about a year later. We're no longer up north in Caesarea Philippi, but we are now farther south in the Holy City of Jerusalem. The religious leaders of Israel and the civil leaders of Rome have condemned Christ to death on a cross. But, just as He promised His disciples, Jesus rose from the dead on the third day! Though His enemies did their best to explain away the empty tomb, there He stood, and His presence rejuvenated His followers. Days later, just before the Lord ascended and returned to heaven, He told His followers to wait in Jerusalem for the promised Holy Spirit (see Acts 1:4–5). On the day of Pentecost, the Holy Spirit came and transformed that small group of followers—a group of about 120 women and men—and they began to do what Jesus said they would do when the Spirit of God came upon them. Boldly and courageously, they became His witnesses in Jerusalem (see Acts 1:8, 15; 2:5–11). Their witness spread quickly. Soon followers of Jesus emerged hundreds of miles beyond Jerusalem. What was happening? Just as He had promised in Caesarea Philippi, Jesus had begun to build His church!

The apostle Peter stood up and delivered a powerful message to the multitudes of Jerusalem, introducing them to the Messiah Jesus. I love it that the Lord used *Peter* to share the message. Peter was the one who first called Jesus "the Christ, the Son of the living God"; he was the one to whom Jesus spoke when He first promised to build His church; and remember, it was Peter who had denied Christ just a couple of months before. What grace! Jesus used *Peter's* message to reach those first converts in Jerusalem on the day the church began. And what a response!

> So then, those who had received his word were baptized; and that day there were added about three thousand souls. (Acts 2:41)

Notice that when the people heard the good news about Jesus, they "received" Peter's message. The original term means they recognized the truth for what it was and believed it. That's how a person becomes a Christian. That's how the church is "built." You *hear* of Christ's death for your sins, and you *believe* in Him—you receive Him by faith. Those who believed Peter's message were baptized that day. We read that they numbered about three thousand people. Remarkable! John R. W. Stott observed, "The body of Christ in Jerusalem multiplied twenty-six times, from 120 to 3,120."[4] Suddenly, there are three thousand brand-new sheep in God's flock. And to think *I* felt uneasy with our church's rapid growth! Can you imagine Peter? I've sometimes called that baptism the first sheep dip in the history of the church.

But in spite of the numbers and all the demands of a group that large, there was still simplicity. There was no tradition, there were no church constitution and bylaws, no programs, no senior pastor, no "board of elders," no marketing plan, no splinter groups, no corruption—and no erosion... not yet. Instead, we see 3,120 people living their lives with the Spirit of God now living within them and directing their steps. So what did that look like? We're told precisely what those early believers did when they met together. Look closely:

> They were continually devoting themselves
> to the apostles' teaching and to fellowship,
> to the breaking of bread and to prayer.
> (Acts 2:42)

In this one verse we have the lowest common denominator of a church. This is ground zero. It would help greatly if God's people reminded themselves of this single verse of Scripture every day. When the first body of believers gathered together, they devoted themselves to four essentials. Did you notice them? Here are the four essentials: *teaching, fellowship, breaking of bread,* and *prayer.* This verse is not only *descriptive* of what the early church did; it is also *prescriptive* of what all churches must do.

For a church to be the kind of church Jesus promised to build, there must be *teaching,* which, of course, includes preaching. Teaching is not the same as mere talking, or reading poetry, or motivational speaking, or delivering a positive-thinking-type devotional. We are told here what type of teaching it means: they devoted themselves to the *apostles'* teaching. Today the church has the apostles' teaching represented in the complete Word of God—the Bible. A church must continually be devoted to the teaching of the sacred Scriptures. Teaching God's truth gives a church deep roots that provide nourishment and stability. I'll have a lot more to say about that in the chapters that follow.

For a church to be the kind of church Jesus promised to build, there has to be *fellowship* as well. If we had teaching without fellowship, the church would be a school—a place that simply dispenses information. The original term for fellowship is *koinonia,* which referred to close, mutual relationships where people share things in common and remain involved with one another. That doesn't mean potluck suppers, dinners on the grounds, and Christmas concerts. *Koinonia* represents close relationships that involve sharing life with one another—the bad times as well as the good. Those in fellowship with one another cultivate an intimate harmony with others. In church, the Word of God is not only *learned* through teaching...it is *lived* through fellowship.

The *breaking of bread* is included along with teaching and fellowship. That refers to the Lord's Table, which was observed when the church gathered. Because baptism was mentioned just before this verse, we understand that the early church devoted themselves to the two ordinances commanded by Jesus: baptism and the Lord's Table. The first represents our conversion to Christ, and the second, our lifelong communion with Him. An acceptable, all-inclusive term would be *worship*. For a church to be the kind of church Jesus promised to build, there must be worship.

Finally, they devoted themselves to *prayer*. They spent time as a body of believers adoring their Lord, confessing their sins, interceding for others, petitioning God to provide, and thanking Him for His blessings—just as Jesus taught them to pray. For a church to be the kind of church Jesus promised to build, there must be prayer.

You can't have a church if you take away any of the four essentials recorded in Acts 2:42. You can have *more* than these four, but you cannot have *less* and still be a church. And if you have more—and most churches do—those things added must never contradict or obscure the importance of the essentials. When they do, count on it, erosion occurs.

Remarkably, the simple setting of the original church provided room for the Spirit of God to work and guide. Don't misunderstand; a simple setting does not suggest perfect people. These new believers were far from flawless. But by the empowerment of the Spirit of God as He worked and controlled their lives, there was integrity, trust, joy, confidence, unity, generosity, forgiveness, compassion, harmony, stability, and, of course, grace (to name only a few). It must have been magnificent! Was it working? Just look at the verses that follow:

> Day by day continuing with one mind in the temple, and breaking bread from house to house, they were taking their meals together with gladness and sincerity of heart, praising

God and having favor with all the people. And the Lord was adding to their number day by day those who were being saved. (Acts 2:46–47)

Read that again, and this time, observe the vertical as well as the horizontal. Also notice that, as a result of the believers' devoting themselves to the essentials, the church continued to expand and grow. Truth be told, the growth was off-the-chart remarkable—even in an era of persecution. Look at how the church continued to enlarge as the months and years unfolded:

But many of those who had heard the message believed; and the number of the men came to be about five thousand. (Acts 4:4)

And all the more believers in the Lord, multitudes of men and women, were constantly added to their number. (Acts 5:14)

The word of God kept on spreading; and the number of the disciples continued to increase greatly in Jerusalem, and a great many of the priests were becoming obedient to the faith. (Acts 6:7)

So the church throughout all Judea and Galilee and Samaria enjoyed peace, being built up; and going on in the fear of the Lord and in the comfort of the Holy Spirit, it continued to increase. (Acts 9:31)

And the hand of the Lord was with them, and a large number who believed turned to the Lord. The news about them reached the ears of the church at Jerusalem, and they sent Barnabas off to Antioch. Then when he arrived and witnessed the grace of God, he rejoiced and began to encourage them all with resolute heart to remain true to the Lord; for he was a good man, and full of the Holy Spirit and of faith. And considerable numbers were brought to the Lord. (Acts 11:21–24)

In Iconium they entered the synagogue of the Jews together, and spoke in such a manner that a large number of people believed, both of Jews and of Greeks. (Acts 14:1)

So the churches were being strengthened in the faith, and were increasing in number daily. (Acts 16:5)

Therefore many of them believed, along with a number of prominent Greek women and men. (Acts 17:12)

Again, the growth was remarkable! In spite of intense opposition and persecution—and sometimes *because of it*—Christ continued to build His church. Theologian and historian F. F. Bruce calls this phenomenon "the spreading flame."[5] The growth continued to crescendo, just as Jesus promised. And the adversary, as hard as he may have tried, could not stop it, hinder it, or overpower it!

Looking Around ... and Realizing Some Timeless Truths

Let's step out of that imaginary time tunnel and return to today. In light of what we have discovered, let me suggest three principles and three imperatives I believe all churches should examine and apply.

28

The first principle: *clear, biblical thinking must override secular planning and a corporate mentality.* And the imperative? *Think spiritually!* However well organized our churches become, we must give priority to biblical, rather than secular, thinking. I've taken the time to write about what *was* present in the early church, but let me also mention some of what *wasn't* there. There were no secular organizational structures or church politics. There was no guru of authority or "chairman" of anything. There were no power grabs from control freaks. There were no personal maneuverings, infightings, financial squabbles, or turf protection. Instead, we see a place where a spiritual emphasis took precedence over the world's way of doing things.

What does this look like when applied today? For starters, our teaching needs to be biblically based and spiritually inclined. Our Sunday school classes, adult fellowships, and small-group instruction gatherings need to center on the teaching of the Bible and spiritual lessons. Our songs and hymns should have spiritual content. Our counseling ministry needs to be derived from the Spirit's revelation in the Scriptures. Our relationships with one another need to have spiritual priorities—intimate fellowship where people can trust one another. The church ought to be the one place where spiritual thinking overrides everything else—all those battles we fight within the marketplace. Why? Because Jesus Christ is the Head of the church. Remember, the church is a *spiritual* entity.

Second, *studied, accurate decisions must originate from God's Word, not human opinions.* A true, spiritual mind-set comes from meditation on the Scriptures. So the imperative would be: *stay biblical!* The Word of God ought to be central to every worship service on Sunday. Furthermore, every elders' meeting and every staff meeting should have the Scriptures as the basis of the decisions that are made. God's Word is to be the church's guide; it shapes our current thinking and future planning by giving us principles we can understand, believe, and apply.

If our churches are committed to these essential dimensions and distinctions, we'll have the most contagious body of individuals in the community. I remember the words of one of my mentors, the late Ray Stedman: "If the church was doing what it is supposed to be doing, people couldn't stay out." Why? If nothing else, curiosity would bring them in! They would witness our love and our excitement and think, *Why on* earth *are so many people flooding into that place? How in the world is there such a spirit of harmony and joy among that many people with such diverse opinions?* What they don't realize is *our* opinions don't matter. What matters is God's opinion.

I love the words of A. W. Tozer: "The world is waiting to hear an authentic voice, a voice from God—not an echo of what others are doing and saying, but an authentic voice."[6] As those in the church who follow Christ as our Head, our words must come from the living God, and not be an echo of human words or works, certainly not the words from our culture! As wise and intelligent as human opinions are, the church isn't guided by the thinking of any fallen human being. (By the way, that includes the pastor!) *Christ* is the Head. Our thinking is shaped by a study of Scriptures—by *God's* thinking. This is about building the church God's way, and God's way is found in God's Word. Nowhere else can we find such an authentic voice.

A church that's working is a church that's growing. I believe that. But be careful of the order of that statement, because a church that is growing is *not necessarily* a church that is working. I found that out the hard way, which leads me to the final principle.

Third, *wise, essential changes must occur to counteract any sign of erosion.* Please notice I did not use the word *easy.* Change is not easy when erosion has occurred, but it is essential. The imperative? *Be flexible!* Be ready and willing to make some changes—essential changes—especially if you hope to arrest the slow, silent, subtle slide of erosion. And stand alone through those changes, if necessary. The poet and artist E. E. Cummings wrote, "To be nobody-but-yourself—in a world which is doing its best, night and day, to make you everybody but yourself—means to fight the hardest battle which any human being can fight, and never stop fighting."[7]

You may find yourself standing alone against erosion in your church. If so, I commend you. And believe me, that's *not* an easy place to be. When I realized the erosion that had already begun to occur in our church...when I realized how far we had drifted from God's original, simple plan, I prayed, "Oh, God Almighty, give us that original vision again. Give me the courage to lead this flock back to the essentials. Make it happen again! *Please...* give us a church awakening." And He has begun to do so. It's been marvelous!

But I repeat, it has not been easy.

Course correction requires changes. It demands a devotion to the four essentials of a church. Let's review them again.

They were continually devoting themselves to the apostles' teaching and to fellowship, to the breaking of bread and to prayer. (Acts 2:42)

It isn't enough simply to *have* the four essentials in our churches. We must *continually devote ourselves* to them. In the original language, that phrase translates a single Greek term that means "to continue to do something with intense effort, with the possible implication of [doing so] despite difficulty."[8] Will there be difficulty? Absolutely! Open your New Testament and revisit the early church. Just look at *any* church! The adversary will stop at nothing to overcome the work of Christ. You can count on it. We'll look at that more closely in the next chapter.

*   *   *

I often call to mind that day my grandfather drove a stake into the ground to measure the erosion beside his little bay cottage. In the same way, all who love (and especially all who *lead*) the church must regularly evaluate where we are against the eternal, immovable standard of the Word of God. We must periodically pause and honestly question whether or not any drifting is taking place. Knowing that erosion is always slow, always silent, and always subtle, we must remind ourselves that it is the primary means by which the church drifts from God's original intent. The casual eye will never see erosion occurring. The corporate mind will not detect erosion. It takes a keen and disciplined mind-set to recognize it...and decisive, deliberate action to stop it.

In spite of the challenges the church faces today, erosion does not *have* to occur. Not if we wake up and *devote ourselves* to doing God's work God's way.

CHAPTER 2

Challenges, Struggles, Solutions, Priorities

What the church needs today is not more or better machinery, not new organizations or more novel methods. She needs men whom the Holy Spirit can use—men of prayer, men mighty in prayer. The Holy Spirit does not flow through methods, but through men. . . . He does not anoint plans, but men—men of prayer!

—E. M. Bounds

Challenges, Struggles, Solutions, Priorities

How can a church building suddenly turn up missing? Well…it did. Stolen!

Last seen in July 2008, the two-hundred-year-old Russian church had disappeared just a few months later. Orthodox officials in a village northeast of Moscow intended to reopen the abandoned two-story Church of the Resurrection and begin services again. Imagine their surprise when they came to the place where the church had stood and saw…nothing! It's a common occurrence in rural areas of Russia for vacant churches to have their gilded icons and other valuables stolen by thieves. But now the entire church building itself had been stolen! How did it happen?

Brick by brick.

Nearby villagers dismantled the structure in October 2008 and sold each brick to a local businessman for one ruble each (which amounts to about four cents per brick). "Of course, this is blasphemy," a local priest blathered. "These people have to realize they committed a grave sin."[1] To which I think, *Oh, really? What about the leadership that neglected the church for so long?* But more on that later.

When I saw the date of the church's deconstruction, it struck a personal nerve. October 2008 represented Stonebriar Community Church's tenth anniversary. It was a pivotal milestone in our church's history as we determined to stop the erosion our local body had begun to experience. Spiritually speaking, we resolved to put a halt to the dismantling of our internal walls and to begin rebuilding the spiritual foundation of the biblical essentials for a church: *teaching, fellowship, breaking of bread,* and *prayer* (see Acts 2:42). I am so grateful that God intervened. He graciously granted us the opportunity to get back on track! His grace rescued us. Even though we were only ten years old, signs of erosion were beginning to appear.

Jesus promised to build His church, adding the declaration, "and the gates of Hades will not overpower it" (Matt. 16:18). That's a good-news/bad-news statement. The good news is that the adversary will not spoil the growth of Christ's church. It *will* prevail. The bad news? Satan will do all he can to dismantle the church. If he can't bring it about suddenly, then he will chip away at it brick by brick.

Every church will face challenges. In fact, the New Testament tells us that struggles are a *normal* part of the Christian experience:

Beloved, do not be surprised at the fiery ordeal among you, which comes upon you for your testing, as though some strange thing were happening to you. (1 Peter 4:12)

What's true of us as individuals is also true of our churches. No need to be surprised when challenges come. We *will* struggle! No need to scramble around, wring our hands, and wonder what to do in the midst of the enemy's insidious attacks. Rather than take our cues from the world, the Scriptures offer us a clear path to follow in the midst of any trial. But that doesn't mean it will be easy.

Let's Recall Three Valuable Principles

We concluded chapter 1 with three principles I have found of inestimable value. Let's review them. You may even find it helpful to read them aloud.

1. Clear, biblical thinking must override secular planning and a corporate mentality. *Think spiritually!*
2. Studied, accurate decisions must originate from God's Word, not human opinions. *Stay biblical!*
3. Wise, essential changes must occur to counteract any sign of erosion. *Be flexible!*

I encourage you to return often to these principles. You may even want to memorize them. Why? Overwhelming challenges and fierce struggles lie ahead in your path and in the path of your church. Believe it. Expect it. But for sure, *prepare* for it. Only through devotion to biblical principles such as these will we retain our values when the adversary starts chiseling away at our walls.

Years ago I read of an article from the *Smithsonian* magazine about a fascinating experiment:

Dr. John Calhoun, a research psychologist at the National Institute of Mental Health, built a nine-foot-square cage for selected mice and observed them as their population grew from 8 to 2,200. The cage was designed to contain comfortably a population of 160. Food, water, and other resources were always abundant. All the mortality factors except aging were eliminated. As the population reached its peak at 2,200 after about two and one-half years, the colony of mice began to disintegrate. There was no physical escape from their closed environment. Adult mice formed natural groups of about a dozen individual mice. In the groups each mouse performed a particular social role, but there were no roles in which to place the healthy young mice. This totally disrupted the whole society. The males who had protected their territory withdrew from leadership. The females became aggressive and forced out the young. And the young grew to be only self-indulgent. They ate, drank, slept, groomed themselves, but showed no normal aggression and failed to reproduce.

Dr. Calhoun observed that courtship and mating—the most complex activities for mice—were the first activities to cease. After five years all of the mice had died, despite the fact that they had plenty of water, food, and no disease. What result would such overcrowding have on humanity? Calhoun suggests that we would first of all cease to reproduce our ideas, and along with ideas, our goals and ideals. In other words, our values would be lost.[2]

If Dr. Calhoun is correct, what's true of mice could also be true of men and women (sounds like a John Steinbeck novel, doesn't it?). Overpopulation presents a real threat. Look again at the last five words in the report: "our values would be lost." That statement troubles me most of all. Haunting words. Not just for humanity... but for the church.

Our whole reason for existence as a body of believers can somehow get lost in the rat race and maze of misplaced priorities. It happens all the time. The church concentrates on buildings and programs, seating and parking, choirs and offerings, staff and signs, and... *wait a minute!* If we're not careful, we get so distracted by growing numbers and doing all it takes to maintain them, we overlook the most important issues. When that happens, we lose our values, our purpose, and our objectives.

I made a list of a few problems that can occur

as a result of rapid growth in the church. It's not exhaustive by any means, but it's enough to get your attention. When a local church grows quickly, it is in danger of these problems:

- uncertainty of purpose
- blurred vision
- fuzzy priorities
- compromised values
- replacing volunteerism with professionalism

All these problems are potential dangers from rapid growth. It's the last one that really sticks in my craw. The church was *never* meant to be a "professional organization." We'll let the world have all of those. The church is not a slick, efficient corporation with a cross stuck on its roof. It is a *ministry*. We do not look to the government for support or to the state for direction. We don't seek the counsel of Wall Street for financial suggestions. We have one Head, the Lord Jesus Christ. We do not rely on any earthly organization or some rich individual to sustain the ministry. The church is a *spiritual entity*, built up and supported by its Founder, Jesus, who promised to build His church.

I agree with and applaud the words of the late

Richard C. Halverson, former chaplain of the U.S. Senate:

> In the beginning the church was a fellowship of men and women centered on the living Christ. Then the church moved to Greece, where it became a philosophy. Then it moved to Rome, where it became an institution. Next, it moved to Europe, where it became a culture. And, finally, it moved to America, where it became an enterprise.[3]

The church can get slick. Its ministers can become perfunctory in their tasks. I guess that's why I love Pastor John Piper's excellent volume *Brothers, We Are Not Professionals* (great title!). Read his words carefully:

> We pastors are being killed by the professionalizing of the pastoral ministry. The mentality of the professional is not the mentality of the prophet. It is not the mentality of the slave of Christ. Professionalism has nothing to do with the essence and heart of the Christian ministry. The more professional we long to be, the more spiritual death we

will leave in our wake. For there is no professional childlikeness (Matt. 18:3); there is no professional tenderheartedness (Eph. 4:32); there is no professional panting after God (Ps. 42:1)....

Our business is...to deny ourselves and take up the blood-splattered cross daily (Luke 9:23). How do you carry a cross professionally? We have been crucified with Christ; yet now we live by faith in the one who loved us and gave Himself for us (Gal. 2:20). What is professional faith?

We are to be filled not with wine but with the Spirit (Eph. 5:18). We are God-besotted lovers of Christ. How can you be drunk with Jesus professionally? Then, wonder of wonders, we were given the gospel treasure to carry in clay pots to show that the transcendent power belongs to God (2 Cor. 4:7). Is there a way to be a professional clay pot?[4]

Not long ago I spent some time with a pastor who serves in a church more than one hundred years old. As we sat down to have lunch together, I couldn't help but notice his slumping shoulders and frequent sighs. He seemed weary and burdened.

I asked him to describe the church where he has served for many years. After a pause, and another deep sigh, he looked me in the eyes: "Chuck, I can sum it up in one word—*dysfunctional.*" He continued, "The ruts that have been formed are so deep and so long, it's hard to imagine I could have *any* influence in pulling the church out...and getting it back on track."

As I listened to his words, I found myself nodding in sympathy. "How tragic," I responded. His joy was gone. His hope was fading. His exciting dreams of yesteryear had turned into boring and predictable reruns.

That conversation reminds me of Ray Stedman's words regarding the moment he crossed the border into Alaska: "I saw a hand-painted sign on the side of the road that read 'Choose your rut carefully. You'll be in it for the next 200 miles.'" The same can be said of many a church. Obviously, the preference is to avoid the ruts altogether. But what if you find yourself stuck in one, as my pastor friend did? You need to take the difficult, but necessary, steps to begin climbing out. Climb alone, if necessary. But climb! In his case, he resigned...and is now in a church that's refused to kick back and stay disengaged.

I have discovered, both by experience and by an examination of the Scriptures, that there are a number of ways the adversary tries to get us off track and stuck in a rut. In this chapter we'll look very specifically at two of these strategies, from different angles. Thankfully, the early church withstood both of these challenges...and overcame them. By following their inspired example, we can also succeed.

Let's Return to the First Church on Record

Sometimes we idealize the first church on record as a model of perfection. Perhaps the setting *was* more ideal, but it certainly wasn't idyllic. It was more pristine, but not perfect. They had challenges, just as we do. However, some of their struggles were far greater than ours.

I usually smile when I hear people say, "We want our church to be a first-century church!"

I want to answer, "Oh? You want persecution?" We tend to forget *that* part of the early church, don't we? The first church on record understood and victoriously endured fierce persecution. Martyrdom was commonplace. Mistreatment was a way of life. As the author of the book of Hebrews wrote to some second-generation Christians,

You have not yet resisted to the point of shedding blood in your striving against sin. (Hebrews 12:4)

How's that for perspective? We think we have it tough, but we have yet to spill our blood for the sake of our testimony. Notice the words *not yet*. Interesting phrase. The day may be coming when we're more like the early church than we would ever wish!

But differences notwithstanding, the first-century church faced challenges similar to our twenty-first-century context. In spite of the many contrasts in geography, culture, and language, some threats to the Christian experience remain universal. The good news? The solutions are timeless as well. Let's examine both.

The early church had experienced rapid growth. Following the day of Pentecost in Acts 2, the body of believers in Jerusalem numbered just over three thousand. A mere two chapters later, that same book records their ranks had swelled to about five thousand (see Acts 2:41; 4:4)! The flame was spreading. The numbers were increasing. The power of the gospel had taken hold. The growth was exponential. The church was being built, just as the Lord Jesus Christ had promised He would do.

But as we learned from the nine-foot-square cage of mice, if growth is not handled wisely, values begin to disintegrate. And wouldn't you know it? The Lord had barely begun to build His church before the adversary began to dismantle it.

One day Peter and John went up to the temple in Jerusalem around 3:00 p.m. in order to pray. While passing through the eastern gate, called the Beautiful Gate, they healed a lame man begging for spare change from the passersby. Peter used the occasion to preach a powerful message to the Jews who witnessed the healing (see Acts 3). As a result of many who heard Peter's message, the church grew to "about five thousand" (Acts 4:4).

But those who believed were not the only ones who heard the message. There were also religious leaders in the group. They had a completely different reaction:

As they [Peter and John] were speaking to the people, the priests and the captain of the temple guard and the Sadducees came up to them, being greatly disturbed because they

were teaching the people and proclaiming
in Jesus the resurrection from the dead. And
they laid hands on them and put them in jail
until the next day, for it was already evening.
(Acts 4:1–3)

Enter the professionals. Obviously they didn't
want Peter and John telling the people Jesus had
been raised from the dead. It's important to remember that these were the same religious leaders who
sentenced Jesus to die. Their desire? To silence
these spokesmen for Christ. To squelch the plans
of these ignorant upstarts. To stop all this growing
enthusiasm! So they threw Peter and John in the
slammer for good measure. The next day, the leaders assembled and interrogated the two disciples
about the healing miracle.

Picture the scene in your mind. Remember
whom Peter is addressing. These were the leaders who had condemned Jesus only a few months
earlier (see Matt. 26:57–66). Could they not do
the same to Peter and John? Absolutely! Peter may
have remembered these same angry faces as they
condemned the Savior, spit in His face, and beat
Him with their fists (see Matt. 26:67). Truth be
told, these were professional thugs, more than

spiritual leaders. It was Peter's fear of their brutal treatment of Jesus that caused Peter to deny even knowing Christ (see John 18:22–25). And now, those religious professionals who condemned Jesus have Peter and John in their crosshairs.

But this is a different Peter now. The bitter tears are past. The crows of the rooster haunt him no more. He is fearless. Why? The big fisherman has seen the resurrected Christ. Peter is filled with the power of the Holy Spirit. Therefore, Peter speaks to these professional thugs without intimidation:

Rulers and elders of the people, if we are on trial today for a benefit done to a sick man, as to how this man has been made well, let it be known to all of you and to all the people of Israel, that by the name of Jesus Christ the Nazarene, whom you crucified, whom God raised from the dead—by this name this man stands here before you in good health. He is the STONE WHICH WAS REJECTED by you, THE BUILDERS, but WHICH BECAME THE CHIEF CORNER stone. And there is salvation in no one else; for there is no other name under heaven that has been given among men by which we must be saved. (Acts 4:8–12)

Now *that*, my friends... is *guts*!

No hesitation. No intimidation. No fear. No concern whatsoever for the consequences. Just honesty mixed with passion and conviction. *How good is that!*

As a preacher, I can relate to the courage of Peter and John. When you are filled with the Spirit and empowered to speak for Christ, there is an accompanying sense of invincibility. There is no fear of what people might say or do. Sometimes I get so fixed on the message I am bringing that it seems I am simply a conduit for the Word of God. (Don't worry, now... Swindoll isn't getting weird on you.) In those moments, that sense of invincibility takes over the declaration of the message. I assure you, there is no greater confidence than knowing you are correctly declaring and applying the truth of God's Word!

That is what Peter and John experienced.

Meanwhile, the religious professionals were listening to Peter's bold words. Their reaction?

Now as they observed the confidence of Peter and John and understood that they were uneducated and untrained men, they were amazed, and began to recognize them as having been with Jesus. And seeing the man who

had been healed standing with them, they
had nothing to say in reply. (Acts 4:13–14)

Unlike the professionals, Peter and John were
uneducated and *untrained.* I love those words!
The first comes from the Greek term *agrammatos,*
and refers to one without a formal education.[5] We
might call this person "unlettered." The second
word, *untrained,* translates the Greek term *idiotes.*
I'm tempted just to leave that one as it is! In that
day the term meant, simply, a "nonprofessional."[6]

No wonder these religious leaders were "amazed"!
No wonder they "had nothing to say"! What *could*
they say? Before them stood, in their opinion, two
unlettered idiots, and yet, Peter and John spoke
articulately and with confidence. Also standing
there was the living result of supernatural power,
the man who had been healed in the name of Jesus.

After a private consultation among themselves—in which even *they* admitted that a miracle
had taken place—these professionals called Peter
and John back before them:

And when they had summoned them, they
commanded them not to speak or teach at all
in the name of Jesus. (Acts 4:18)

Now, Peter and John *could* have said nothing and walked away. But remember, they knew the truth about Jesus. They had no reason to keep quiet. So Peter's confidence burst forth again with strong emotion:

> Whether it is right in the sight of God to give heed to you rather than to God, you be the judge; for we cannot stop speaking about what we have seen and heard. (Acts 4:19–20)

How invincible! I love their courage! Let's look further:

> When they had threatened them further, they let them go (finding no basis on which to punish them) on account of the people, because they were all glorifying God for what had happened; for the man was more than forty years old on whom this miracle of healing had been performed. When they had been released, they went to their own companions and reported all that the chief priests and the elders had said to them. And when they heard this, they lifted their voices to God with one accord. (Acts 4:21–24)

Upon obtaining their freedom, did Peter and John immediately exit Jerusalem? On the contrary, they made their way to the other Christians in Jerusalem for the purpose of prayer. Notice one part of their prayer in particular:

And now, Lord, take note of their threats, and grant that Your bond-servants may speak Your word with all confidence. (Acts 4:29)

Don't think for a moment that Peter and John's calm and cool demeanor came from themselves. Not at all. They communicated the situation to the church...so that other Christians could bear the burden with them before the Father. The body of Christ prayed to the Lord as one body, "with one accord," asking that the apostles might continue to speak with confidence. Prayer was their natural response, not their last resort.

One of my favorite comic strips was *The Far Side* by Gary Larson. (Why do good cartoonists *ever* have to retire?) One particular strip I love shows two deer standing in a forest. One of these bucks has a big, bold bull's-eye across his side, near his shoulder. The other buck stares at the target while giving a great one-liner: "Bummer of a birthmark, Hal."

Let me pause for a moment and remind you that any pastor who is doing the hard work of communicating the truth—and also living it—lives with a big, bold bull's-eye on his chest. Every courageous pastor who speaks the truth is under the gun. He is in the direct line of fire from the adversary, who would like nothing more than to ruin his reputation or, preferably, take him out. Don't think that because he preaches with the confidence of Peter and John that he doesn't need your prayer support. *Pray for your pastor!* He needs it more than you can imagine. I urge you also to let him know of your commitment to pray for him. The encouragement he will receive through your words will be surpassed only by the strength God will give him through your prayers. Once again, *pray* for your pastor.

Peter and John weren't obsessed with fear. They simply understood that the cross of Christ has enemies. In writing to the Corinthian believers from the city of Ephesus, the apostle Paul noted:

A wide door for effective service has opened to me, and there are many adversaries. (1 Corinthians 16:9)

Later Paul would explain to a young pastor named Timothy that challenges and struggles are to be expected by believers:

Indeed, all who desire to live godly in Christ Jesus will be persecuted. (2 Timothy 3:12)

I don't mean to suggest we should be paranoid. As one wag put it, "Just because you're not paranoid doesn't mean they're not out to get you!" *Please.* Paul wasn't paranoid; he was a realist. He understood threats are overcome by the prayers of the saints and the resulting courage of those who share the good news. Because Peter and John also understood, they solicited the prayers of their fellow believers.

When told by the authorities to keep quiet, Peter and John refused to stand mute. "We cannot stop speaking about what we have seen and heard," they replied (Acts 4:20). They stood their ground because they knew they had to answer to a higher power. The puny rules of the professionally religious thugs meant nothing to them. Clearly, they had a higher authority. There was a greater power they must obey.

I have a friend who is a federal judge and lives in the Washington, D.C., area. He sent me a fictional story that always reminds me of Peter and John and why they could respond as they did:

Two California Highway Patrol Officers were conducting speeding enforcement on I-15, just north of the Marine Corps Air Station at Miramar. One of the officers was using a hand-held radar device to check speeding vehicles approaching the crest of a hill. The officers were suddenly surprised when the radar gun began reading 500 miles per hour. The officer attempted to reset the radar gun; it would not only not reset, it shut down. Just then a deafening roar over the treetops revealed that the radar had in fact locked on to a United States Marine Corps F-18 Hornet, which was engaged in low-flying exercises near the location. Back at the CHP Headquarters, the Patrol Captain fired off a complaint to the Marine Corps Base Commander. The reply came back in true Marine Corps style:

Dear Sir:
Thank you for your letter. We can now complete the file on this incident.

You may be interested to know that the tactical computer in the F-18 had detected the presence of, and subsequently locked on to, your hostile radar equipment and automatically sent a jamming signal back to it, which is why it was shut down.

Furthermore, an Air-to-Ground missile aboard the aircraft had also automatically locked on to your hostile equipment location.

Fortunately, the Marine pilot flying the Hornet recognized the situation for what it was, quickly responded to the missile system alert, and was able to override the automated defense system before the missile was launched to destroy the hostile radar position.

Our pilot also suggests you cover your mouths when cussing at them, since the video systems in these jets are very high resolution. Sergeant Johnson, the officer holding the radar gun, should get his dentist to check his left rear molar. It appears the filling is loose. Also, the snap is broken on his handgun holster.

Thank you for your concern.

Semper Fideles[7]

It's easy for those in authority on earth to forget that there is a higher authority that hovers above them. There is a sovereign God, who presides over our times and our seasons...who does whatever He pleases...whose authority is supreme. He answers to no one. We answer to Him. Therefore, those who serve their sovereign God have nothing to fear!

But (I repeat) where God is at work—count on it—the enemy is equally active. Where Christ is building His church, never forget, the adversary is laboring to dismantle it brick by brick. Satan chisels away at the church from the outside, as we've seen from these worldly religious leaders. We are not surprised when the world's system takes its shots against the church and its purposes. That's obvious. That's expected. But what shocks us, very often, are those bricks that get chiseled out *from the inside.* What do I mean? I'm referring to those times when Satan uses *Christians* (often they are counterfeit Christians) to tear down what Christ is building. Sounds incredible, I know. Unfortunately, it happens regularly.

An Internal Threat: A Lack of Integrity

Even within the first church on record, depravity was alive and well. Immediately after this issue occurred with the religious leaders, a threat arose from inside the first-century church:

> But a man named Ananias, with his wife Sapphira, sold a piece of property, and kept back some of the price for himself, with his wife's full knowledge, and bringing a portion of it, he laid it at the apostles' feet. (Acts 5:1–2)

Now, there's nothing wrong with owning property. And there's nothing wrong with selling property. While I'm at it, there's also nothing wrong with holding back some of the profit for yourself. So what was the problem? The problem occurred when this couple kept some of the profit but let on as if they were giving it *all* to the Lord. That's called hypocrisy. Watch how Peter exposed their lack of integrity as he confronted the husband:

> Ananias, why has Satan filled your heart to lie to the Holy Spirit and to keep back some of the price of the land? (Acts 5:3)

Talk about a confrontation! When's the last time someone challenged you to your face, claiming that Satan has filled your heart? Chances are, never. What gave Peter the gumption to speak so boldly? He may have remembered an episode just more than a year earlier when *he* was the one being confronted. It's true, Jesus' words were aimed at the devil...but the Lord spoke them directly to Peter:

> Get behind Me, Satan! You are a stumbling block to Me; for you are not setting your mind on God's interests, but man's. (Matthew 16:23)

You may remember the context of this scolding. Jesus had just promised that He would build His church on Simon Peter's foundational, rocklike confession that Jesus is the Christ. The Savior went on to predict His own death and resurrection, but Peter would have none of it! *How could the Messiah die? Unthinkable!* So Peter took Jesus aside and began to rebuke Him (see Matt. 16:13–22). Can you imagine rebuking Jesus? Satan had tempted Peter to set his mind on man's interests rather than on God's. No sooner had Jesus promised to build His church than the adversary went to work trying to crumble its foundation. Remarkable! Jesus immediately confronted the threat with those strong words to Satan, and Peter never forgot them.

Peter also had another incident to remember, much more recent. When Jesus and His disciples ate the Last Supper in the Upper Room, Jesus turned to Peter and predicted that three times he would deny even knowing Jesus. Again, Peter set his mind on man's interests rather than God's. And the source of this temptation? Jesus' words to Peter send a chill up my back every time I read them:

Simon, Simon, behold, Satan has demanded permission to sift you like wheat. (Luke 22:31)

It's no surprise, then, that it was Peter who would later write and warn his fellow Christians of the hard lesson he himself had learned:

Be of sober spirit, be on the alert. Your adversary, the devil, prowls around like a roaring lion, seeking someone to devour. (1 Peter 5:8)

How ironic that the Lord would use Peter to confront the same issue in the book of Acts that Peter himself had learned. Now that Jesus had begun to build His church, the adversary employed the same tactic as when Jesus had first promised to build it. When Ananias and his wife, Sapphira, kept back some of the price of the land and then lied about it, they were setting their hearts on man's interests rather than on God's. Peter must have shaken his head in amazement.

I've always pictured Peter's words to Ananias as strong, bold, and even loud. But, in light of Peter's own rebukes by Jesus, I wonder if the apostle's words carried a more compassionate tone. Try reading them again in that light:

Ananias, why has Satan filled your heart to lie to the Holy Spirit and to keep back some of the price of the land? While it remained unsold, did it not remain your own? And after it was sold, was it not under your control? Why is it that you have conceived this deed in your heart? You have not lied to men but to God. (Acts 5:3–4)

Peter had learned that the most significant presence was the Lord's presence. Rather than focusing on man's interests—as we've seen Peter do more than once—it is the Lord's interests we pursue. We magnify Christ. It is Jesus we exalt and serve. We answer to a higher authority than to people. "You have not lied to men," Peter declared to Ananias, "but to God."

And as he heard these words, Ananias fell down and breathed his last; and great fear came over all who heard of it. The young men got up and covered him up, and after carrying him out, they buried him. Now there elapsed an interval of about three hours, and his wife came in, not knowing what had happened. And Peter responded to her, "Tell me whether you sold the land for such and such a price?" And she said, "Yes, that was the price." Then Peter said to her, "Why is it that you have agreed together to put the Spirit of the Lord to the test? Behold, the feet of those who have buried your husband are at the door, and they will carry you out as well." And immediately she fell at his feet and breathed her last, and the young men came in and found her dead, and they carried her out and buried her beside her husband. And great fear came over the whole church, and over all who heard of these things. (Acts 5:5–11)

Before you think of calling this unfair, remember, God is holy. He takes sin seriously. In our postmodern culture that diminishes the significance of sin—that humanizes God and deifies man—it doesn't surprise me when some people frown and ask, "How could a holy, loving God do such a thing?" My answer to that is, *how could a holy God do anything else?* Thank God He doesn't deal with all of us as He dealt with Ananias and Sapphira! "If God dealt with people today as He did in the days of Ananias and Sapphira," the old country preacher Vance Havner once said, "every church would need a morgue in the basement."[8] God takes seriously issues of integrity. Have we forgotten that?

Don't think for a moment that because Christians don't fall over dead after sinning that God turns a blind eye from sin in the lives of His own. He still disciplines His children, but in His timing and in His way. Think about it: *do we really want immediate accountability as a norm?* I sure don't! Again, Peter's writing comes to mind:

> The Lord is not slow about His promise, as some count slowness, but is patient toward you, not wishing for any to perish but for all to come to repentance. (2 Peter 3:9)

Too many people these days are relying on too few to walk in integrity. Your personal integrity matters more than I can put into words. As Christians, we can't play fast and loose with our money and expect it not to affect us. It's God's money. We can't play fast and loose with our morality either. A believer can't sleep around and get away with it as a Christian. There's a terrible price to pay, because God holds His own directly accountable. We are not our own. We answer to Him, remember, not men.

Your personal integrity is not a private matter. Why? As a Christian, you represent Christ. You live for the honor of His name and the reputation of His church. You can't compromise your integrity without it affecting others. Remember, the church is a body. If one part suffers, we all suffer.

But when you trust in a holy God with fear and trembling, you're extremely careful with your lifestyle. You realize, as Alexander Whyte once wrote, that you're "hanging very heavy weights on very thin wires."[9] You purpose to set your mind on God's interests...which, after all, are really your best interests.

God Himself solved the problem of a lack of integrity in Acts 5. He took the lives of those who compromised. And rather than this divine discipline dividing the church, the body of Christ became more than ever united and operated under a heightened fear of God and hatred for sin. *That was healthy.* And it further strengthened the apostles to speak boldly, regardless of the consequences. That brings us to the next event.

An External Threat: Ungodly Authorities

Like a lumberjack who saws a tall tree one direction and then another, Satan tried to fell the church by chipping away from multiple angles. We've seen an attack from the outside through the threats of local leaders. We've observed an internal threat from the enemy through a lack of integrity. Now the enemy adjusts yet again for another assault from the outside. Those religious leaders refused to back off.

Because the church continued to increase in number, and because the people of Jerusalem held the apostles in high esteem, the religious leaders were filled with jealousy. They had the apostles arrested and thrown into prison and then threatened them to stay silent about Jesus. Their response? It hadn't changed from the last time they were bullied.

We must obey God rather than men. (Acts 5:29)

Their courageous response is what the church father John Chrysostom, Archbishop of Constantinople, had in mind when he wrote, "We must not mind insulting men, if by respecting them we offend God."[10]

Believers of all eras have squared off against those in authority who would demand disobedience to God. Moses' parents resisted the order of the Egyptian pharaoh to kill their baby son, because "they were not afraid of the king's edict" (Heb. 11:23). Daniel and his friends resisted their government's decrees that outlawed the worship of their Creator God (see Dan. 3; 6). The apostle Paul stood firm in the face of those who could take his life for preaching Christ (see Acts 25–26). As history unfolded, we saw the likes of Martin Luther, John Knox, Jon Hus, and many others who clung to the Word of God in spite of the threats of earthly authorities.

Even in modern history, those passionate for Christ stand strong. During the reign of the brutal dictator Idi Amin, an Anglican bishop named John Rucyahana served as a pastor in Uganda. Amin targeted thousands of political opponents for extermination, including many Christian leaders. On one occasion, government soldiers came for Pastor John and put a gun to his head. After intimidating and threatening John, they released him, assuming he would no longer speak the name of Christ. Two days later John walked into the cathedral and, to his shock, he found it full of people who had heard what happened. Boldly, John continued to speak to them about Jesus—in spite of the threats he had endured.[11]

Please don't misunderstand. Believers *are* to obey the government. Peter himself would later affirm this fact (see 1 Pet. 2:13–17). Keep in mind, the government in Peter's day was the brutal caesar Nero! Christians are to be model citizens and to submit to the governing authorities…unless doing so requires disobedience to God. At that point, to quote Peter, "We must obey God rather than men"—and also be prepared to bear the consequences.

Rather than letting the apostles walk free with only a warning, as the religious leaders had done earlier, they now added injury to insult:

They flogged them and ordered them not to speak in the name of Jesus, and then released them. (Acts 5:40)

Don't move too quickly over those initial words: *they flogged them.* The original term means that they were struck or beaten repeatedly. Try to picture that. Line up the apostles in your mind and imagine each one mercilessly beaten again and again. Let me ask you, have you ever been flogged? Probably not. Have you ever been struck even once because of your faith? Most in our Western world haven't. Look at the apostles' amazing reaction:

> So they went on their way from the presence of the Council, rejoicing that they had been considered worthy to suffer shame for His name. And every day, in the temple and from house to house, they kept right on teaching and preaching Jesus as the Christ. (Acts 5:41–42)

Rejoicing…in beatings? No, rather, they rejoiced over the privilege of suffering shame for Jesus. This was the first time the apostles had experienced physical pain as a result of following Jesus, yet they rejoiced. "This is an instance of what rhetoricians style an *oxymoron*," wrote the late Marvin R. Vincent, Baldwin Professor of Sacred Literature at Union Theological Seminary. "The apostles are described as *dignified by indignity*."[12] What amazing character those men displayed. What enormous stature!

For many years our radio ministry, *Insight for Living*, has had the privilege of participating in the annual conference of the National Religious Broadcasters (NRB). Recently the members of the NRB drafted a document that represented the rededication of its commitment to the historic Christian faith. Of all the essential declarations listed, my eyes were drawn particularly to the final one:

> *We fully accept* our charge to faithfully obey the command of Christ to preach the Gospel, even if human governments and institutions attempt to oppose, constrain, or prohibit it.[13]

After I read those words, I recalled the apostles who "kept right on teaching and preaching Jesus as the Christ" (Acts 5:42). I also remembered J. Vernon McGee's quip about the prophet Daniel, who suffered persecution for his faith: "The reason the lions didn't eat him is because he was three-fourths backbone and the rest gristle!"

The apostles had that same tenacity. You could *not* intimidate them. You could threaten them and beat them repeatedly, but you could *not* silence them or stop them. Remember why? They reported to a higher authority. They answered to the living God. Thus, they were not afraid of the authorities of the world system.

Let's Examine a Specific Issue

As we have made our way through Acts 4–5, we have seen the adversary assault the church from a number of fronts. First, he hacked from the outside, then from the inside, and then again from the outside. Take a guess what's next in Acts 6: not surprising, it was another *internal* attack. But this one was far more subtle.

The previous internal threat came from a greedy couple. It was an issue of right versus wrong. The solution in those cases will always be to find out what is right...*and then to do it.* Period. But what do you do when the threat comes not from evil things, but from too many *good* things? How do you respond when the ministry grows so large, and the opportunities to minister are so immense, that you can't balance it all? Great question.

Before we examine this specific issue, let's reread my list of potential dangers that can come from rapid growth:

- uncertainty of purpose
- blurred vision
- fuzzy priorities
- compromised values
- replacing volunteerism with professionalism

It's not difficult to understand how expansion can usher in these threats. Like too many mice in a cage, we can lose our values, our purpose, and our objectives—our very influence as a church can be threatened.

All of the dangers I've listed—every one of them—are addressed with the internal threat we're about to examine. When the struggles we grapple with stem from too many good obligations, what is the solution? The Scriptures answer that for us in one word: *priorities.*

First-century Jerusalem was steeped in Jewish culture. So, not surprisingly, the first believers in Christ had Jewish roots. But some of these new Jewish Christians hailed from Gentile countries and could not speak Aramaic, the native language of the Jews in Israel. From many different backgrounds, the church gathered around the unity of faith in Jesus Christ as the Messiah. Using today's terms, the church was a blended family. These diverse backgrounds cultivated the seedbed for dysfunction. *In the church?* Precisely.

> Now at this time while the disciples were increasing in number, a complaint arose on the part of the Hellenistic Jews against the native Hebrews, because their widows were being overlooked in the daily serving of food. (Acts 6:1)

Perhaps the needs had grown so large that it was impossible for the leaders to stay aware of them all. That can happen. (Remember my experience in the previous chapter?) Even in an environment where "all things were common property" (Acts 4:32), preferential treatment crept in. And with it, naturally, complaining. Some things never change! The original Greek term for "complaint" is *goggusmos,* a word that grammarians call an onomatopoeia. That is, *goggusmos* is a term that sounds like what it means: to grumble.[14] Try mumbling *goggusmos* under your breath a few times quickly, and you'll see what I mean. The Hellenistic Jews were grumbling...complaining...whining. (There's an additional way to translate the word, which I learned in the Marine Corps, but I won't go there!)

Watch how the apostles dealt with this complaint. Their response is instructive:

So the twelve summoned the congregation of the disciples and said, "It is not desirable for us to neglect the word of God in order to serve tables. Therefore, brethren, select from among you seven men of good reputation, full of the Spirit and of wisdom, whom we may put in charge of this task. But we will devote ourselves to prayer and to the ministry of the word." (Acts 6:2–4)

Let's not misunderstand the apostles' words. There's nothing wrong *per se* with serving tables— with meeting physical needs. Actually there's everything right about that. The problem comes when meeting those needs requires a *neglect of the Word of God*.

Jesus experienced this as well. When His ministry enlarged so much that the physical needs of the people became all-consuming, Christ withdrew by Himself to pray. The apostles searched for Him and told Him that everyone was looking for Him. Why? They wanted healing. Christ responded by modeling for His disciples the importance of priorities:

Let us go somewhere else to the towns nearby, so that I may preach there also; for that is what I came for. (Mark 1:38)

Jesus knew the priority of keeping prayer and preaching central to His ministry. The apostles applied that same standard when the needs of the church increased.

Do you see how rapid growth can threaten our purpose, vision, priorities, and values? No one will *ever* demand that you pray and give priority to the Word of God. Physical needs will always bring the louder complaint. And the predictable will occur: we'll spend so much time greasing those squeaky wheels that we neglect prayer and the Word of God. In a fine volume titled *The Courage to Be Protestant*, David Wells asks several penetrating questions:

What is the binding authority on the church? What determines how it thinks, what it wants, and how it is going to go about its business? Will it be Scripture alone, Scripture understood as God's binding address, or will it be culture? Will it be what is current, edgy, and with-it? Or will it be God's Word, which is always contemporary because its truth endures for all eternity?[15]

We can become so absorbed with trying to "do church" (whatever *that* means) on our own that we turn to impressive marketing techniques and corporate organizational strategies, instead of keeping first things first. (I'll have much more to say about this in the next chapter.) But wait a minute; doesn't Jesus want the church to grow? Absolutely. In fact, *He* has promised to do it. So what is our task? What are our priorities? A properly functioning church, we have learned, stays committed to its four biblical essentials: *teaching, fellowship, breaking of bread,* and *prayer* (see Acts 2:42). In the first church on record, it was Christians who planted the seeds and watered them, as the apostle Paul reminded his readers, "but God was causing the growth" (1 Cor. 3:6). It remains the same with us today.

If we let the demands of ministry determine the priorities of the church, then the tail of "the urgent" will wag the dog of "the important." That's how erosion occurs. That's how bricks disappear one by one until, at last, the church's original purpose is forgotten, and its spiritual influence is completely removed. The needs of ministry will always be greater than your ability to meet them. *Always.* Don't let them distract you.

Does that mean we ignore the needs? Not at all. It's a matter of recognizing one's calling. By confirming their priorities, the apostles also provided the opportunity for laymen to get involved in ministry. They told those who complained about the unmet needs to "select from among you seven men of good reputation, full of the Spirit and of wisdom, whom we may put in charge of this task" (Acts 6:3). This wise response curbed the temptation to replace volunteerism with professionalism.

If church leaders attempt to meet all of the church's needs themselves, then two effects will occur. First, as we've seen, the spiritual leaders will neglect their priorities of prayer and the Word of God. Second, the body of Christ will cease to function as a body! God has gifted every Christian to serve in some way (see 1 Cor. 12:7). It's a matter of calling. Moreover, it's a matter of obedience.

Some churches today have adopted a professional mind-set entirely. Like the consumer culture they live in, the people pay the pastors to do the work of the ministry, while they sit and watch and offer critiques. Where is *that* in the Bible? A pastor who allows this approach to occur has fallen for what I call the

"Superman syndrome." I'm not talking about pulling on a pair of blue tights and a red cape and putting a fancy "S" on his chest—though I heard of a pastor who did *exactly* that on Easter Sunday (I wish I were kidding). I'm talking about an attitude that says, "I am self-sufficient," "I need no one else," or "I will show no weakness or admit any inadequacy." These words betray the presence of the Superman syndrome—that particular peril for pastors who go it alone and become "the stars of the show."

Funny thing is, I've rarely seen anyone lose ground by admitting inadequacy or weakness. The best professors I ever had would admit, "I don't know, Chuck, but when we come back together I'll try to have that answer for you." I deeply respect that attitude in a person. Kids acknowledge weakness all the time and never feel as if they've lost confidence. Pastors set themselves up for letting people down when they pose as Superman.

One of the greatest privileges of my early ministry was to know a man named Jim Petersen. Through his capable leadership and sterling character, the ministry of the Navigators expanded greatly in São Paulo, Brazil, where he and his wife, Marge, served for more than twenty years. Cynthia and I first met Jim and Marge at Glen Eyrie, the Navigators' headquarters in Colorado Springs. I was new to ministry at the time—and far too naive—and I was looking for a formula for success in God's service.

"How do you do it, Jim?" I asked him. "Tell me the secret of ministering to people." I expected him to say, "Always set the pace," or "Be strong no matter what," or "Model the truth and stand against the gale as it attacks you." I got none of that.

Jim just smiled in his inimitable way and answered, "Chuck, let people see the cracks in your life, and you'll be able to minister to them." That's it. That's the distilled essence of all he told me.

As we left their cabin that day, I felt somewhat like the deflated rich young ruler, who had just asked Jesus how to inherit eternal life (see Mark 10:17). Like Jesus' surprising answer to the ruler, Jim's reply was *not* what I expected. It convicted me. It ripped the "S" off my chest and cut the tie strings to my cape. I was looking to minister from my strengths. Jim challenged me to serve in weakness. He made that statement to me more than fifty years ago, and it remains one of the greatest lessons I have learned in ministry. I have never forgotten it. I never will.

I remembered it once when a young believer in our church approached me and gushed, "I don't know of *anybody* I admire as much as I do you—"

"Stop right there," I interrupted. "I appreciate your admiration, but always remember: when it comes to one another on this earth, never put anyone on a pedestal."

"I never thought about that before," she replied.

"Only one person deserves to be on a pedestal, and He'll never fall off. That's Jesus. You can respect me," I continued, "but please don't put me in that place where I'm sure to let you down."

As the apostle Paul asked in 2 Corinthians 2:16, "Who is adequate for these things?" Obvious answer: nobody! By asking this question, Paul showed us the cracks in his life. He takes himself off any would-be pedestal and lands in the ranks of humanity. I thank God for the transparent apostle that he really was. His writings are permeated by vulnerability.

But we have this treasure in earthen vessels, so that the surpassing greatness of the power will be of God and not from ourselves. (2 Corinthians 4:7)

"Who is adequate for these things?" Obviously, the appropriate attitude is to embrace this fact: pastors are not self-sufficient. We have cracks. We need other people.

Let's get practical. If you're a pastor, *ask for help!* Never leave the impression that you don a cape and tights. Hardly a day passes that I don't ask someone to assist me in doing something. Also, make sure when someone does help with a project and it succeeds, *that* person gets the credit. If an individual comes up with a great idea, and the whole church applauds it, let the people know it was his or her idea. Why leave any other impression? By the way, this reminds me of what the mother ape said to her baby ape: "Watch out when climbing on those high poles. The higher you get, the more they're gonna see your rump." In other words, remember, when you're up high you're a big target. You're on display. So it's essential to say, "I can't handle this myself" or "I need you guys right now." Didn't Jesus do this at Gethsemane? Admit weaknesses and failures. Acknowledge your own fallibility. Don't buy into the Superman syndrome. You can't carry the weight of the whole world (or even the whole church) on your shoulders. Someone else already has that distinction.

If you're a layperson, *help your pastor!* I've already mentioned that he needs your prayers and support. He's a target for the adversary. But your pastor also needs your companionship and your involvement. Moreover, *you* need it! God has not called the pastor to be an independent professional who does it all while the consumers watch. Rather, the pastor is to be a teacher and a shepherd. He is to equip "the saints for the work of service, to the building up of the body of Christ" (Eph. 4:12). *That's you.* Do you allow him to teach and equip you? Are you available for works of service? Have you told him? Remember, the ministry has far more responsibilities than can be done. God has prepared ahead of time many good works for you (see Eph. 2:10). Don't miss them.

If the first-century church had adopted a professional model for ministry, they would have hired Distributors-R-Us, whose slogan would be "We specialize in cultural conflicts, griping Christians, and whining widows." But the church doesn't do that. You know why? The church is a family—a blended one. That's by God's design. That's how we learn to grow in grace with one another. When you're a church family, you don't hire everything done. Everybody pitches in! Professionalism and a consumer mentality rob the body of Christ of the privilege of serving Christ. Instead, the church should say, "We have a need, and some of you can help us with the need." That's what the apostles did.

Obviously, not every layperson is fit for every place of service. In this case, the early church chose seven individuals who were filled with the Spirit—because when walking in fellowship with Christ they wouldn't steal. (The church had had enough of that already!) They chose people who were full of wisdom—so that the distribution of food to the Hellenistic widows would be fair and impartial. Look at how a church that was sensitive to the leading of God's Spirit responded to leaders who had their priorities straight:

> The statement found approval with the whole congregation; and they chose Stephen, a man full of faith and of the Holy Spirit, and Philip, Prochorus, Nicanor, Timon, Parmenas and Nicolas, a proselyte from Antioch. (Acts 6:5)

One wag has said that this was the first and last time in all of history that the entire congregation found approval in one decision! Interestingly, if you check the names of these individuals, you'll find they are all of Hellenistic origins. Smart decision. What wisdom!

You know what else is interesting? While we see two of these men, Stephen and Philip, again in the book of Acts, five of them are never mentioned again. I love that because you don't *have* to hear about them or see them. They're servants. They're content to work in the shadows. They're part of a group in the Bible I call the "Willing Unknowns." These are the servants who find delight in serving without recognition or fanfare or applause. They are faithful without demanding tangible rewards. Believe me, these individuals are rare.

The only time in the book of Acts the phrase "the twelve" is used is here in chapter 6, verse 2. Judas had already died, remember, so there were only eleven original apostles remaining. Do you recall who replaced Jesus' betrayer? More important, do you remember the qualifications he had to fill? Let's take a quick look back at Acts 1 where Peter gave the credentials required to replace Judas:

"Therefore it is necessary that of the men who have accompanied us all the time that the Lord Jesus went in and out among us— beginning with the baptism of John until the day that He was taken up from us—one of these must become a witness with us of His resurrection."...And they drew lots for them, and the lot fell to Matthias; and he was added to the eleven apostles. (Acts 1:21–22, 26)

If you search the Gospels, you'll not find Matthias's name anywhere. Many Christians today have never heard of him. He was a man just as qualified as the other apostles, but whose name never appears in the ministry of Jesus. *Never.* And yet, he was there the whole time! Never demanding attention. Not hung up on his position. In no way insisting on a particular rank or title. (How's *servant* for a job title?) He didn't stay faithful in order to get a pat on the back or in hopes of replacing anybody. Matthias had none of that. I *love* that kind of humble integrity in one who serves in ministry.

The church today still needs that kind of quiet modesty and availability among its servants. If you are one of those willing unknowns, and sometimes feel discouraged because you're overlooked, remember a promise the Lord has made to you:

For God is not unjust so as to forget your work and the love which you have shown toward His name, in having ministered and in still ministering to the saints. (Hebrews 6:10)

An individual with that kind of selfless commitment to the ministry of Jesus was *exactly* who was needed to serve the Hellenistic widows. That's why the congregation chose these seven faithful servants.

> And these they brought before the apostles; and after praying, they laid their hands on them. The word of God kept on spreading; and the number of the disciples continued to increase greatly in Jerusalem, and a great many of the priests were becoming obedient to the faith. (Acts 6:6–7)

By now it isn't surprising that the number of the disciples continued to expand. What's amazing is that a "great many" of those in the church's growing ranks were priests! Can you imagine seeing one who had persecuted the apostles come walking into your assembly on Sunday morning? Talk about a blended family!

Let's Always Remember Two Specific Principles

Ours is a world that wants to squeeze us into its mold. And its architect? Your adversary, the devil.

He hates everything you love...and he loves all that you hate. While Christ has promised to build up the church, the adversary is equally committed to tearing it down.

Let's conclude this chapter with two specific principles we would be wise to remember. One is about the adversary, and one is about our Lord. First, *the adversary will stop at nothing to disrupt and, if possible, destroy the church.* Always remember that. We know he can't completely tear it down, for Christ has promised, "the gates of Hades will not overpower it" (Matt. 16:18). But Satan will take it as far as he possibly can! He will use officials on the outside for his purposes. He will make use of Christians on the inside as well...carnal Christians, ornery Christians, pseudo-Christians. He will use *anything* to disrupt and destroy a ministry. In his mind, the end justifies the means...so he plays by no rules but his own. Hypocrisy. Wrong motives. Mishandling of funds. Sexual scandal. Biblical error. Bullying techniques. Caustic criticism. Unsigned letters. Discouragement. Disharmony. Anything goes. The adversary will stop at *nothing*. By introducing compromise and chaos into the church body, he tries to distract us from the spiritual erosion he has introduced. While we

focus on numbers and budgets and needs and com-
plaints and gripes, we can fail to notice the bricks
that have begun to disappear from our walls...one
by one.

The enemy of our souls tries to preoccupy us
with the physical struggles and causes us to miss
the spiritual conflict that rages in our lives. A. W.
Tozer, an outstanding scholar of yesteryear, quite
vividly described the delusion we experience:

> It is not a cheerful thought that millions of
> us who live in a land of Bibles, who belong to
> churches and labor to promote the Christian
> religion, may yet pass our whole life on this
> earth without once having thought or tried
> to think seriously about the being of God....
> We prefer to think where it will do more
> good—about how to build a better mouse-
> trap, for instance, or how to make two blades
> of grass grow where one grew before. And
> for this we are now paying a too heavy price
> in the secularization of our religion and the
> decay of our inner lives.[16]

The most spiritually bloodthirsty, vile creature on earth, our adversary the devil, wages a

bloodless, invisible war against you, your family, your church, and every other person who has been redeemed by the blood of the Lamb. Remember Peter's warning:

> Be of sober spirit, be on the alert. Your adversary, the devil, prowls around like a roaring lion, seeking someone to devour. (1 Peter 5:8)

We stay of sober spirit when we remember that we fight on the front lines of a relentless, brutal, invisible war. Sadly, many in the church do not realize that. They may have been taken hostage and not know it. They could be wounded, but nobody notices because they don't bleed. The apostle Paul knew this conflict well and wrote of it often:

> For though we walk in the flesh, we do not war according to the flesh, for the weapons of our warfare are not of the flesh, but divinely powerful for the destruction of fortresses. (2 Corinthians 10:3–4)

We are engaged in a battle, not for our bodies, but for our minds. Please don't think of the mind as a brain inside the cranium. Think of the mind as the inner person, with emotions and will and intellect all interconnected. It involves the way we think and how we react in life.

It is in these vulnerable and unseen areas that Satan focuses his attention. He battles through people or without people. He battles in events, in depression, in success, or in failure. He battles in money or in poverty, when numbers increase or decrease, among elders who aren't qualified to lead and parishioners who aren't submissive to the Holy Spirit. He is constantly at work, bent on our destruction. Why does he despise God's people and fight so insidiously against us? The answer must not be overlooked: he has a consuming *hatred* for the mission of Christ. Knowing that he can't overthrow it—because the gates of Hades will never do that—Satan plays a wicked game of spiritual chess. He knows he's doomed, but he'll get your last man if he can. He knows Christ has already won, but he won't give up without an ugly and continuing fight.

How can we be on the alert with a sober spirit? We can defend ourselves against the enemy's schemes by "taking every thought captive to the obedience of Christ" (2 Cor. 10:5). Isn't that a great verse! Since Satan makes our minds his battlefield, our best defense is to surrender our thoughts to Jesus Christ and ask Him to guard and protect us. When we release ourselves to Him, He takes charge, and Satan backs off. I make this practical in my own life by regularly telling God, "Lord, I need You right now; take charge of this. I need Your thoughts, I need Your strength, I need Your grace, I need Your wisdom, I need specific truths from Your Word, and I need Your very words. Protect me from fear. Hold me near. Give me resilient courage. Get me through this stormy time." He will; He'll get you through—victoriously.

It is only by focusing on the Word of God that we can set our minds on God's interests instead of man's. It is only through His Spirit that we can find divine enablement. It is only through prayer to God that we confess our vulnerabilities, our weaknesses, and our total need of God's strength in life and ministry. That brings me to my next point.

Second, *the Lord will honor and bless any plan that upholds prayer and promotes His Word.* Please read that again, for I have crafted those words very carefully. Granted, that game plan doesn't square with today's church-marketing techniques and seven-step plan for rapid church growth. The world's ways see such dependency as weak and foolish...

and yet, this reliance drips with the wisdom of God (see 1 Cor. 1:20–21). *God*—not people—gets the glory in a ministry that upholds prayer and promotes His Word. Why would He not bless that?

In the midst of a growing church and urgent needs, the apostles maintained their priorities. How? By devotion "to prayer and to the ministry of the word" (Acts 6:4). May I again point out something obvious? Notice which one came first. Prayer is to be a priority. *"First of all*, then," the apostle Paul wrote to young pastor Timothy, "I urge that entreaties and prayers, petitions and thanksgivings, be made on behalf of all men" (1 Tim. 2:1, emphasis added). I can imagine Paul's stylus pressing hard into the parchment as he penned those words: "First of all, then, I urge..." Prayer should have a place of priority among the leadership of our churches. In yours as well as mine.

I have the privilege of pastoring a church whose elders and other church officers are leaders of prayer. Our meetings are punctuated by prayer. Before one agenda item gets discussed, we pray. As the meeting proceeds and issues arise that are too difficult for us, or that require special wisdom, we lift them up to the Father. When we look over the financials and witness how God has provided, we pause and give Him our praise in prayer. We never conclude a meeting before giving thanks for the congregation, the staff, and all in leadership. We spend valuable time in prayer, minutes that a professional model for ministry would balk at as a huge waste of time. Once again, read John Piper's perceptive words, written in a prayer of his own:

> Banish professionalism from our midst, Oh God, and in its place put passionate prayer, poverty of spirit, hunger for God, rigorous study of holy things, white-hot devotion to Jesus Christ, utter indifference to all material gain, and unremitting labor to rescue the perishing, perfect the saints, and glorify our sovereign Lord.[17]

I love the writings of the Civil War chaplain E. M. Bounds. His insightful words, written more than one hundred years ago, still read today as if the ink were wet on the page. Read them slowly and thoughtfully:

> We are continually striving to create new methods, plans, and organizations to advance the church. We are ever working to provide

and stimulate growth and efficiency for the gospel. This trend of the day has a tendency to lose sight of the man. Or else he is lost in the workings of the plan or organization. God's plan is to make much of the man, far more of him than of anything else. Men are God's method. The church is looking for better methods; God is looking for better men.... What the church needs today is not more or better machinery, not new organizations or more novel methods. She needs men whom the Holy Spirit can use—men of prayer, men mighty in prayer. The Holy Spirit does not flow through methods, but through men. He does not come on machinery, but on men. He does not anoint plans, but men—men of prayer![18]

But in addition to prayer itself, let me quickly add that it matters greatly *what* we pray. For example, at the fifth annual Planned Parenthood Interfaith Prayer Breakfast (now there's a contradiction in terms!), held in Washington, D.C., the Bishop V. Gene Robinson, a homosexual Episcopal cleric, made this startling claim:

We have allowed the Bible to be taken hostage, and it is being wielded by folks who would use it to hit us over the head. We have to take back those Scriptures.... What an unimaginative God it would be if God only put one meaning in any verse of Scripture.[19]

Incredible words...but hang on. Bishop Peter James Lee, one of the sixty Episcopal bishops who approved the appointment of Robinson, stated to the annual diocesan council in 2004:

If you must make a choice between heresy and schism, always choose heresy. For as a heretic, you are only guilty of a wrong opinion. As a schismatic, you have torn and divided the body of Christ. Choose heresy every time.[20]

Because of ecclesiastical nonsense such as this, I worded the principle as specifically as I did: "The Lord will honor and bless any plan that upholds prayer *and* promotes His Word." If your prayers contradict the Holy Scriptures, why in the world would God bless it? What audacity to think He would! What confusion that creates!

The Word of God tells us that it alone remains our guide for life and godliness (see 2 Pet. 1:2–4). That includes what we need to know about prayer. Only the Scriptures tell us what to pray, when to pray, why to pray, how to pray, whom to pray for, whom to pray to, and what to pray through! A prayer by any means other than submission to the objective, historical body of truth revealed in the Scriptures is a heretical prayer. A "wrong opinion" is just that—wrong. And as such, it will never be the right path to pursue for those who call themselves part of the body of Christ. Unity was never to be sought after at the exclusion of truth. In fact, Jesus saw no contradiction between the two pursuits (see John 17:17–23). Rather, they are part of the same Christian walk.

Just as we would starve without food on our tables, so we could not survive spiritually without the Word of God. It's not surprising, therefore, that it is the Word of God—and especially the inerrancy of the Scriptures—that continues to be the watershed issue of every generation. Recently, pollster George Barna discovered that only 55 percent of Christians in America have a strong belief in the accuracy of the Bible's principles.[21] That's only slightly more than half! Our belief in the inerrant

Scriptures is the essential issue of our day...and of every day. If we weaken the Word, we have immediately begun to starve the church spiritually. Satan applied this tactic in the Garden of Eden with our original parents (see Gen. 3:1–4), and he has not once deviated from his effective strategy...outside as well as inside the church.

Our dedication to the Word of God is not rooted just in the reading of it, or in the believing of it, or even in the preaching of it...but in *living it.* Author and pastor Eugene Peterson writes of the church:

When Christian believers gather in churches, everything that can go wrong sooner or later does. Outsiders, on observing this, conclude that there is nothing to the religion business except, perhaps, business—and dishonest business at that. Insiders see it differently. Just as a hospital collects the sick under one roof and labels them as such, the church collects sinners. Many of the people outside the hospital are every bit as sick as the ones inside, but their illnesses are either undiagnosed or disguised. It's similar with sinners outside the church. So Christian churches are not, as a rule, model communities of good behavior. They are, rather, places where human misbehavior is brought out in the open, faced, and dealt with.[22]

Dealing with error in both behavior and belief is part of the pursuit of truth. But addressing error is also part of the pursuit of unity in the church. Peter had no misgivings about rebuking Ananias and Sapphira. Not only that, remember, but God Himself had no qualms about taking their lives! The results? The body of Christ was strengthened...the cause of Christ was clarified...the Word of God was honored...the glory of God was upheld.

*   *   *

Will the church that Jesus is building have challenges? Absolutely! Whether from the outside or from the inside, the adversary will stop at nothing to try to disrupt and dismantle the church...brick by brick. But these struggles are not the demise of the body of Christ. On the contrary. They are our opportunities to apply biblical principles and priorities—the only solutions to the challenges we face.

We must keep our fingers on the pages of Scripture like a boat moored to the pier in a raging storm. While we do not worship the print on the page, the paper and ink lead us to the knowledge of the One whom we do worship—Jesus, our Master and Savior.

We need to stay on our knees. Prayer is a radical interference with the status quo. It is the means by which God grants power to those who rely on Him. This dependence never changes. Even as a sixty-something-year-old man who had been preaching faithfully for years, the apostle Paul continued to walk in a state of dependence on God. You have to love Paul's humility:

> Devote yourselves to prayer, keeping alert in it with an attitude of thanksgiving; praying at the same time for us as well, that God will open up to us a door for the word, so that we may speak forth the mystery of Christ, for which I have also been imprisoned; that I may make it clear in the way I ought to speak. (Colossians 4:2–4)

There was no pretense with Paul. No degree of success or number of years in the ministry gave him a false sense of ultimate accomplishment. He knew he had not yet arrived. He remained dependent on the Spirit of God. And so, with a genuinely thankful heart, he entreated his fellow believers for their prayers. Can you see the power of that kind of attitude? Very refreshing in the first century. And very *rare* in the twenty-first.

No wonder the man made such a lasting impact for Christ! The Lord honored and blessed Paul's ministry because he upheld prayer and promoted God's Word.

Rather than trying to ape the world's system, God points us in another direction. It's a way of life that stays out of step with the world, and yet not aloof from those in the world. J. Wilbur Chapman, an evangelist and pastor of the late eighteenth and early nineteenth centuries, observed, "It's not the ship in the water but the water in the ship that sinks it. So it's not the Christian in the world but the world in the Christian that constitutes the danger."[23]

The early church didn't ask God to bless their gimmicks. The church doesn't need gimmicks to attract people—it needs biblical truth taught consistently, preached passionately, and lived out authentically.

That's the next chapter. It's a chapter I've wanted to write for a long, long time.

Fasten your seat belt.

Distinctives of a Contagious Church

Most of us don't need to know more nearly as much as we need to be known more. We don't need a set of principles to practice nearly as much as we need another person to help us. We need someone to believe in us, stand by us, guide us, model Christ for us. We need another's encouragement, wisdom, example, and accountability.

—Howard Hendricks

Distinctives of a Contagious Church

I wish I could have been there to see it.

It was 7:51 a.m. on January 12, 2007. L'Enfant Plaza in Washington, D.C., a busy subway station, had its usual morning rush of commuters.

A young man wearing a baseball cap, T-shirt, and faded jeans entered the plaza and quietly removed his violin from its case. He tossed in some seed money to bait the passersby and lifted the violin to his chin. The player? Joshua Bell, possibly the finest violinist of our generation. His instrument? The rare Gibson ex Huberman, handcrafted in 1713 by Antonio Stradivari, one of the most coveted and expensive violins in existence. The music? Bell began with "Chaconne," from Bach's Partita No. 2 in D Minor, hailed by some as one of the greatest pieces of music ever composed in history. The response? You'd be surprised.

Of the 1,097 commuters who passed Bell that morning, only seven stopped to listen. That's right... *seven*. Just three days earlier, Bell had played to a sold-out crowd at Boston's Symphony Hall where the average seat cost $100. His earnings that morning in the subway? A little over $32. Bell usually earns around $1,000 a minute.[1] (I should have stayed with the violin!)

The *Washington Post* sponsored Bell's incognito performance in order to evaluate the public's taste, priorities, and perception. But for me, the experience remains a powerful lesson on the importance of something else.

Context.

No matter how beautifully Joshua Bell played his Stradivarius, and no matter how exquisite his musical selection may have been, it took more. His giftedness wasn't enough. It took a *context* that was conducive and favorable to it.

I find the same true of preaching.

Excellent exposition of the Scriptures alone isn't enough to cause people to continue attending and to stick together as a church. It takes more.

Please don't misunderstand. I'm certainly not diminishing the importance of preaching God's Word. I simply mean there are preachers all around the world who faithfully declare the truth...and yet their local church is not growing. In fact, I used to serve at such a church. I preached just as passionately there as I do in my current ministry. But there was no growth. The marks of an attractive church weren't present. In fact, I remember one Fourth of July weekend when there were seven people in the entire place...and four of them were Swindolls! That was *not* an inviting context. I might as well have been preaching in the subway.

Why is it we will drive past any number of churches in order to worship at one particular church located farther from our house than all the rest? What is it that draws us in, causing us to stay excited about, invest our time and money, and become an active participant of that church instead of some other? How can one ministry become so attractive, so meaningful to us, that we're willing to adjust our lives to fit its schedule, rear our children in it, and even invite other people to come with us?

The best word to describe such an attraction is *contagious*. Webster defined the root word, *contagion*, as "an influence that spreads rapidly."[2] When a church is in this category, word quickly travels. People witness the passion in our enthusiasm. They hear the excitement in our voices.

They see characteristics that set our church apart. They finally become so curious they come to see for themselves. One thing is for sure: they observe a set of distinctives being modeled like nothing the world around them has to offer. A contagious church is unique.

Some movies have quotes that have become so inimitable, so distinctive, that you could say the first part of the line, and most folks could finish it for you. Let's try a few:

"Houston, we have _____."

"Go ahead, make _____."

"Of all the gin joints in all the towns in all the world, she _____ _____."

"Frankly, my dear, I don't..." (Well, let's not go there!)

The movie *Field of Dreams* has one of those lines as well: "If you build it"—can you finish the quote?—"he will come." Some people think it's "*they* will come." In fact, when I graduated from seminary, long before the movie came out, I thought a similar line would be true in the church: *if you preach it, they will come.* Wow! Was I wrong.

I have lived to realize that, while a strong pulpit is essential, a contagious church also requires a context of other distinctives. There must be more than preaching. More than one gift at work. More than the conviction of one person. A contagious church has a number of individuals living out clear, biblical principles with the result that people pause in the midst of their busy lives. They realize this is a place worth their coming and participating.

When you look across the landscape of churches today, you find many congregations that have experienced phenomenal growth. Unbelievable growth. But upon closer examination, you discover that they have not committed themselves to the four biblical essentials for a church as prescribed in the book of Acts: *teaching, fellowship, breaking of bread,* and *prayer* (see Acts 2:42). The church may have more than these four...but it must not have less.

It is precisely these four areas the adversary will attack so he can disrupt and, if possible, destroy the church. That's why it's important to keep our priorities straight. It's essential that we not get distracted by all that we *can* do as a church...and stay focused on only what we *must* do as a church. Otherwise, we may be attracting a crowd for the wrong reasons.

This emphasis on the essentials is what the apostle Paul had in mind when he passed on the torch of ministry to a young pastor named Timothy:

I solemnly charge you in the presence of God and of Christ Jesus, who is to judge the living and the dead, and by His appearing and His kingdom: preach the word; be ready in season and out of season; reprove, rebuke, exhort, with great patience and instruction. For the time will come when they will not endure sound doctrine; but wanting to have their ears tickled, they will accumulate for themselves teachers in accordance to their own desires, and will turn away their ears from the truth and will turn aside to myths. (2 Timothy 4:1–4)

Notice both the command and the reason for it. The command is clear: "preach the word"— followed by an explanation of *when* and *how* to do it. But there's also a *why*, a reason to proclaim boldly the Bible on a consistent basis: there will come a time when biblical truth will be rejected in favor of what people want to hear. The biblical alternative? We learned in the last chapter that the Lord will honor and bless any plan that upholds prayer and promotes His Word. This is what Paul was affirming to Timothy.

Large numbers don't necessarily reveal God's

blessing. They could, in fact, reveal error. They could reflect an ear-tickling ministry that panders to people and tells the crowds what they *want* to hear, instead of what they *need* to hear. A growing number of churches and denominations today have found the four essentials unnecessary—burdensome, you might say. Archaic traditions of a bygone era. So they have hired what I call "pulpit whores," or put more mildly, "teachers in accordance to their own desires"—to affirm them in their selfish and carnal lifestyles. No wonder the crowds expand... it's as if God has officially approved their sin!

But even a calloused conscience eventually aches with the emptiness that only God—the true God—can fill. The tragedy is that these empty individuals think they have already tried God... and He has left them just as unfulfilled as the world has. It's downright tragic.

Our culture is driven by marketing. There's no escaping it. Consumerism and materialism have wormed their way into our lives, and marketing spreads the disease. For instance, how can I know which of the eight hundred cereals in the store is most healthy? Which car should I purchase? What vacation should we take this summer? See the dilemma? Consumers must make decisions. How can we possibly determine what to buy with so many options to choose from, with so little money to spend, and with such limited time to spare? Marketing informs us which choices will make us most comfortable... bring the most satisfaction... cause the least inconvenience... give us the biggest bang for our buck... and the like. You get the picture.

I've learned through the years that perception overshadows reality. I hate that, but it's true. From political candidates to polyester carpet, how people perceive things is, to them, more convincing than a truckload of evidence. Unfortunately, most people draw their opinions from the shallow stream of perception instead of the deep reservoir of truth. I find that strange and disappointing.

Marketing works. That's why each year businesses spend billions of dollars trying to get us to spend just as much. In his book *The Brand Gap*, marketing guru Marty Neumeier offers a number of strategies to help companies develop and protect their unique brands. But he also offers a witty insight into a deeper motivation for consumer purchases:

Depending on your Unique Buying State, you can join any number of tribes on any number

112

of days and feel part of something bigger than yourself. You can belong to the Callaway tribe when you play golf, the VW tribe when you drive to work, and the Williams-Sonoma tribe when you cook a meal. You're part of a select clan (or so you feel) when you buy products from these clearly differentiated companies. Brands are the little gods of modern life, each ruling a different need, activity, mood, or situation. Yet you're in control. If your latest god falls from Olympus, you can switch to another one.[3]

This example was written tongue-in-cheek, of course, but it taps a profound need. Often we make decisions—both large and small—in an attempt to satisfy something deep within ourselves. This truth motivates more than spending. Even our critical life decisions are often made based on a consumer mind-set. Scary thought, isn't it? Perception actually overshadows reality.

It's even more frightening when we realize that our culture doesn't market Christianity very well. Have you ever noticed it's usually the aberrant "Christian"—preferably an evangelical—the media displays to represent the rest of us? Like William

Jennings Bryan at the Scopes Monkey trial, this poor individual is revealed in all his or her pitiful naïveté, promptly vilified, pigeonholed, and finally, dismissed with a laugh. Christianity looks foolish. Perception overshadows reality.

Then, at other times, when controversial subjects like abortion, homosexuality, evolution, or the inerrancy of the Scriptures find their way to prime-time debates, the "Christian" view is usually defended by some theological liberal who couldn't tell the book of Genesis from Boy George. He or she only quotes verses about the love of God and calls no one to any standard. It's the theological liberal the world embraces in a politically correct culture. It's the Bible-believing, evangelical Christian, however, whom our tolerant world cannot tolerate.

Our culture has branded evangelicals as narrow exclusivists, hypocritical killjoys, and religious fanatics. In short, we're oddballs. (Not a great brand.) Who wants to be an oddball? Moreover, who wants to go to an oddball church?

So here's the problem: How do I know which church to attend? What helps me identify which ministry is best for me? Aware of our stereotype, we evangelicals find it tempting to fight fire with fire... or marketing with marketing. "Our church is not boring," we promise. "This is *not* your grand-mother's church," we assure the younger genera-tion. But we need to be careful with our words... fighting fire with fire could be dangerous. Tyler Wigg-Stevenson, a Baptist preacher and author, writes in an article titled "Jesus Is Not a Brand":

Marketing is not a values-neutral language. Marketing unavoidably changes the mes-sage—as all media do. Why? Because mar-keting is the particular vernacular of a consumerist society in which everything has a price tag. To market something is therefore to effectively make it into a branded prod-uct to be consumed....And we market the church at our peril if we are blind to the criti-cal and categorical difference between the Truth and a truth you can sell. In a marketing culture, the Truth becomes a product. People will encounter it with the same consumerist worldview with which they encounter every other product in the American marketplace.[4]

Most people would never intentionally compare Jesus to Coca-Cola or Chevrolet. But in a consum-erist society, we run the danger of implying that the good news of Jesus is just one of many similar choices, all of which are equally valid. Just choose your flavor of Savior. But Jesus never gave us that option. He claimed that He was the *only way* to God the Father (see John 14:6). In a world that's bound for hell, Jesus' claim isn't selfish exclusivism. It's grace.

Our world has lost its way. So it's no surprise that when the church takes its cues from the world, the church begins to go astray as well. But must we resort to gimmicks for people to come to church? Is biblical reinterpretation the new essential for church growth? Must we dumb down historic Christianity into shallow entertainment in order to pamper consumers? May it never be! I am convinced that the church doesn't need marketing devices, worldly strategies, live entertainment, or a corporate mentality to be contagious. Not if the glory of God is the goal. Not if the growth of God's people is in view. Rather, the church needs biblical truth taught correctly and clearly...and lived out in authenticity.

One of the worst things we can do in our churches is to take our eyes off the essentials— to take our cues of how to "do church" from our postmodern world instead of determining our distinctives and priorities from the Scriptures. It's a great temptation to try that these days, because there are so many churches doing it. They look like they know what they're doing. The crowds swell. The ratings soar. The money pours in. They speak in such a convincing way that we are tempted to think, *Well, maybe they're right and we're beginning to miss it.* Please. Don't go there.

As we're thinking about the awakening needed for the church, we need to define what it is that makes it contagious. How should a church grow biblically? What environment causes a community to take notice? It isn't just the building, or the sound system, or the music. It's not even the preaching. I repeat, it's the context that makes a church contagious.

It's the people.

And it's more than a curiosity at the numbers of people. It's their passion. It's their Spirit-directed enthusiasm. It's the obvious work of God engaging the lives of believers in a meaningful connection, a genuine compassion, and an almost electric excitement about reaching out into the community and investing themselves wholeheartedly into places of ministry.

Having laid a solid foundation of what the Scriptures require as essentials for a church, let's consider some distinctives of what makes a church contagious. We'll find them in the same letter from which we read earlier—the letter from Paul to Timothy.

A Mentor's Last Letter to a Friend

It is often true that a person's final words are among his or her best words. At that point, life seems to have distilled into its most significant thoughts, and knowledge has been tempered to wisdom. We seem to listen more closely when a person is just about to pass off this earth's scene, especially when it's someone we have known well and loved.

Before we look at Paul's words to Timothy, I want to share with you a letter from a grandmother to her grandchildren. It's the letter she wrote to them after she discovered she had cancer. I share it with you with their permission.

Packing for the Trip of a Lifetime

I am in my car driving home from the doctor and am trying to digest the news I received over a routine biopsy on what the ENT thought was an infected gland. I had gone in because I thought I had a sinus infection but he diagnosed me too, as having acid reflux. Infected sinuses I had experienced several times over the years and although acid reflux was something new, I could deal with it. I might have to make some changes in my eating habits, but I certainly could handle that. I have never been one of those that "live to eat." I am more an "eat to live" kind of person. To say I was shocked at the news I had just received is putting it mildly. It seems the biopsy was labeled with that dreaded word, malignant. *Stunned, surprised, and even shaken, are way too mediocre to express the feelings I had. Perhaps unbelief can best sum up the mixture of emotions that surged through my body.*

All of a sudden (like instantly), I was jolted into facing the reality that my head had known for years but had never been embraced by my heart: we are mortal, and we are going to die. When I was young, I thought of death as something for old people, and now that I am old it still seemed like it was always out there in the future somewhere.

It was at that point that I remembered a verse I had memorized only a few days earlier. It jumped off the page at me as though God was speaking to me. "THIS IS THE ATTITUDE I WANT FROM YOU," He said to me through Luke 1:38. The verse was originally Mary's response to the angel, and I had often admired her reply. She said, "I am God's servant, and I am willing to accept whatever He wants." Never in a million years did I think this would be what He wanted from me and ask me to accept. Peace flooded my soul though, as I acknowledged God and was willing to submit to His will. I knew in my heart it was time to get ready to go.

Grand Dad and I have traveled a lot in our 58 years of married life together. I have loved each and every trip because basically I am a "Go-er." Part of the fun of each trip was the anticipation and preparation. I loved to plan just what to take, and, of course, that always depended on where we were going, what we would be doing, and whom we might be meeting or seeing. Getting ready for this trip, however, was of a completely different nature. This trip was the trip of a lifetime and was the most important, most momentous trip I would ever make. I would be meeting the King of kings and Lord of lords, the God of all creation. How do you pack for that?

As I began to think about it, I realized I had one major problem. I couldn't take anything with me. No suitcase, no change of clothes, no makeup or jewelry. I was all that was going. *I thought it was difficult when the airlines came up with their new rules that you were allowed only one checked bag and one carry-on. This was even more of a challenge. I would be allowed to carry with me only what was already packed in my spirit and soul. I could take with me any of the changes the Holy Spirit had made in my life, any of the things that were of eternal value, and the verses I had committed to memory would certainly come along. Those were the very words of God.*

Then, I thought of what God said about Himself. He said, "I am the high and holy One that inhabits eternity. I live in that high and holy place with those whose spirits are contrite and humble." Isn't it interesting that God did not choose to live with the wise people, the rich people, or the super-strong people? As great as

God is, you would have thought He would have enjoyed their company more. On earth we tend to gravitate to people who think like we do and have similar ideas. But then it occurred to me that maybe that is the whole reason. Who could be more humble than God? In addition to everything else God is that makes him so great, He is also humble. What could be more humbling than to take upon yourself the likeness of a mere human being, walk among us with all our limitations, and then die for us? That is why He dwells with the ones who know what they are (corrupt to the core) and who they are (a complex human created by Him). Everything we have or are comes from God alone.

First Corinthians 4:7 states it plainly: "What makes you better than anyone else? What do you have that God hasn't given you? And if all you have is from God, why boast as if you have accomplished something on your own?" And 2 Corinthians 10:17 adds, "The person who wishes to boast should boast only of what the Lord has done." So, in reality, the only things worth packing or that are packable for me are the things God Himself has done. The things He has done IN me and THROUGH me. I can only hope there are a few of those there. I can't go back in time and relive the wasted moments that I sought things for myself and aspired to self-praise and glory, or erase all the times I was busy feathering my own nest; but I can relate this truth to you: you have a lifetime ahead of you. My parting words to you would be to change your focus today and set your affections on things above, not on things on the earth (Colossians 3:2). For the things which are seen are temporal and the things that are unseen are eternal (2 Corinthians 4:17–18). This is not easy when you are young because everything seems to be screaming the opposite and appealing to your ego to make a name for yourself or to achieve so you can have more. I know, because I have been there, but if anyone can do it, if anyone can live life with an eternal perspective, I am betting on the best 13 grandchildren God ever made.

Remember, heaven is home. I'll be waiting for you and will see you when you get there.

With all my love,
Noney[5]

If it's true that a person's final words are often his or her most significant, that only adds to the value of the book of 2 Timothy. This little letter represents the apostle Paul's last letter, written to an individual he considered a "kindred spirit" and a "true child in the faith" (Phil. 2:20; 1 Tim. 1:2). Paul and Timothy were like father and son. They had grown close through many years of ministry, friendship, and mentoring. How would you feel if you were Timothy, knowing that the great apostle personally penned his final letter to you? Well, in a way, he has. The truths of this letter are timeless. The mentor's last letter to his friend represents his final words to us as well.

I've said for years that what helps 2 Timothy come alive is to remember it is dungeon talk. Paul doesn't write while relaxed in a rocking chair by a fireplace. He isn't sipping tea as he watches the surf of the Mediterranean. He's alone...in a dark, stinking dungeon...beneath Rome. Chances are good you have never even seen a dungeon, much less been imprisoned in one. Look at a brief, but rich, description of Rome's Mamertine Prison from author John Pollock's fine volume *The Apostle: A Life of Paul*:

Paul was once more seized, shackled, and this time placed in rigorous confinement in Rome, not as an honorable citizen on remand but "chained like a criminal."...He was among the felons in the Mamertine or equally obnoxious dungeon, reached only by rope or ladder let down through a hole in the floor above. His weary body must lie on rough stones. The air was foul, sanitation almost nonexistent.[6]

I seldom turn to 2 Timothy without trying to picture myself as a silent observer in the same cell as Paul. I imagine hearing him cough and watching him wheeze and sneeze as the rats scurry into the cracks in the stones. Perhaps I step forward to help the old man light a candle for the evening. Or I wrap him in a cloak to stay warm for the night. I watch him weep as he writes. He knows his days are numbered.

The trial that would follow would be a hearing where he would stand manacled, bearing the marks of age and torture, before a godless caesar named Nero. Author James Stalker does a good job describing the irony of the scene that would occur:

On the judgment seat, clad in the imperial purple, sat [Nero,] a man who in a bad world had attained the eminence of being the very worst...and in the prisoner's dock stood the best man the world contained, his hair whitened with labors for the good of men and the glory of God. Such was the occupant of the seat of justice, and such was the man who stood in the place of the criminal.[7]

T. R. Glover, the English classicist of Cambridge, made an unforgettable comment about the paradox of history as he contemplated Nero serving as Paul's judge: "The day was to come when men would call their dogs Nero...and their sons Paul." *I love that line!*

Here sits the aged apostle under a flickering flame, committing to parchment his final words. He's cold. He's lonely. He's come to the end. It's dungeon talk. It's time for him to pass along to a younger man some guidelines for ministry. It's as if Paul uses his pen as a baton to pass along vital principles to Timothy and then tells him, "Run with this baton!" When you realize you're reading a letter that was written by a condemned man in a dungeon, the letter carries with it a great deal more impact than it otherwise would.

Why is this letter so insightful? Not just because it's dungeon talk. Not only because it's Paul's final words. Not just because of the wisdom it offers. But it's also because it is *Scripture*. These first-century guidelines are still inspired of God...still relevant...still trustworthy. The principles worked then; they work now; they will *always* work.

Timeless Characteristics of a Contagious Ministry

When considering church growth, we must think strategically, we must preach creatively, and our worship must connect. Absolutely. But we must also be careful. A marketing mentality and a consumer mind-set have no business in the church of Jesus Christ. By that I mean, Jesus is *not* a brand... human thinking does *not* guide God's work... and the church is *not* a corporation. The church of Jesus Christ is a *spiritual entity*, guided by the Lord through the precepts of His Word.

If we sacrifice the essentials of *teaching, fellowship, breaking of bread,* and *prayer* on the altar of strategy, creativity, entertainment, and "relevancy," we have abandoned the main reasons the church exists. We should build *on* those essentials, not attempt to replace them.

Let's examine four characteristics of a contagious ministry, all from Paul's last letter to Timothy.

A Place of Grace

Paul underscores the principles of a contagious church with four verbs. As we interpret the Scriptures, we should always pay attention to the verbs in a passage. Verbs are the backbone of literature. They hold thoughts together. When there is action to be taken, verbs reveal the steps we must walk to align ourselves with truth. In this case, the verbs appear as commands required to nurture a church environment that is both biblical and attractive. Here's the first one:

> You therefore, my son, be strong in the grace that is in Christ Jesus. (2 Timothy 2:1)

From the verb *be strong*, we glean the first distinctive for a contagious church: *it is always necessary to be strong in grace.* That sounds simple, but it will be one of the most difficult principles to apply in a consumerist culture.

Where does the application of this principle begin? With church leaders. Paul could write this command because he himself modeled it. He proclaimed grace. He promoted grace. His message was the gospel of grace. He relied on grace. Paul never forgot the importance of God's unmerited favor in his own life...and it permeated his entire ministry. Read a sampling of his own words:

For all have sinned and fall short of the glory of God, being justified as a gift by His grace through the redemption which is in Christ Jesus. (Romans 3:23–24)

For by grace you have been saved through faith; and that not of yourselves, it is the gift of God. (Ephesians 2:8)

But when the kindness of God our Savior and His love for mankind appeared, He saved us, not on the basis of deeds which we have done in righteousness, but according to His mercy, by the washing of regeneration and renewing by the Holy Spirit, whom He poured out upon us richly through Jesus Christ our Savior, so that being justified by His grace we would be made heirs according to the hope of eternal life. (Titus 3:4–7)

Isn't it amazing that this former legalistic Phari-see—this violent man whose life was once charac-terized by making sure that Christians were wiped out—was stopped in his tracks by grace? While on the road to Damascus, Paul was made blind by a light from heaven as the Lord Jesus spoke to him and called him (of all people!) into His work. That changed him from the inside out: the long-standing legalist was transformed into a messenger of grace! Paul's ministry emphasized grace to the lost as well as to those in God's family. As I've studied the life of Paul, I find grace woven like a silver thread through the colorful tapestry of his ministry. Paul became the preeminent spokesman for grace:

> Let it be known to you, brethren, that through Him forgiveness of sins is proclaimed to you, and through Him everyone who believes is freed from all things, from which you could not be freed through the Law of Moses. (Acts 13:38–39)

Paul's message offered the good news of grace to the lost. This is the first part of Christ's Great Commission to the church (see Matt. 28:18–20). Imagine the impact our churches would have on our communities if each Christian committed to sharing the gospel of God's great grace once a week with someone who expresses a need. The lost need to hear how they can cross the bridge from a life filled with emptiness and guilt to a life flowing with mercy and peace and forgiveness...all because of His grace. We help build this bridge when we lovingly and patiently communicate the gospel.

You don't need a seminary degree. You don't have to know a lot of the religious vocabulary or the nuances of theology. In your own authentic, honest, and unguarded manner, simply share with people what Christ has done for you. Who knows? It may not be long before you will know the joy of leading a lost person from the darkness of death's dungeon across the bridge to the liberating hope of new life in Christ. How exciting...how *contagious!*

There's another reason being strong in grace makes a church attractive—the absence of legalism. Just as the lost don't understand the good news of Christ, so the saved rarely understand the remarkable reality of grace. I know of no activities more exhausting and less rewarding than Christians attempting to please the people around them by maintaining impossible legalistic demands. What a tragic trap, and the majority of believers are caught in it. When will we ever learn? Grace has set us free! That message streams throughout the sermons and personal testimonies of the apostle Paul.

Author Steve Brown says that some people think legalistic churches are as bad as grace-oriented churches. As he put it, they are no more alike than saying a taxidermist is like a veterinarian. Some would claim, "Well, either way you get your dog back!" True, but one of them collects dust and never moves. The other one is busy and barking and eating and jumping...he's *alive!* He's the real thing! The point? Let's choose to be veterinarians. Let's determine that our churches will be places of grace. A church of grace is alive, anticipating God's work, willing to risk, free of judgmentalism...but make no mistake—they're not free of holiness. There's a vast difference.

Once someone has trusted in Jesus for the forgiveness of sins, we need to release them. Release them into the magnificent freedom grace provides. I don't mean leave them alone without biblical instruction or guidance. (We'll talk about that later.) I mean, rather, don't smother them with a boatload of *nonbiblical* rules and regulations that put them on probation and keep them in some holding tank until they "get their lives straightened out." Rules about what to wear, what to look like, what to eat and drink, what entertainment to enjoy, what movies Jesus would watch...et cetera. *Please.* That's a straitjacket of religious bondage. That's not a contagious place. It's a frightening place. The day a church stops being strong in grace is the day the church loses its magnetism. Truth sets people free (see John 8:32). Tragically, legalistic churches incarcerate them behind bars of fear.

When Paul stood on Mars Hill in Athens and proclaimed the grace of God to the lost, he preached to a crowd of skeptics, critics, and those we might call sophisticated eggheads. Rather than beginning with the Scriptures, Paul began with the created world in which these nonbelievers lived in order to introduce Jesus to them. He began with their spiritual hunger and pointed them to Jesus as the satisfaction for their longings...and the payment for their sins. Paul even quoted a pagan poet as a means of building a bridge between the lost and the Lord (see Acts 17:16–33).

A number of ministries and movements have adopted for their churches what I call a "Mars Hill philosophy of ministry." Modeled after Paul's message on Mars Hill, their goal is to connect with the nonbeliever, or the postmodern, or one they would call a "seeker." In recent years the "emerging" church movement has attempted to "do church" (or *be* the church) in a new way amid our postmodern world. Their purpose is "missional living," that is, to get involved in the world in hopes of transforming it. This style of ministry engages the culture in a "conversation," rather than preaches to people as a prophet. A wide range of theologies and strategies exist within this current movement. Some individuals hold to orthodox beliefs but have adopted very unorthodox ways of communication. I have read of sermons that use language that would make most believers cringe...and cover their children's ears.[8]

Are we to minister as those *in the world*? Absolutely. That's an answer to Jesus' own prayer for His followers (see John 17:14–16). But let's be very discerning here. Does this mean we must minister as those *of the world*? Do we have to adopt postmodern thinking in order to minister to the postmodern mind? *Absolutely not.* Such behavior and words are not fitting in the life of a Christian (see Eph. 5:4). They are obviously, then, not fitting in the context of worship.

Please understand, grace does not mean anything goes, which includes biblical theology. One author, who likens the emerging church to the Protestant Reformation, writes,

> The actual nature of the Atonement ... or the tenet of an angry God who must be appeased on the question of evil's origins are suddenly all up for reconsideration. If in pursuing this line of exegesis, the Great Emergence really does what most of its observers think it will, it will rewrite Christian theology— and thereby North American culture—into something far more Jewish, more paradoxical, more narrative, and more mystical than anything the Church has had for the last seventeen or eighteen hundred years.[9]

Is this what grace requires of us? Since when was the nature of the Atonement determined by anything other than a close, careful examination of the Scriptures? As I said in the last chapter, when the inerrant Word of God is not our standard for truth, erosion will creep in. It will eventually crowd out truth. David Wells offers a helpful reminder:

> Scripture is divine revelation. It is not a collection of opinions of how different people

see things that tells us more about the people than the things. No. It gives us God's perfect knowledge of himself and of all reality. It is given to us in a form we can understand. The reason God gave it to us is that he wants us to know. Not to guess. Not to have vague impressions. And certainly not to be misled. He wants us to know. It is not immodest, nor arrogant, to claim that we know, when what we know is what God had given us to know through his Word.[10]

I need to make this clear: I don't intend to erect an "emerging" straw man and then light him on fire. I realize, in the same way our culture unfairly pigeonholes evangelicals, there is a risk of stereotyping the emerging church—or any similar movement. The danger of a broad stroke of analysis is to fail to represent everyone fairly or to recognize the exceptions. I'm certain that not all of those who number themselves among the "tribe" of the emerging church favor liberal theology with no belief in absolutes or traditional, orthodox convictions. However, my concern is for those churches *in any movement* that, in an attempt to connect with the culture, actually embrace a compromise of biblical truth. Paul had the same concern as he wrote with urgency to Timothy:

I solemnly charge you in the presence of God and of Christ Jesus, who is to judge the living and the dead, and by His appearing and His kingdom: preach the word; be ready in season and out of season; reprove, rebuke, exhort, with great patience and instruction. (2 Timothy 4:1–2)

In other words, stick with the plan God has promised to bless and use: preaching the timeless, ever-relevant, always-powerful Word. Deliver the biblical goods! Stick with Scripture. Be strong in the grace that is in Christ Jesus. It's worth noticing that this exhortation is not addressed to the hearer; it's for the speaker. The one who is to obey this command is the one proclaiming the message. That's your pastor. That's me. That's every elder who teaches. That's all who are called to stand and deliver. It is to be the commitment of every church. That's a crucial part of being a place of grace... a contagious church. Being strong in grace always begins with the leadership.

Methods may differ, and taste in music may

fluctuate. But there's an appropriate limit churches must recognize. Churches don't need to try so hard to be so creative and cute that folks miss the truth. No need for meaningless and silly substitutes that dumb down God's Word. These may entertain people—even encourage them—but rarely will they convict the lost or bring believers deeper in their maturity. Teaching the truth takes care of all that. Remember Paul's words: "reprove, rebuke, exhort" (2 Tim. 4:2). Those are not politically correct terms. Why? Because God is not politically correct. He never intended to be.

Sadly, in an alarming number of churches today, God's people are being told what they *want* to hear rather than what they *need* to hear. They are being spoon-fed warm milk, not challenged to digest solid meat. A watered-down teaching ministry will usually attract crowds (for a while), but it has no eternal impact. Jesus chose and appointed us that we may bear fruit that lasts (see John 15:16). Even Jesus, by teaching the politically *incorrect* truth (but the truth nonetheless), lost some followers (see John 6:66). Nothing wrong with that. I've not been able to find any place in the Scriptures where God expresses the least bit of concern for enlarging the size of an audience as the goal of the church.

Satisfying the curious, scratching the itching ears of our postmodern audiences, is an exercise in futility. Like eating cotton candy, the experience may be delightful...but there's no food value. David Wells offers another helpful insight:

> The truth is that without a biblical under-standing of why God instituted it, the church easily becomes a liability in a mar-ket where it competes only with the greatest of difficulty against religious fare available in the convenience of one's living room and in a culture bent on distraction and enter-tainment.... The evangelical church, or at least a good slice of it, is nervous, twitchy, and touchy about consumer desire, ready to change in a nanosecond at the slightest hint that tastes and interests have changed. Why? Because consumer appetite reigns.[11]

There is a major problem with adapting a church to fit the lost person, rather than the church follow-ing God's design for what He intended it to be. Here it is, plain and simple. The church is a body of people *called out* from among the world for the distinct and unique purpose of glorifying their

Savior and Lord. Nowhere in the book of Acts or the Epistles do we see a church called to provide a subculture for nonbelievers. The lost don't need to find at church a world that's like their world outside the church. The church is not competing with the world. Jesus is not a brand.

The church needs to guard against compromising the Word of God so that it tastes more palatable to newcomers. Christians suffer when we do that. I've said for years, "Sermonettes are for Christianettes." If our churches give a little eight-minute sermon, we are not feeding the flock. Instead of teaching them, we're tantalizing them. Instead of stretching and challenging them, we're entertaining them. Our congregations need pastors who study hard, pray hard, and prepare well-balanced meals, then open the Scriptures and teach people how to study the Word for themselves. That's what gives them stability in hard times, discernment in the midst of deception, and the strength to stand alone.

But like Joshua Bell in the subway, it takes more than a gift expressed with skill to make a church contagious. It takes a context. It takes an entire church functioning as a place of grace . . . with leaders setting the pace.

In late 2007, Pastor Bill Hybels and the

leadership team of the Willow Creek Community Church shared the startling results of a study they conducted of their own church—as well as other so-called seeker churches. The results, Hybels said, were "the greatest wake-up call of my adult life." Among other findings, they discovered that their ministry to "seekers" was very effective for introducing Christ to those who were new to church. No big surprise. But they had not been as successful in fulfilling their mission statement to turn "irreligious people into fully devoted followers of Christ." That is, they had not been as strong in developing the spiritual lives of those who had trusted Christ. In a conversation Hybels had with his executive pastor, Greg Hawkins, they realized this:

> We should have started telling people and teaching people that they have to take responsibility to become self-feeders.... We should have taught people how to read their Bibles between services, how to do the spiritual practices.... What's happening to these people [is that] the older they get, the more they're expecting the church to feed them, when, in fact, the more mature a Christian becomes, a Christian should become more

of a self-feeder.... We're going to up the level of responsibility we put on the people themselves so that they can grow even if the church doesn't meet all their needs.[12]

I admire Bill for his vulnerability and candor. I applaud any church that takes spiritual growth seriously enough to evaluate its effectiveness and to modify its methods of discipleship to the biblical model. If only *all* churches would periodically take a long look into the mirror of God's Word! In fact, if evaluation is not done on a regular basis, erosion *will* occur. It can happen anywhere; I know that for a fact.

Let me urge you who are considering adopting the emerging church philosophy, or the "seeker church" strategies, to take a good look at what you are trying to do—*and why.* Be sure to look at it biblically. Be certain you can support any change you plan to implement from the Scriptures. Don't look to Mars Hill in Acts 17 while ignoring the essentials of Acts 2. Instead of searching for justification in the Bible, search and pray for direction from the biblical text. Then follow it. I would say the same thing to *any* church, including my own.

A place of grace releases and affirms; it doesn't

smother. Grace values the dignity of individuals; it doesn't destroy. Grace supports and encourages; it isn't jealous or suspicious. In the church, grace is the means by which the gospel is preached. But it also becomes the *context* where God's written commands are taught. Here's how Paul puts it:

> For the grace of God has appeared, bringing salvation to all men, instructing us to deny ungodliness and worldly desires and to live sensibly, righteously and godly in the present age, looking for the blessed hope and the appearing of the glory of our great God and Savior, Christ Jesus, who gave Himself for us to redeem us from every lawless deed, and to purify for Himself a people for His own possession, zealous for good deeds. These things speak and exhort and reprove with all authority. Let no one disregard you. (Titus 2:11–15)

Did you notice, "the grace of God has appeared ... instructing us to deny ungodliness"? I repeat it only to underscore: grace doesn't mean anything goes. Rather, grace motivates our behavior. Grace frees us to obey. Being strong in grace goes hand in hand with being committed to living the truth. There is no contradiction in those two commitments. After all, "grace and truth were realized through Jesus Christ" (John 1:17). Grace provides the context for God's commands to be taught. Truth equips our minds and shapes up our lives. Truth therefore *must* be taught! That brings us to the second characteristic of a contagious church.

A Place of Mentoring

Jesus gave the church its marching orders in practical terms. You're probably familiar with His words:

> Go therefore and make disciples of all the nations, baptizing them in the name of the Father and the Son and the Holy Spirit, teaching them to observe all that I commanded you; and lo, I am with you always, even to the end of the age. (Matthew 28:19–20)

Here in Jesus' Great Commission to His followers, we find no greater challenge...and no more comforting promise. But you probably have never considered the Great Commission as part of what makes a church contagious. The command to "make disciples" has two parts. The first, "baptizing them," assumes that we'll share our faith with the lost. The second, "teaching them to observe," directs us to share our lives of faith with those who have believed in Jesus. Returning to the second chapter of Paul's final letter to Timothy, we see the practical outworking of how the Lord intends this "teaching" to occur:

> The things which you have heard from me in the presence of many witnesses, entrust these to faithful men who will be able to teach others also. (2 Timothy 2:2)

This verse offers us our second distinctive: *churches that are contagious faithfully mentor those who are coming along in the Christian life.* The verb that gives us this direction is *entrust.* The term literally means to hand over "something to someone... for safekeeping."[13] I like that image. We invest the truth like a trust in the lives of others. We have a valuable message we pass along to others.

Paul's words to Timothy outline a process of multiplication that can be visualized in a simple chart:

Paul → *Timothy* → *faithful men and women* → *others also*

145

Paul the apostle entrusted his heart, soul, truths, confrontations, encouragements, affirmations—his very life—to Timothy. Timothy was a recipient, much like the second runner in a relay receives the baton from the first runner. Timothy then looked for others to pass that baton on to—those who would be faithful to pass it along to others also. This process has been occurring since Jesus began it with His apostles, including Paul. In fact, we are all recipients of Paul's baton. Duane Litfin, president of Wheaton College, calls this "the endless chain of Christian discipleship." The Navigators call this "the ministry of multiplication." Both are correct. It is an essential part of a contagious church.

A church is not just a gathering of people who sit and listen to one person preach. As important as the message is, it is only part of the passing of the baton. One person's life touches the life of another, who then touches the lives of people in his or her sphere of influence—those whom the originator would never have known. To make it even more exciting, those recipients, in turn, touch the lives of others also. *That* is a contagious ministry.

The medical profession models the idea of multiplication very well. They don't just educate and graduate medical students and then cut them loose, saying, "Okay, folks, lots of luck. Carve away!" How would you like to be a patient lying on the bed, about to go in for surgery, and the doctor blurts, "You know, I've never really actually done surgery, but hey, we'll give it the ol' college try. Turn on the anesthesia, Doc…and let's get 'er done!" You'd explode, "*Wait! Stop!*" Why? You want somebody who's been trained. *Really* trained. You want a skilled surgeon, one who has traveled across the country to study under the most outstanding doctor in his or her field. You want a professional, who has learned specific, tried-and-true techniques of doing medical work correctly—one who has spent years being shaped, observed, confronted, reproved, rebuked, and corrected. In a word, you need someone who has been *mentored*.

Any education is most effective when the teachers are more than mere dispensers of information. Students need a school where the professors care about the *lives* of their students, where a student is not just number 314 in the class. That's why I don't believe a theological education can take place online. (You don't learn surgery online, by the way.) *Information* can go on the Web, but an *education* requires more than data. It involves the touch of a mentor—one seasoned life poured into another inexperienced life.

Why do I say this with such conviction? I am the product of mentoring. There have been men in my life, some of whom you would not know if I mentioned their names, who have made a major difference in my life. They saw potential where I did not. They encouraged me to become something more than I was. They reproved and corrected me. They modeled what I longed to become. One of the first of these men saw the most potential in me where I saw the least.

When I began high school, I stuttered so badly I could not finish a sentence. With that speech impediment came a very low self-esteem. I learned to keep my mouth shut and maintain a low profile. The *last* place I wanted to be was in front of an audience! I managed to get through the first weeks of my freshman year without embarrassing myself too often when, one day, Dick Nieme found me at my hall locker and shocked me with his words: "Chuck, I want you on my debate team. I'd also like you to take one of my elective courses in dramatic arts."

"Who, m-m-m-m-m-m-me?" I looked over my shoulder at the guy standing behind me. I thought for sure Dr. Nieme was talking to him. "Y-y-y-y-y-y-you want hi-him. You d-d-don't want m-me."

"No, I know who I want. I want you. You've got the right stuff, young man. We just need to tap into it." I finally gave in...very reluctantly. Starting the very next week, Dr. Nieme met with me from 7:15 to 7:45 each morning before school for speech therapy sessions. Very common now. Almost unheard of back then. He helped me understand that my mind was running ahead of my ability to form the words in my mouth properly. My mind was running ahead of my mouth. (I have the *opposite* problem now.) He taught me to slow down, pace my thoughts, and concentrate on starting the words I wanted to say. He gave me exercises to hone my enunciation and give a rhythm for each syllable to follow. I joined the debate team...and, ultimately, I loved it! That led to my participating in school plays. Our drama team jelled into a top-notch bunch of young actors. We went on to enter the finals of the Texas state one-act play competition. What a blast! I hardly need to tell you, Dick Nieme was there all the way. When I failed, he coached and encouraged. At each triumph, he applauded louder than anyone else in the audience. He challenged me and inspired me, and we continued to set goals just beyond my reach.

Finally, I auditioned for the lead role in the senior

play...and landed it. When the curtain rose that night, Dick Nieme sat front row, balcony. When I came out for my bow, he was the first to stand... again, he cheered the loudest. He really embarrassed me...but I loved it. Today, more than fifty-five years later, I look back and realize how much I owe that man. He believed in me. He respected me. He started me down the path to becoming the man—the preacher—that God intended. I'm glad I was able to express my deep gratitude to him before he died. I'm glad he knew the impact he had on at least one life. I'm honored to have been invited to write his eulogy. I still give God thanks for that mentor.

The church becomes a place of mentoring when we stop seeing people as heads to count and money to collect. Instead, we view people as opportunities to build into their lives. In Paul's letter to Titus, the apostle spoke in similar terms of multiplication, just as he did with Timothy. Notice how more than information is passed on from person to person. Mentoring involves the modeling of character:

Older women likewise are to be reverent in their behavior, not malicious gossips nor enslaved to much wine, teaching what is good, so that they may encourage the young women to love their husbands, to love their children, to be sensible, pure, workers at home, kind, being subject to their own husbands, so that the word of God will not be dishonored. (Titus 2:3–5)

Another of my mentors, Howard Hendricks, says that every Christian needs at least three individuals in his or her life. We need someone who has come before us who mentors us. We need another beside us who shares our burden. And we need someone beyond us whom we're mentoring. Otherwise, we grow stagnant. The church then becomes a place where Christians sit, soak, and sour. They take notes, walk out, and come back next week… to sit, take notes, walk out, and return again next week…to sit, take more notes, and walk out… until (ho-hum) Jesus comes back. What's wrong with that picture? *Virtually everything!* There's no contagion. No application and change, personally. No passing of the baton. No multiplication. Just stagnation. I know of no one who says it clearer than Dr. Hendricks in his fine volume *Standing Together: Impacting Your Generation.* See if you catch a glimpse of yourself in his words:

Many of us in the church are under the mistaken impression that the way to produce spiritually mature Christians is to enroll people in a course on spiritual maturity. We give them books on the subject. We take them to passages of Scripture. We hand out assignments and worksheets. Nothing wrong with these activities. But has it ever occurred to you that spiritual growth is rarely the product of assimilating more information? If it were, we could have transformed the world several million books ago. But inasmuch as knowing Christ involves a *relationship*, growing in Christ also involves relationships. One of the most helpful of these involves a mentor. That's because most of us don't need to know more nearly as much as we need to *be known* more. We don't need a set of principles to practice nearly as much as we need another *person* to help us. We need someone to believe in us, stand by us, guide us, model Christ for us. We need another's encouragement, wisdom, example, and accountability. We need his smiles, his hugs, his frowns, his tears.... People will forget most of what you say; they will forget almost nothing of what you do. Therefore, whatever behavior you model for your protégé is the pattern he will tend to follow—or, in some cases, reject.[14]

Make no mistake, we all need mentors. Furthermore, we all need those we are mentoring. The church is the ideal place to connect both. When it does, it becomes a contagious place. Just as the home is the place where life training takes place, so the church is another family of sorts—a spiritual family. I read an article that mentioned the fact that 90 percent of the ministries that target a younger generation—for example, Generation X—ran into trouble after only three years.[15] Why? For one reason, because these age-targeted ministries often separate young adults from other age-groups in the church.

A contagious church comprises a body of caring women and men who see value in others and take the time to cultivate those lives. That must become a goal in our churches. Otherwise the church becomes a dusty old museum full of stuffed Christians, straight from the taxidermist. When the church fails to reproduce...it dies.

Webster defines a *mentor* as "a trusted counselor or guide; tutor, coach."[16] This describes a man I knew during a vulnerable time in my life as a young man. I was serving in the Marine Corps, stationed on the island of Okinawa…separated from my newlywed wife for about seventeen long, lonely months. I arrived at that island disheartened and disillusioned. I left transformed. The difference-maker? A mentor.

To my surprise, Bob Newkirk, a representative for the Navigators, took an interest in me as a person. We regularly played handball, ate meals, prayed, and played together. I stayed in his home on occasion. I spent holidays there when I was off duty on liberty. Bob and I did street meetings together. At those gatherings, I would lead singing, and Bob would preach. We ministered as a team. I went through an advanced Scripture-memory program, thanks to Bob. He confronted me. He pointed out blind spots. He built into my life. He loved me. I decided to return to advance my education, enter seminary, and pursue a lifetime of ministry through his influence. *That* is mentoring.

The sermons I preach, the books I write, the life I model to my family and congregation all are a direct result of mentors who have poured their lives into my life. It's their lives and the truth of Scripture that they passed on to me in mentoring that I pass along to others in my life.

I've discovered when individuals are young and unusually gifted, the most common tendency is to drift toward arrogance and, sometimes, raw conceit. Almost without exception when I detect conceit in an individual, I say to myself, *They haven't been mentored.* I have never met a self-important, arrogant individual who has been well mentored. Truth be told, arrogance doesn't survive mentoring. A mentor will point out blind spots and will reprove you appropriately when you need to be confronted about your pride. And a mentor won't back off. He or she relentlessly presses for excellence.

A church that's contagious cares enough about people to build into their lives. Never forget that. As a result of being mentored, an individual learns the value of being vulnerable, open, unguarded, honest, and, ideally, a person of authenticity.

A Place of Hardship . . . and Fellowship

There's a third distinctive of a contagious church. It involves the realities of life we often mask behind pride and—may I say it?—hypocrisy. Everybody hurts. But not everybody lives an honest and vulnerable life that admits the pain. Why? Very often, there isn't a safe place to do so. The church should be that place (second only to the home).

I heard of a research study where psychologists discovered the top three places where average people "fake it." First, we tend to put on airs when we visit the lobby of a fancy hotel. Next, we typically fake our true feelings alongside the salesperson at a new-car showroom. And the third place we wear a mask? You guessed it. In church!

Tragically, in church, where there should be authenticity, we'll paint on the phony smiles, slap backs, and masquerade to hide what is inside our hearts—the fact that in reality...we're hurting. I've often said if you could know the pain in the lives of those sitting in front of and behind you in church, you'd be shocked. Everybody hurts. We've all been shot...we're all bleeding within, including the one behind the pulpit. I love the insightful words of Dietrich Bonhoeffer:

> The pious fellowship permits no one to be a sinner. So everybody must conceal his sin from himself and from the fellowship. We dare not be sinners. Many Christians are unthinkably horrified when a real sinner is suddenly discovered among the righteous. So

we remain alone with our sin, living in lies and hypocrisy. The fact is that we *are* sinners! But it is the grace of the Gospel, which is so hard for the pious to understand, that it confronts us with the truth and says: You are a sinner, a great, desperate sinner; now come, as the sinner that you are, to God who loves you. He wants you as you are; He does not want anything from you, a sacrifice, a work; He wants you alone. "My son, give me thine heart" (Prov. 23:26). God has come to you to save the sinner. Be glad! This message is liberation through truth. You can hide nothing from God. The mask you wear before men will do you no good before Him. He wants to see you as you are, He wants to be gracious to you. You do not have to go on lying to yourself and your brothers, as if you were without sin; you can dare to be a sinner. Thank God for that; He loves the sinner but hates sin.[17]

Part of what makes a church an attractive place is when Christians aren't afraid to live transparent lives with one another. Paul's challenge to Timothy pushes past the facade and reminds us to live in reality:

Suffer hardship with me, as a good soldier of
Christ Jesus. (2 Timothy 2:3)

I like the simplicity of Paul's words...though
they are not simple to live. In the original Greek
language, the phrase "Suffer hardship with me"
translates a single verb, *sugkakopatheson,* which
means, "to endure the same kind of suffering as
others."[18] It's not a command we can obey on our
own. It requires the application of a third distinctive of a contagious church: *when tested the body
pulls closer together.* What a blessing it is when this
actually occurs! See the word *with* in the verse?
That's what makes a church attractive to others.
When one hurts, we all hurt. Nobody hurts solo.

I am privileged to be a part of a church that
has people who care. We even have a group called
Soul Care—it's made up of everyday, garden-
variety folks who come alongside others in times
of extreme difficulty. Some in our congregation are
struggling through ugly, unwanted divorces. Others are victims of rape. Some have been abused.
There are some gripped with lingering, debilitat-
ing addictions. A number have loved ones who
have special needs. Many churches will help you
find the exit when you have these challenges. (I'm

not kidding; I've seen it occur!) Instead, we welcome them. We want to help them work through the difficulties. We suffer *with* them. I don't mean to sound like we've got it all together. No, it's not that...but we do pull together, albeit imperfectly. How can that happen? We're back to that great truth: grace. Grace constantly reminds us that the ground at the foot of the cross is level.

It's like what occurred in the early church. Who would have ever thought so many Christians would have been martyred? Because of the persecution, the church pressed right on. Because they suffered together, their ranks grew. You don't find that in the world's system. When testing comes, folks usually scatter like rats on a sinking ship; it's every man for himself! There's competition. There's envy. It's all about the almighty dollar. But in the church? Grace pulls us together. It's about considering others more important than ourselves. When someone is going through a tough time, a phone call is made. Somebody shows up at his or her door. Someone brings a bag or two of groceries...sometimes a hot meal. You cannot suffer hardship with someone from a distance. In a contagious church, everybody hurts. But nobody hurts or heals alone.

This is one reason I find the prosperity gospel

movement so heretical. Nowhere in the New Testament do you find God promising health, wealth, and prosperity to those who have enough faith. That way of thinking is a direct result of consumerism-Christianity. You don't see it in the early church or anywhere in the New Testament Letters. Even the life of Jesus—One who had *complete* faith—was a life of struggle that ended with crucifixion! He was "a man of sorrows and acquainted with grief" (Isa. 53:3). How's that for prosperity? "When Christ calls a man," writes Dietrich Bonhoeffer, "He bids him come and die."[19] The normal Christian life is a cross-bearing life. It's the *next* life that promises health and prosperity. To say otherwise is to misrepresent the message of Christ, personally, and the New Testament as a whole.

The apostle Paul illustrates what he means by suffering hardship together by using three metaphors:

No soldier in active service entangles himself in the affairs of everyday life, so that he may please the one who enlisted him as a soldier. Also if anyone competes as an athlete, he does not win the prize unless he competes according to the rules. The hard-working farmer

ought to be the first to receive his share of
the crops. (2 Timothy 2:4–6)

What great analogies! A soldier...an athlete...
a farmer. The soldier reminds us that we're in a
battle, and the battle requires a serious dedication to God alone. Whoever heard of a soldier
working in the business world while carrying a
weapon on foreign soil? He or she can't do that.
There's a fight to fight. In his *Address to Martyrs*,
the church father Tertullian wrote, "No soldier
comes to the war surrounded by luxuries, nor goes
into action from a comfortable bedroom, but from
the makeshift/narrow tent, where pleasantness is to
be found." I love the way author Warren Wiersbe
puts it:

> Christian service means invading a battle-
> ground, not a playground; and you and I are
> the weapons God uses to attack and defeat
> the enemy. When God used Moses' rod, He
> needed Moses' hand to lift it. When God
> used David's sling, He needed David's hand
> to swing it. When God builds a ministry, He
> needs somebody's surrendered body to get
> the job done.[20]

In a way similar to a soldier, an athlete focuses and devotes himself or herself to the task. Evidently, Paul was a sports fan, for he used this metaphor more than once (see 1 Cor. 9:25). While every event had its prize, each one also had its rules. The athlete had to compete "according to the rules." The original term for *rules* refers to "lawfully" participating. God has left us with boundaries, and we're to live within them. Holiness. Purity of motive. Discipline. Self-control. A servant's heart. Integrity in private as well as in public. Perseverance to the end. Just like an athlete running. Tough stuff!

Paul's illustration of the farmer emphasizes the labor that accompanies any meaningful ministry. It never just happens. Blessings from God rest upon ministries that remain actively engaged in serving Him. That calls for hard work. And it often goes unnoticed. I've never seen a group of people out in a farmer's field applauding and yelling, "Great job on the tractor! Wow, look how straight that row is! Keep it up; it will be worth it!" No, instead he does all the plowing and planting, but nobody's there to see it. He wipes the sweat off his brow with a bandanna, walks inside, washes up, and eats a huge meal...and never gains a pound. Why? He's a hardworking farmer. He diligently maintains his crops.

I stayed at the home of a farmer years ago when I was ministering in the San Joaquin Valley. Behind his home he had an orange orchard with trees *loaded* with oranges. One quiet morning we walked out back together and made our way into his orchard. I reached out and plucked a huge orange off a tree. "Man, look at that orange!" I said. "To think that just happened on its own."

The farmer reached and grabbed it out of my hand. "Give me that orange. That did not 'just happen.' Chuck, I pruned this tree. I sprayed this tree. I watered this tree. I watched this tree. I prayed over this tree. This orange did not 'just happen.'"

We had a good laugh over my stupid comment.

The hardworking farmer gets the job done. Is it any wonder why so many in our generation don't want to farm? It's terribly hard work...nothing easy about it. Neither is the suffering together that ministry requires. John R. W. Stott writes,

This notion that Christian service is hard work is so unpopular in some happy-go-lucky Christian circles today that I feel the need to underline it....The blessing of God rested upon the ministry of the apostle Paul in quite exceptional measure.... I find myself wondering if we attribute it sufficiently to the zeal and zest, the almost obsessional devotion, with which he gave himself to the work.[21]

We have hard work ahead of us as the body of Christ. That includes praying together as we've not prayed before. That includes laboring to make our fellowships places of grace. That includes pouring our lives into one another, mentoring those younger in the faith. It also means that we endure hardship with one another. Show me a church that is contagious, attracting people from far and wide, and I'll show you a group of Christians devoted to hard work—regardless of the cost. That brings us to the fourth and final distinctive.

A Place of Selfless Endurance

The last characteristic we'll examine can be summed up this way: *because of Jesus Christ, the church must endure every difficulty for the benefit of others.* I find this principle again in Paul's writings to Timothy:

For this reason I endure all things for the sake of those who are chosen, so that they also may

obtain the salvation which is in Christ Jesus
and with it eternal glory. (2 Timothy 2:10)

The key to this principle is found in the verb
endure. The term *hupomeno* is a compound word—
from *hupo,* meaning "under," and *meno,* meaning,
"to abide."[22] We are expected to "abide under."
The idea is that we continue to stand firm underneath the difficulty and suffering that faithfulness requires. We endure every difficulty. We hold
together. We don't whine. We don't quit. Leaders
don't resign just because things get tough. We keep
our word. We aren't self-serving. We maintain our
integrity. The reason? Paul tells us: "for the sake of
those who are chosen, so that they also may obtain
the salvation which is in Christ Jesus and with it
eternal glory" (2 Tim. 2:10). We don't cave in to
the culture or soften and lower the standard. We
stay on message, and we consistently share that
message with others. We don't drift from making
Him known.

I like the story Charles Paul Conn tells in his
book *Making It Happen*:

When I lived in Atlanta, several years ago, I
noticed in the *Yellow Pages*, in the listing of

restaurants, an entry for a place called, Church of God Grill. The peculiar name aroused my curiosity so I dialed the number. A man answered with a cheery, "Hello! Church of God Grill!" I asked how his restaurant had been given such an unusual name, and he told me: "Well, we had a little mission down here, and we started selling chicken dinners after church on Sunday to help pay the bills. Well, people liked the chicken, and we did such a good business, that eventually we cut back on the church stuff. After a while we just closed the door to the church altogether and kept on serving chicken dinners. We kept the name that we started with, and that's the Church of God Grill."[23]

I am committed that Stonebriar Community Church will not someday become Stonebriar Community Grill. I pray the same is true of your church. *Grace...mentoring...fellowship...endurance.* If our churches added these distinctives to the essentials of Acts 2:42, we couldn't contain the crowds. Our churches would be incredibly unique, amazingly attractive. In a word, *contagious*.

It's one thing to agree that a church needs to have

these qualities. But how do we sustain them? How do we maintain our focus while living in a consumerist, postmodern culture? Here's the answer: *we must remember these distinctives and resist any sign of erosion.* Easy to say... but challenging to do. We must commit as a local church that we're not going to drift from the essentials of Acts 2:42 or from the distinctives of a contagious church.

If we drift, we change our whole identity. And when that happens we look and sound just like any other office building in town.

* * *

In our marketing-driven culture, many churches struggle with staying on task. A desire for church growth often overrides a commitment to biblical principles. How tragic... and unnecessary. A growing, contagious church includes each part of the body functioning as a healthy, caring, growing, and maturing whole. It's all about context. But as important as it is, even being a contagious church is not the *primary* purpose for the body to gather together on Sunday mornings. It's still something else.

That mound of stone Paul once stood on named Mars Hill was not the church. Paul's message to the intellectuals in Athens was never intended to be a model for our worship services. It *is*, however, a great example for personal *evangelism*. Does evangelism occur in the church? Absolutely! I can't remember a single Sunday morning service when I haven't shared the gospel message in some way. But evangelism isn't the *primary* purpose for believers to assemble on the Lord's Day. The reason isn't even "teaching them to obey"—though that, too, occurs. The Great Commission is the purpose of the universal church, lived out in the *daily* lives of the local church members. Even the essentials of Acts 2:42—*teaching, fellowship, breaking of bread,* and *prayer*—are but the means through which Christian assemblies pursue their primary purpose on Sundays.

Then, what's the main reason for the church to gather?

Read on...

Worship: A Commitment... Not a War

Most middle-class Americans tend to worship their work, to work at their play, and to play at their worship. As a result, their meanings and values are distorted. Their relationships disintegrate faster than they can keep them in repair, and their lifestyles resemble a cast of characters in search of a plot.

—Gordon Dahl

Worship: A Commitment... Not a War

Though small in size, the book *Tyranny of the Urgent* packs a wallop. In order to help remind myself of its message, I carried this booklet so long it became torn and tattered. Its warning became permanently etched in my brain. The little book addresses the difference between the things that are urgent in life and the things that are important. It cautions us against allowing the urgent to crowd out the important. They are not the same. The author, Charles E. Hummel, describes the problem:

> When we stop long enough to think about it, we realize that our dilemma goes deeper than shortage of time; it is basically a problem of priorities.... We sense uneasily our failure to do what was really important. The winds of

other people's demands, and our own inner compulsions, have driven us onto a reef of frustration.[1]

When our thirty-fourth president, Dwight D. Eisenhower, began his administration, he instructed his aides and his executive assistant that there should be only two stacks of papers placed on his desk in the Oval Office. The first would be a stack of those things that were urgent, and only the extremely urgent. The other was to be a stack of the important, and only the extremely important. He said years later that it was interesting to him how rarely the two were one and the same. He was right.

The conflict between the urgent and the important is inescapable. How easy to get the two confused! It is common for us to think that by staying busy and working hard we're dealing with the important things. But that is not necessarily the case. Those things most urgent *rarely* represent the things most important. And therein lies the reason so many people today feel such a lack of satisfaction after working so hard and for so many hours each day.

Not only is that frustration true in the world in

which we live, it is all the more true in the church we attend. When we substitute the urgent for the important in the church of Jesus Christ, we emphasize work, activity, involvement, doing, producing, impressing, and accomplishing. But it leaves us feeling flat and empty. Exhaustion replaces satisfaction. Furthermore, it smacks of the secularized world in which we work. Who knows how many people have been turned away from Christianity, longing for the true, living God but encountering at their church a secularized substitute?

Perhaps this helps explain why so many activities in so many churches distract from the one essential ingredient that makes a church unique in this postmodern society: *worship*. Author Gordon Dahl analyzes the issue better than anyone I've heard in years:

> Most middle-class Americans tend to worship their work, to work at their play, and to play at their worship. As a result, their meanings and values are distorted. Their relationships disintegrate faster than they can keep them in repair, and their lifestyles resemble a cast of characters in search of a plot.[2]

What a profound statement! Worshiping our work...working at our play...playing at our worship. *It was never meant to be that way.*

When we look at life with a horizontal perspective, the urgent takes center stage. It is loud. It is popular. It is product-oriented. The horizontal highlights all things human...like human achievement, human importance, human logic, human significance, human opinion, human efficiency, human results. It demands our time and attention. As that ever-present tyranny screams at us, the most natural reaction is to yield, giving it our first priority. After all, *it's urgent!* We're very familiar with its voice.

The important things, however, are different. They are quiet and deep. They are vertical in their perspective. They highlight the things of God— God's Word, God's will, God's plan, God's people, God's way, God's reason for living, God's glory, and God's honor. And the goal of all these? God's *worship.*

The underlying objective of a church committed to the important things—rather than the urgent— is the cultivation of a body of worshipers whose sole focus is on the Lord our God.

The Irreplaceable Priority

Not surprisingly, Jesus addressed the subject of worship on a number of occasions. The first instance that comes to mind is tucked away in the fourth chapter of John's Gospel. In the context, Jesus is talking to a Samaritan woman in the geographical region of Samaria. Two things are scandalous about that scene. First, it was unthinkable that a Jewish man, particularly a rabbi, would talk to a Samaritan woman as Jesus did—with words of dignity and honor. Second, it was extraordinary that a Jew would even be *found* in Samaria! The racial tension between Jews and Samaritans was centuries old, and no geographical spot was more avoided by the Jews than Samaria. Jesus ignored those long-standing scruples and spoke to her at the point of her deepest need:

> "Go, call your husband and come here." The woman answered and said, "I have no husband." Jesus said to her, "You have correctly said, 'I have no husband'; for you have had five husbands, and the one whom you now

have is not your husband; this you have said truly." (John 4:16–18)

She didn't even know this man, and suddenly He revealed the dark secrets of her life. She was embarrassed. Her heart beat faster. She felt the weight of her guilt. So she quickly shifted the subject from her...to Him—and to matters of worship. People do strange things when their lives are exposed.

Sir, I perceive that You are a prophet. Our fathers worshiped in this mountain, and you people say that in Jerusalem is the place where men ought to worship. (John 4:19–20)

On a recent trip to the Holy Land, I heard this comment spoken by modern Jews: "If you want to party, go to Tel Aviv. If you want to do business, go to Haifa. If you want to worship, go to Jerusalem." Interesting, isn't it? Even today, as in the first century, Jews say that Jerusalem is the place for worship. But Jesus clarified that this is not true:

Woman, believe Me, an hour is coming when neither in this mountain nor in Jerusalem will you worship the Father. You worship what you do not know; we worship what we know, for salvation is from the Jews. (John 4:21–22)

Jesus took the time to teach her that worship is not connected to a *place* but to a *Person*. The problem she had wasn't a lack of knowledge about where to worship, but a lack of connection with the One whom she was worshiping. Jesus declared that worship is not some mystical groping in the dark after an unknowable deity. Rather, it begins with a clear, definitive, conscious connection with the living God. Jesus had the audacity to claim she lacked that connection! "Salvation," He emphasized, "is from the Jews." Now, notice Jesus didn't say, "*for* the Jews." Salvation isn't exclusively Jewish. But the *source* of salvation is exclusive: it came from the Jews through Jesus Christ. To worship God the Father, an individual must come *through* Jesus. That includes both Jews and Gentiles (see John 14:6; Rom. 1:16).

Sound pretty narrow? *It is.* Don't be afraid of the narrowness. We're living in a pluralistic, postmodern era when people don't care what your god is, as long as you're sincere. (There's a great Hebrew word for that way of thinking: *hogwash!*) It *does* matter in whom you believe. Let's be very clear about that.

177

Through *Jesus* you came to know the living God. Salvation is by faith alone through Christ alone. *Jesus* is why you have peace in your heart. *Jesus* is the reason you're ready to live and also, when necessary, ready to die. *Jesus* is why you can worship the living God. It is not politically correct, but it is biblically accurate to say that the Lord Jesus Christ is the only mediator between God and humankind (see 1 Tim. 2:5). Make no mistake: the means of salvation *is* narrow. Jesus said that "the gate is small and the way is narrow that leads to life" (Matt. 7:14). Clearly, Jesus is that way. The fact that there is a way to God *at all* is because of His amazing grace.

Jesus went on to tell the Samaritan woman how those properly connected with God will worship Him:

> But an hour is coming, and now is, when the true worshipers will worship the Father in spirit and truth; for such people the Father seeks to be His worshipers. (John 4:23)

If I'm not mistaken, this is the only place in the Bible where we read that God seeks something from us. And what is it He seeks from His followers? *God seeks our worship.* He loves it when we connect with Him . . . when we are preoccupied with Him alone. We're not to "play at our worship." The Father wants us to worship Him with our spirits fully engaged. We also worship Him according to the truth found in the Scriptures. Stay with that thought. It will unlock the door to our understanding of what true worship is.

What Worship Represents—Its Essence

When we think of worship in the context of church, we usually think of praying and singing. Although worship often does occur when we do these things, its meaning lies much deeper. The Hebrew term for *worship* has at its root the action of bowing down.[3] Interestingly, the root Greek word for worship, *proskuneo*, refers to the custom of "prostrating oneself before a person and kissing his feet," which carries the idea of giving honor.[4] Our English word *worship* comes from the old Anglo-Saxon term *weorthscipe*, or "worth-ship." It means to attribute worth to someone or something.[5] Therefore, when referring to the worship of our God, it is attributing supreme worth to Him who alone is worthy of our praise and honor. Go back and read that again.

Worship is significant because it turns our full attention to the only One worthy of it. Worship underscores our celebration of everything that brings honor to our God. In giving Him honor—when we have truly worshiped—there is something so deeply satisfying and gratifying that words cannot describe it. Its importance eclipses all things urgent.

During the journey to Israel I mentioned earlier, our group of more than six hundred sat around patio tables alongside the Sea of Galilee. The sun had set behind the hills above us as a full moon rose on the far side of the sea and reflected across the water. It was an unforgettable visual feast. Almost impromptu, our worship leader rose and led our group in singing. One of the songs was Lanny Wolfe's "Surely the Presence of the Lord Is in This Place." I closed my eyes as I listened to what we were singing. To borrow from the words of Charles Wesley's hymn, I was "lost in wonder, love and praise."[6] It was marvelous. But it wasn't because I was in the Holy Land (remember, worship isn't connected to a *place*). For a moment, in fact, I forgot there was a full moon. I forgot that I was on the Galilean shore where Jesus once walked. What was happening? True worship. I was focused fully on

God. My thoughts were of Him and Him alone. In various ways I reflected on how much He means to me…how magnificent He is…and I wanted Him to know that I meant every word I was singing.

Because God seeks our worship, it stands to reason that the church is to represent both a place of worship…and a place that cultivates worshipers. It isn't a place to make business contacts. Church isn't about being entertained. It isn't even about being a place that makes you feel good. It is, first and foremost, about *worship*.

Let's go further. The *essence* of worship does not refer to external, localized actions we perform. Worship is inward. It has to do with the mind, the heart. Worship is the personal contemplation and adoration of God. It is the natural response of those who recognize who God is and what He has done on our behalf. The *essence* of worship has to do with our internalizing our adoration. When we worship we affirm a deep, personal commitment. That is what God seeks.

The *expression* of worship, on the other hand, moves us into the outward forms of worship…the ways we express our praise to God. *That* may be as varied as whatever culture is expressing it. Some are quite effusive and expressive; others are more reserved. But let's never forget, the essence remains the same. A correct understanding of the *essence* of worship is integral to a correct *expression* of worship. The first always lays the groundwork for the second.

How Worship Connects—Its Expression

Worship is a verb. It is something we *do*. With that understanding, worship in the church can occur in many different ways. We have looked before at the essentials of a church, but let's consider them again in the context of worship:

> They were continually devoting themselves to the apostles' teaching and to fellowship, to the breaking of bread and to prayer. Everyone kept feeling a sense of awe. (Acts 2:42–43)

If the essence of worship is internal, we see the expression of worship in these external actions. How do we know these represent acts of worship? "They were *continually devoting* themselves." Worship's expression is not some halfhearted, haphazard religious activity we do with a shrug. Rather, it's a matter of devotion. It's from an internal passion. It stems from the essence of worship.

When you hear a message from your pastor, rather than passively listening, you are actively engaged. You are devoting yourself wholeheartedly to truths that are worthy of your time and attention. As he preaches through a passage of Scripture, you have your finger on the text—if not literally, at least mentally. You are serious about the Word of God. Your participation replaces false information—or maybe traditional information, half true and half not—with accurate information. The teaching of the Word becomes your nourishment. It points you to critical reminders about God. When we learn about our God through the faithful and passionate preaching of His Word, our worship of Him grows increasingly deeper, more meaningful, and understandable. Listening and responding to biblical teaching in this way is an act of worship.

Worship also adds a dimension to relationships that go beyond common friendship. And why is that? The presence of the Lord is in the fellowship, making it invigorating and magnetic. That's why, when a service of worship is over, many say, "I don't want to leave." There's nothing magical or magnetic about the seats. It's the "sense of awe" we just read about in Acts 2:43. It's the invisible, magnificent presence of God. When that awe occurs in fellowship, it becomes worship at its best. Or to quote my youngest granddaughter, "It's *awe-some!*"

In chapter 1 we generalized the ordinance of breaking of bread, as well as the ordinance of baptism, by the all-inclusive term *worship*. You will recall that in the Lord's Table, or Communion, we are completely focused on Him as we remember the Savior's body and blood. Such worship is deeply satisfying and cleansing to our souls.

Church worship also includes protracted times of silence. True worship includes prevailing and purposeful intercession. No clichés. No empty repetitions. No mindless mantras. We remember families in prayer...those who grieve, who struggle, who rejoice. We intercede for the women and men in the military who serve in dangerous and lonely places. We pray for those who are in prison for their faith. Prayer in church is a worshipful act.

See the connection? The essence of worship forms the foundation of its expression in *teaching, fellowship, breaking of bread,* and *prayer.* Worship is not an agenda item in the Sunday bulletin. Worship doesn't end when the songs cadence. Worship is as much what you bring to the service as what you do there. It is an *inclination of the heart* to glorify God.

But worship isn't limited to these four expressions. Not at all! We're most familiar with corporate worship expressed in music. Paul even commands that we do so:

> Let the word of Christ richly dwell within you, with all wisdom teaching and admonishing one another with psalms and hymns and spiritual songs, singing with thankfulness in your hearts to God. (Colossians 3:16)

Even instrumental music can be used to praise the Lord:

> *Praise Him with trumpet sound;*
> *Praise Him with harp and lyre.*
> *Praise Him with timbrel and dancing;*
> *Praise Him with stringed instruments and pipe.*
> *Praise Him with loud cymbals;*
> *Praise Him with resounding cymbals.* (Psalm 150:3–5)

When we sing, we sing for Him alone. When we listen to someone singing or playing a solo—although we may be impressed with the person's musicianship and grateful for the voice—our focus is on the worship of our God. When one plays an instrument, he or she plays for God's glory. Music is a marvelous vehicle through which we can express our praise to Him, our gratitude, and our expression of His value because He alone is worthy.

Now is a good time for me to mention that, if you find a congregation where music has a proper and prominent place, centering its message on the Word of God, you have found a rare church. Don't lose that place. Music is not seen as some preliminary or a warm-up act to what's "really important" in the pulpit. Music is not squeezed in at the beginning. It's not filler until the preacher stands up. Music is a vital part of worship. God has given us song, and He wants us to sing! Music is but one means—a powerful one—through which we can worship God as a congregation. God intends our corporate worship to be a unified voice directed at Him—*for* Him.

But tragically, another word has fastened itself like a barnacle to worship, resulting in an awful oxymoron: *worship wars*. Can you think of any terms more contradictory than these two?

What Worship Was Never
Meant to Be—A War

A war is raging and it's taking a terrible toll. The war began sometime back in the 1980s . . . it intensified as the 1990s arrived . . . and it seemed to reach its zenith around the turn of the century. There isn't bloodshed, but there are casualties. Countless people have been wounded. Disillusioned, disenchanted, and displaced, many people have decided that the conflict proves the church is a joke . . . so they have drifted off. Some of them have yet to return. The battle became too severe.

What is the war? It occurs when Christians clash over the *expression* of worship. Traditional style versus contemporary, organs versus bands, choirs versus teams, coat and tie versus jeans and T-shirts, hymns versus choruses, hymnals versus screens, long messages versus sermonettes, King James Version versus *The Message*—and the list goes on. Get the picture? It's a war of *expression*. Of my expression versus yours. Most wouldn't *believe* the infighting that occurs around these themes!

What God intended for His glory and for our corporate and personal growth—worship—has been transformed from a soul-deep commitment to an ugly, carnal fight. Christ promised that the gates of Hades would not prevail against the church. And yet this war has hurled shrapnel into the body of Christ and pockmarked Christian unity. If there is anything that brings delight to Satan, it is the disruption of the worship of God. Surely this must grieve the heart of our Lord! This is a war that was never meant to be.

Almost every year I take a road trip with our church's interns in order to visit other congregations. On one of those journeys, we spent some time with several churches; all of them were engaged in worship wars. We discovered that in some of them their seats were filled with just the younger generation. When I noticed this, I asked one pastor, "What are your demographics here?" I was interested in the community in which the church was located.

"Well, we don't have many old people," he answered.

"What's old?"

"Oh, I guess we'd say over forty."

"So, where are they?"

"They've left."

"Yes, but *where* are they?"

"I . . . I don't know." You would have thought he had *never* given this question a moment's thought.

"As a pastor, doesn't that bother you?" I pressed the question further: "Doesn't the church include every part of the body—young and old? Aren't both found in your surrounding community? Obviously, you don't want a church of all old folks, but do you really want a congregation with none who are older and more mature? Who will mentor the young if the mature leave?"

He was silent. He had no reply.

"Let me ask you this," I continued. "Why don't you want your church to look like a church?"

"Well, people are turned off by the church," he replied quickly and confidently.

"Of course they are," I said, "by the *wrong kind* of church. But when it's inclusive, and when all ages and stages are welcome, it's like a magnet."

As we were leaving, he put his arm around me and said, "I want to thank you for asking me some hard questions."

"I'm not trying to be ugly or cantankerous; I mean that," I assured him. "But don't keep doing this. You're going to regret it because your flock won't grow. Can you find *any* place in the Scriptures to justify what you're doing?"

"No."

"Then why *on earth* are you doing it?"

I will never forget that blank stare.

The Problem: Self-Serving Traditions

Without wanting to be misunderstood, let me say unashamedly that I love the grand old hymns. Throughout my Christian life I have treasured their historic statement of the church's faith, having committed many of them to memory. They have been my dearest companions in dark hours of loneliness and discouragement and my greatest encouragers in times of celebration and adoration. And while I'm the first to admit that there's nothing holy about a hymnal *per se,* hymns remain an important part of our Christian heritage. Why? Because the theology of hymns is far too rich and beneficial to lose. The hymn writers were wordsmiths and musicians (seldom the same person) who wove theology and melody together into splendid compositions. They gave us words for worship and marvelous music. One of the benefits of music—whatever style you choose—is that it helps cement truth in our brains stronger than memorizing words alone. We remember words easier with a tune attached. Hymns bring to mind deep and practical truths, not only for times of worship, but also for times of trial and distress. I have always loved the old hymns, and I always will . . . because the truths they express are timeless.

However, let me quickly add that the canon isn't closed on music for worship. In addition to hymns, each new generation will continue to compose fresh choruses of worship and new songs of praise . . . and that is as it should be—it's biblical! Those churches who believe we should *only* have hymns have forgotten the words of David, the sweet psalmist of Israel, who wrote: "I will sing *a new song* to You, O God; upon a harp of ten strings I will sing praises to You" (Ps. 144:9, emphasis added). The prophet Isaiah and the apostle John would later use similar words (see Isa. 42:10; Rev. 5:9). The worship of our Creator should stay fresh and creative. David Wells offers this helpful perspective:

It would be quite unrealistic to think that evangelicalism today could look exactly as it did fifty years ago, or a hundred, or five hundred. At the same time, the truth by which it is constituted never changes because God, whose truth it is, never changes. There should therefore be threads of continuity that bind real Christian believing in all ages. It is some of those threads, I believe, that are now being lost.[7]

There is everything right about singing new songs. But we must be certain that the songs we compose and sing express sound doctrine and not man-centered philosophy. Simply claiming, "The Lord gave me this song," doesn't qualify it for public worship. (There have been times I had wished the singer would give the song *back* to the Lord!) Even Christians in the first century were urged to "test" the words they heard (see 1 John 4:1–6). Furthermore, a good melody should never override our critical thinking. Harmony doesn't supercede heresy. Lyrics take on significance only when they are filtered through the inerrant text of the Holy Scriptures. The music can be new…but the truths the music proclaims must not be. I would also add that earsplitting volume doesn't prove sincerity, nor does it replace excellent musicianship.

Some claim that contemporary songs and praise choruses have too much "meaningless repetition." Ever heard that objection? I have. But consider the question: does repetition alone disqualify a song as meaningless? My friend Don Wyrtzen—who composed the theme music for our *Insight for Living* radio broadcast—said he is glad that George Fredric Handel didn't know about the objection to repetition when he wrote the "Hallelujah Chorus." Talk about repetition! But meaningless? Hardly. Repetition of truth is never without meaning, if the worshiper is sincere (see Rev. 4:8!).

I'll say it again: the *essence* of worship drives our *expression* of worship. Whether it's a chorus written two weeks ago, or a hymn written two centuries ago, a statement of genuine, biblical worship set to music is always appropriate in the body of Christ.

I find it interesting that only the words of the Psalms were inspired—and yet they were also set to music...music that fit their ancient culture. They originally had specific tunes, to be sure. For example, in the New International Version, the superscript of Psalm 22 reads, "For the director of music. To the tune of 'The Doe of the Morning.' A psalm of David." (See also Pss. 9; 45; 56; 60; 69; 75; 80.) My point? The accompanying music wasn't inspired, and so Paul's admonition to sing psalms allows for a variety of musical expressions (see Col. 3:16).

I'm amazed at how some hymns have melodies that originally had nothing to do with their lyrics. A number of these tunes started out as secular songs—and yet many folks hold the melody itself on par with the inspired Word of God! *Please.* There's a warning here to remember: sometimes we can misinterpret tradition for inspiration. When *any* man-made tradition or expression of worship—old or new—is held on equal par with the Scriptures, we have gone too far. When we demand our own tradition—be it one of music, dress, a particular translation, you name it—the requirement we insist on results in nothing less than legalism. This brings us to another occurrence when Jesus spoke on worship. But this kind of worship is *not* what God seeks.

> Then some Pharisees and scribes came to Jesus from Jerusalem and said, "Why do Your disciples break the tradition of the elders? For they do not wash their hands when they eat bread." (Matthew 15:1–2)

Jesus' disciples didn't wash their hands a certain way before eating, and the Pharisees and scribes got all hot and bothered. Understand, it wasn't an issue of hygiene but of the tedious rules of tradition. The religious leaders followed a practice that required them to meticulously wash their hands before eating lest they themselves become ritually defiled. The "tradition of the elders" represented the customs and detailed rules of behavior derived from rabbinic interpretation of Old Testament law (see Mark 7:8–9, 13; Gal. 1:14; Col. 2:8). In the time of Christ, these traditions were mostly oral, but they would become codified more than one hundred years later and form what is called the *Mishnah*. In this "tradition of the elders," a single command in the Old Testament may have hundreds of specific applications, such as the way one washed his hands before eating a meal. The Pharisees viewed this oral tradition as having authority *on par with the Scriptures*. Does that tune sound familiar? This is a perfect example of a first-century worship war. "You don't observe our traditions," the Pharisees griped. I love Jesus' answer:

> Why do you yourselves transgress the commandment of God for the sake of your tradition? For God said, "HONOR YOUR FATHER AND MOTHER," and, "HE WHO SPEAKS EVIL OF FATHER OR MOTHER IS TO BE PUT TO DEATH." But you say, "Whoever says to his father or mother, 'Whatever I have that would help you has been given to God,' he is not to honor his father or his mother." (Matthew 15:3–6)

195

Notice how Jesus contrasted their tradition with the Bible: "*God* said…But *you* say.…" Jesus had heard enough. He knew their motive. He could see their hearts. Their minds were filled with judgmentalism. They sounded so righteous, but their actions revealed hypocrisy. Jesus continued quoting Scripture, but this time He applied the text to the religious leaders with a slamming indictment:

And by this you invalidated the word of God for the sake of your tradition. You hypocrites, rightly did Isaiah prophesy of you: "THIS PEOPLE HONORS ME WITH THEIR LIPS, BUT THEIR HEART IS FAR AWAY FROM ME. BUT IN VAIN DO THEY WORSHIP ME, TEACHING AS DOCTRINES THE PRECEPTS OF MEN." (Matthew 15:6–9)

Tradition is not inspired. The precepts of men are not the doctrines of God. They never will be! God doesn't want our lips just to mouth the words or sing the songs. That is not true worship. The Father seeks those who worship in spirit and truth. He wants *all* of us to praise Him: lips, hearts, thoughts, actions, every part of who we are. He wants us to love Him with our *entire* being (see

Deut. 6:5; Matt. 22:37). Otherwise, as God said of the hypocrites, "in vain do they worship Me" (Matt. 15:9). After Jesus offered this stinging rebuke, the disciples asked the obvious:

> Do You know that the Pharisees were offended when they heard this statement? (Matthew 15:12)

You think?

The Pharisees always took offense to truth. (They still do, by the way.) When a sense of personal preference lords over biblical priorities, the worship of God is vain and meaningless. Why? Because it's really the worship of self.

On one hand, the freethinkers in the church today, who stand firmly in favor of worship wars, kick historical tradition in the teeth. They label long-standing practices as woefully irrelevant, out of date, and useless in a postmodern world. And if you happen to be one who still embraces historical tradition, you are considered a dinosaur.

On the other hand, I have seen those who favor traditional worship sing their hearts out in a hymn. But one moment later, they cross their arms and refuse to sing a chorus projected on a screen. "I don't know the song," they scowl. I want to ask them, "Is that the real issue? You can learn, can't you? 'Sing to the Lord a *new* song,' remember?"

Truth be told, the problem at the heart of worship wars lies on *both* sides of the battlefield. Both camps reveal by their words and actions: "I will worship God only *my* way! Moreover, *you* should worship God my way as well." It was this type of hypocrisy that Jesus vehemently exposed. Worship wars are fueled by personal preference (on both sides!), rarely by biblical priorities.

I was serving a church years ago that traditionally had started every worship service with the doxology. No kidding, *every* service. The unstated rule could be summed up in the words of an age-old benediction: "As it was in the beginning... it is now and ever shall be... the doxology must be at the beginning." That's how it seemed! So one morning I said, "Let's sing it at the end of our service for a change." Well, you would have thought I had canceled the Rapture! The backlash was amazing. I even had an older gentleman say to me, "I didn't know it would work at the end." Work? It's a *doxology*, which Webster's defines as "a hymn or form of words containing an ascription of praise to God."[8] It was hard to change that long-standing tradition, to be sure. But it was important that we did because that church's tradition had become our dictator. The expression of worship had been confused for the essence of worship.

Do you serve in church leadership in some way? Let me urge you to examine your worship service. Is it the same order of service every time? Have you always done it the way you do it? Why? Try adding some variety to your services. Sing some songs without any instruments. Try various melodies with familiar words. Risk changing things up! And don't be afraid of silence, where you stand in silence before your God. I promise you that it will enhance your worship. It will scrape the scales off your eyes. It will bring creativity to your gatherings. You'll be surprised how refreshing worship will become if the flock is mature enough—and prepared beforehand—to handle the change. Remember Jesus' words: "You are experts at setting aside the commandment of God in order to keep your tradition" (Mark 7:9). That verse serves as a warning to *all* religious leaders. We should always evaluate what we're doing—and *why*—based on these wise words of Jesus. Tradition should never become our dictator. The truths in God's Word allow for a variety of expressions.

The Solution: Self-Sacrificing Attitudes

One of the things I most appreciate about the Protestant Reformation is its rediscovery of congregational singing. The great Reformer Martin Luther had a passion for the worship of God, and his original hymn, based on Psalm 46, "A Mighty Fortress Is Our God," became the anthem of the Reformation. A number of sixteenth-century historians have claimed that Luther "won more converts to Christ through his encouragement of congregational singing than even through his strong preaching and teaching."[9] Luther, the old Wittenberg monk, was right:

> Next to the Word of God, music deserves the highest praise. The gift of language combined with the gift of song was given to man that he should proclaim the Word of God through music.[10]

Luther's passion for worship was matched only by his zeal for sound doctrine. Often his diatribes against the long-standing, unbiblical traditions of his day spewed venom at the religious leaders.

Luther's close friend, Philipp Melanchthon, was a marvelous balance to Luther and helped soften the rough edges of the passionate Reformer. Melanchthon had a credo, a philosophy of life, which still rings true today. It is as profound as it is brief: "In essentials, unity. In nonessentials, liberty. In all things, charity." (Read that again.) What a helpful maxim to remember when the noisy din of worship wars threatens the unity of our congregations!

Let's examine the three parts of Melanchthon's words. First, "In essentials, unity." In other words, on those issues absolutely fundamental to our Christian faith, we should all agree without deviation. These are the essentials worth fighting for, the doctrines that ignited the Reformation. Around these basic tenets of our faith there should be unity. On the night before Jesus died, He prayed for His disciples . . . and He prayed for us:

> My prayer is not for them alone. I pray also for those who will believe in me through their message, that all of them may be one, Father, just as you are in me and I am in you. May they also be in us so that the world may believe that you have sent me. (John 17:20–21 NIV)

201

Christ's plan for the church is not uniformity...
not unanimity...but *unity*. What a contrast!
When you are connected with the traditions of
men, you are soon being told to get in line. In other
words, "Wear the uniform." "Believe as I believe...
no more, no less. Unless you conform, you can get
out." "Every jot and tittle of my list must become
your list." *That* is uniformity. Jesus didn't pray that
for us. Thank goodness! He didn't even pray that
we might have unanimity. It's doubtful the church
has *ever* been unanimous on *anything*. (Even your
church.) Jesus didn't pray that we would be uni-
formed or have unanimity, but that there would be
unity in the essentials.

Second, "In nonessentials, liberty." That means
that on those issues not fundamental to our faith,
we should extend grace to other believers who have
different opinions. These are the issues we should
not fight over, which would include expressions of
worship. As I've said before, believing in grace is
one thing, but living it is another.

Years ago my good friend Chuck Smith, pastor
of Calvary Chapel in Costa Mesa, California, was
faced with a problem when hippies started attending his church. But the problem wasn't with the
new attendees...it was with the congregation! The

fellowship of believers at that time was serious and a bit...well, rigid. When the hippies in bare feet and torn jeans started pouring in to hear Chuck's simple yet sound teaching of the Word of God, some of the church's board members became concerned. One of them, in fact, got really uptight and said to Chuck, "What in the world are we going do when the rivets on their Levis begin to scratch our pews?"

"We take out the pews," Chuck replied without hesitation.

I love that answer! You know why? Because it's the perfect expression of Melanchthon's words: "In nonessentials, liberty." Some don't like that answer, because they've always had pews...or they've always sung the doxology at the beginning...or they've always read from the King James Version only. They are entrenched in their own comfort zone. Human traditions die hard. When nonessentials threaten unity, they *should* die.

Nonessentials would include expressions of worship, but never the essence of worship. In practical terms, "nonessential" refers to guitars, pipe organs, pianos, a cappella singing, choirs in robes, full orchestra, full band, praise ensembles, pews, or no pews—*any* means of expression. None of these are essentials worth going to the mat for. Each has its place, each can be a meaningful expression of true worship, but each can become a battlefield of controversy. Far too often we are ready to fight as if the nonessentials are essential. This is not the kind of worship the Father seeks.

Finally, "In all things, charity." Regardless of the subject—essentials or nonessentials—Christians' love for one another should be preeminent. As mentioned in the previous chapter, our churches should be marked by grace. Our congregations become contagious fellowships when they are "strong in the grace that is in Christ Jesus" (2 Tim. 2:1). But when we quibble over things like musical styles and church decor, we confirm to a watching world of skeptics that we are no different from anyone else. Grace is hidden. As Paul writes,

> Beyond all these things put on love, which is the perfect bond of unity. Let the peace of Christ rule in your hearts, to which indeed you were called in one body; and be thankful. Let the word of Christ richly dwell within you, with all wisdom teaching and admonishing one another with psalms and hymns and spiritual songs, singing with thankfulness in your hearts to God. (Colossians 3:14–16)

Did you notice how love, unity, peace, and worship are in the same context? That's not a typo. Christian unity and genuine worship can occur only in a context of love. What causes worship wars in the church, then, is exactly the opposite of love. Look how the apostle James expressed it:

What causes fights and quarrels among you? Don't they come from your desires that battle within you? (James 4:1 NIV)

I like the explanation *The Expositor's Bible Commentary* offers for this verse:

Instead of the climate of peace necessary for the production of righteousness (3:18), James's readers were living in an atmosphere of constant "fights and quarrels." These two nouns (*polemoi* and *machai*) were normally used of national warfare, but they had also become common, forceful expressions for any kind of open antagonism. James asks, "What causes fights and quarrels among you?" His answer, with which he expects his reader to agree, is "Don't they come from your desires?" The term *hedonon* (NIV,

205

"desires") means "pleasures." It is the source of the English word "hedonism," the designation of the philosophy that views pleasure as the chief goal of life. James pictures these pleasures as residing within his readers, there carrying on a bitter campaign to gain satisfaction. Pleasure is the overriding desire of their lives. Nothing will be allowed to stand in the way of its realization.[11]

I find it fascinating that the original terms for "fights and quarrels" referred to warfare. And we thought worship wars were a product of the twentieth and twenty-first centuries! They were alive and well in the first century, too. The source of the conflict? It's always the same: the priority of pleasing self. When self-centered desires reign supreme, there will never be unity in the body of Christ, much less in worship. But when self-sacrifice is the priority...unity falls into place.

I believe any expression of music can be used potentially to worship the Lord—but we must stay sensitive to cultural tastes. How? Let me give you an example. Think of a short-term missionary who journeys to a foreign land and fellowships with other believers. Any sensitive missionary would never presume to wag his or her finger at a national congregation's expression of worship. Rather, for the sake of unity, the missionary chooses to embrace their expression, giving up his or her own. I find it wonderful that even Jesus did this on His short-term mission trip to earth. He wore *their* clothes... He donned *their* hairstyles... He even sang *their* songs! In words that referred to His life as well as to His death, Jesus said,

> For even the Son of Man did not come to be served, but to serve, and to give His life a ransom for many. (Mark 10:45)

So why do we have such a problem when our own churches attempt to strike a balance of expression by offering a style of music we may not prefer? Just like that missionary—just like Jesus—can we not give up our own preferences for the sake of others? Consider Paul's warning to a local church whose worship wars were dividing the church into factions:

> But take care that this liberty of yours does not somehow become a stumbling block to the weak....Therefore, if food causes my brother to stumble, I will never eat meat

again, so that I will not cause my brother to stumble. (1 Corinthians 8:9, 13)

Don't get distracted because Paul is writing about meat. Look deeper at the principle behind the application. Paul knew that there was nothing inherently wrong with eating meat sacrificed to idols. But weaker Christians had scruples over the act. The stronger believer, therefore, should be mature enough to tolerate the weaker believer until he or she grows to a mature understanding of Christian liberty. That may mean refraining from a worship style you prefer.

Personally, I have my preferences like anybody else. But I've grown to recognize that's *all* they are—personal preferences. The apostle John didn't play the pipe organ. Peter didn't play drums. There's nothing in the book of Acts about either choir robes or praise bands. And Paul never read the New American Standard version of the Bible. So when someone else's expression of worship takes center stage, I have to ask myself: *Is God more glorified by my preferred style of worship... or by my response to another's preferences? Does my being a servant stop when the worship service begins?*

I believe what feeds our corporate worship wars on Sundays is a failure to worship God personally during the week. We can't do corporately what we don't do privately. When we don't have the daily attitude of self-denial but rather self-fulfillment, Sunday naturally becomes an extension of that mind-set. Such thinking prompts an unavoidable clash. As consumers in a consumer-driven society, we want worship to be a reflection of *our* musical tastes, *our* personal preferences, confirming *our* likes and dislikes, *our* pleasures and prejudices. When it doesn't occur, we cross our arms, shake our heads, and convince ourselves that what is happening is wrong. What is wrong is occurring in our hearts. *That* is what needs to change.

All who fight over the expression of worship are revealing their view of the essence of worship. It's all about *them*.

Don't go there. There's a better way.

An Invaluable Reminder

I have found that it's impossible to lead a group of people in something that is not a part of me personally. So I have had to cultivate a life of private worship. I urge you to do the same. Sunday is simply a corporate expression of what we do all week.

209

I love the crescendo that builds in the book of Romans and culminates in the marvelous expression of praise at the end of chapter 11. Paul begins that powerful letter by revealing that we are sinners who are lost, undone, and without hope. There's no way we're going to reach God on our own, because our sin separates us from Him. In fact, no one even seeks God. Not one! So God must intervene, and in Christ He did just that. He offered His grace through Jesus' death on the cross. He reached down and loved us when we weren't lovely. As a result, because of His grace we came to know Christ by faith alone. That's the first five chapters of Romans. But salvation from the penalty of sin doesn't remove our struggle with sin. So in the next three chapters of Romans Paul reveals in practical terms how Jesus has given us freedom from the power of sin in our lives. The security of our salvation, revealed at the end of chapter 8, is illustrated in chapters 9–11 where God promises a future for Israel...in spite of their sins. What grace! What mercy! How great and awesome is our God! All of this is like a crescendo mark on a musical score. It gets louder and louder until finally Paul bursts forth into praise as he inserts this doxology at the end of chapter 11:

Oh, the depth of the riches both of the wisdom and knowledge of God! How unsearchable are His judgments and unfathomable His ways! For WHO HAS KNOWN THE MIND OF THE LORD, OR WHO BECAME HIS COUNSELOR? OR WHO HAS FIRST GIVEN TO HIM THAT IT MIGHT BE PAID BACK TO HIM AGAIN? For from Him and through Him and to Him are all things. To Him be the glory forever. Amen. (Romans 11:33–36)

Amen, indeed! Aren't those great words? No one has the wisdom to advise God. No one gives anything to Him that He needs (and, for sure, He needs nothing). As finite creatures, we can't begin to understand the infinite mind of God. We can't even explain last week, much less why the last five years of our lives have been the way they were. We only know that life—with all its pains and challenges—has been for our good and for His glory. God's plan is to do a profound work in our sinful, lost lives. He is unsearchable, unfathomable, and all-knowing. That puts the Lord in a category completely different from all others. We look to no president. We turn to no king or queen. We call on no military general. We depend upon no statesman, no physician, no pastor. None of these are in the category of unfathomable and unsearchable. He is the One and only God. That's why we worship Him and no other.

I regret the break between chapters 11 and 12 of the book of Romans. (Remember, the chapters and verses are not inspired.) Paul climaxes his grand crescendo with an urgent plea:

> Therefore I urge you, brethren, by the mercies of God, to present your bodies a living and holy sacrifice, acceptable to God, which is your spiritual service of worship. (Romans 12:1)

Do you teach a class of children or teenagers or adults? That is a "spiritual service of worship." Do you play an instrument? That's also an act of worship. Perhaps you work behind the scenes, cleaning the church or folding the handouts. Or you give regularly to the work of God, a generosity marked by sacrifice and consistency. That, too, is an act of worship. It will revolutionize your idea of Christian service when you see it as an act of worship— something you do for the glory of the Lord, not to receive the praise of others.

When is such worship paramount? Whenever the focus is *fully* on our Lord and Savior, such as the time we spend with Him at the Lord's Table. It is when we take Communion that we bring our deepest needs and wounded hearts to the surface. It is there we come just as we are, and meet Him in pure and simple worship. We concentrate on Him and Him alone, remembering His Son's sacrifice on our behalf.

This further emphasizes that worship is not, and never has been, something people do in order to be entertained or fed. Worship *can be* entertaining and personally nourishing—but these are by-products of true worship. The Bible calls worship a "sacrifice of praise," words that stem from gratitude (see Heb.13:15). Praise is a *sacrifice* to God; it's something we give *Him* . . . it's not done for ourselves.

By connecting worship to the presentation of our physical bodies to God, Paul reveals that worship is not limited to songs we sing on Sundays. Worship also relates to the lives we live on Mondays. It's a devotion of our whole selves to Christ. We crawl on that sacrificial altar every day and offer God our bodies, our thoughts, our sexual purity, our vocations, our friendships, our work, and each member of our family. We give God our futures, our finances, our worries and concerns, and our joys. We withhold nothing in our worship!

Now, what's the problem here? In a word, again: *marketing.* We're surrounded by a culture that calls us stupid for thinking and living like that. Check the next periodical you receive in your mail. Look at tomorrow morning's news on the Web. Peruse the *Wall Street Journal* or your local newspaper. Scrutinize the words of your company's next motivational seminar. Nothing in our postmodern society persuades us to offer ourselves as living sacrifices. On the contrary, our world feeds us the lies that image matters more than character, that money is more important than people, and that we deserve to have our dreams come true. Truth be told, we deserve hell...but God had mercy. And it's because of "the mercies of God" that Paul urges us to present our lives to Him as a living sacrifice. The next verse tells us how:

And do not be conformed to this world, but be transformed by the renewing of your mind, so that you may prove what the will of God is, that which is good and acceptable and perfect. (Romans 12:2)

I like the way J. B. Phillips paraphrases the first part of that verse: "Don't let the world around you squeeze you into its own mould." To live as Jesus prayed for us, we must choose to dwell on God's thoughts, and so have our minds renewed in the midst of a corrupt world. And the source of God's thoughts? Jesus' prayer reveals it:

I have given them Your word; and the world has hated them, because they are not of the world, even as I am not of the world. I do not ask You to take them out of the world, but to keep them from the evil one. They are not of the world, even as I am not of the world. Sanctify them in the truth; Your word is truth. (John 17:14–17)

To have our minds transformed and sanctified, we take our cues from God's Word, now complete in the pages of Scripture. Look how the apostle Paul repeatedly emphasizes the importance of renewing the mind:

For those who are according to the flesh set their minds on the things of the flesh, but those who are according to the Spirit, the things of the Spirit. For the mind set on the flesh is death, but the mind set on the Spirit is life and peace. (Romans 8:5–6)

Finally, brethren, whatever is true, whatever is honorable, whatever is right, whatever is pure, whatever is lovely, whatever is of good repute, if there is any excellence and if anything worthy of praise, dwell on these things. (Philippians 4:8)

Set your mind on the things above, not on the things that are on earth. For you have died and your life is hidden with Christ in God. (Colossians 3:2–3)

These cannot be mere words on a page. Our minds are transformed when we dwell on God's Word and apply it directly to our everyday lives. In the process of that transformation, we lose our worry list as we replace it with a lifestyle of worship. Stop and think. *That* is what we want to cultivate in our churches. Not a group of selfish people who come together to be entertained, but a body of selfless believers who are learning how to worship God as a lifestyle.

One of the gifted worship leaders I know is

my friend Fernando Ortega. On a recent *Insight for Living* cruise conference, Fernando led all of us with his sensitive and simple arrangement of the old spiritual "Give Me Jesus." Without our planning it, that gentle song became our anthem for the week. I love that song! What tremendous depth is expressed in these original African-American lyrics:

In the morning when I rise . . . give me Jesus.
You can have all this world, but give me Jesus.

When I am alone . . . give me Jesus.
You can have all this world, but give me Jesus.

And when I come to die . . . give me Jesus.
You can have all this world, but give me Jesus.[12]

My love for that song is deep because it illustrates an invaluable reminder: *worship, the one essential ingredient of our corporate gatherings, also takes first place in our private lives throughout the week.* In God's Word, there is no distinction between the sacred and the secular for the Christian. We do all things for His glory.

A friend of mine, Howie Stevenson, has often

217

said, "If you don't love to sing, then why in the world would you ever want to go to heaven?" I've thought about that and asked myself, *Why are there so few who sing?* It's true. Why is it that the song has dried up in our voices? Could it be that the world has squeezed us into its own mold?

Think about it. How many people do you hear singing in your Monday-through-Saturday world? Do you ever notice a coworker humming a song? How often do you see someone singing on a freeway or at a stoplight? One reason this occurs, I believe, is because the tyranny of the urgent has squeezed out their song. Song requires creativity, relaxation, and freedom from tension. Urgent lives have no room for such important things.

Another reason our world doesn't sing is because everything else sings for us! Not long ago, I was sitting in my truck at a stoplight, and the guy three cars away had his radio cranked. *BONG, bam, bam—BONG, bam, bam!* It was so loud I don't know how his ears kept from bleeding. I didn't *want* his song in my truck, but I couldn't shut it out. Music of some sort is everywhere, have you noticed? It's in our cars, offices, homes, grocery stores, department stores, restaurants, and even on elevators. We even have music on airplanes. I once asked a flight attendant why music always comes on immediately after the plane lands. Her answer was depressing: "People can't stand silence." Maybe that's why so many folks have earphones connected to an MP3 player dangling from their ears.

Let me urge you not to allow the world to squeeze you into its own mold. Start to sing again. Add it to your time with God. Wake up with a song on your lips. Before the tyranny of the urgent seizes your agenda, sing a song of praise to God. If you can't create one, get a hymnbook or songbook. Use it with your time in the Scriptures. Worship your Lord in song from the heart. Remember, your God seeks that kind of worship.

In view of "the mercies of God," respond to Him with a lifestyle of praise. That's how I see worship at its essence: a human response to a divine initiative. God has done something for us—in word or deed—and we respond to it. The response may be absolutely silent. The response may be a loud voice. It may be singing. It may be public or private. But when the response is genuine, it's amazing that you aren't concerned about what others think. Whether you are lifting your hands or kneeling in silent awe, it seems like everything else is blocked out. You have been touched by God . . . and you respond. In worship we "connect" with the living Lord on a moment-by-moment basis.

In writing this book, I write with devotion. I labor over terms. I shape the words so that they fit together in ways that make sense. I do it through prayer. I do it through research. I do it over time... lots of time. You, the reader, deserve that. More important, God deserves that... because for me, writing is an act of worship.

True worship begins by realizing that God seeks those who worship Him with *all* of who they are. It's not just a Sunday morning activity. When I awaken in the morning, God seeks my worship. As I'm serving in my vocation throughout the day, God seeks my worship. On Saturday afternoon when I'm at work in my yard, God seeks my worship. The Father wants me to worship Him in all circumstances: as I drive my car... as I rear my family... as I live alongside my wife... when I am alone or when I'm with others... when I'm thinking quietly or laughing loudly. The same is true of your life, whatever the details may be. He wants you to view *everything* as an act of worship.

Even hardships offer us an opportunity for worship. Remember Job? He lost all of his possessions and all of his children in one fateful day. Imagine that for a moment, if you can. Now try to wrap your mind around his marvelous, immediate response of *worship*:

> Then Job arose and tore his robe and shaved his head, and he fell to the ground and worshiped. He said,
>
> > *"Naked I came from my mother's womb,*
> > *And naked I shall return there.*
> > *The Lord gave and the Lord has taken*
> > *away.*
> > *Blessed be the name of the Lord."* (Job 1:20–21)

Yes, it's possible to worship on a hospital bed. We can worship God in a financial crisis. It's also possible to worship at a graveside. Even with everything having been lost, you can still worship God in view of His rich mercies toward you . . . and because of His sovereignty you can say, "Give me Jesus."

You don't need comfortable surroundings or the soft seats of a pew. You don't need a choir or a praise band. You don't need a pipe organ or a drum set. Those elements may assist you, but worship must be a part of your daily walk with God . . . in every part of your personal life. Otherwise, we're just consumers. Or worse, we're opponents in a worship war.

*   *   *

We who tend to worship our work, work at our play, and play at our worship need to realize how the tyranny of the urgent can diminish the significance of the things that are important. If we're not careful we will allow the world to have too much control over us...and it will squeeze us into its own mold. The winds of other people's expectations and demands will drive us onto a reef of frustration, leaving us feeling shallow and desolate.

It's at this point that we need to stop and reconsider what's important—then go there, not only as individuals, but as a church. When we do, it quickly becomes obvious that what we're missing is the one essential ingredient without which we cannot grow deeper and reach that satisfying realm for which we were made: *worship*. God seeks those who will worship Him. Worship focuses on how worthy our God is. Worship is a declaration of His supreme majesty. It is being so preoccupied with the importance of our God that nothing urgent on this earth gains a significant place in our thinking. As this occurs, we discover that there's a dimension to life that is supernatural and unseen...and the invisibility of it only adds to its invincibility.

While we worship the God of heaven, we do so while living in a world that has lost its way. "Behold," Jesus told His disciples, "I send you out as sheep in the midst of wolves; so be shrewd as serpents and innocent as doves" (Matt. 10:16).

It's time to shift our focus from observing the church itself to examining the ravenous world in which we live and minister. If we are to be both shrewd and innocent...there are warnings we dare not ignore.

What Must the Church Realize?

*Tolerance is the virtue of the man
without convictions.*

—G. K. Chesterton

What Must the Church Realize?

I love the spring each year. Around the middle of March, the new growth pushes its way through the winter's dormant branches. In just a matter of weeks, the dull, brown, monochrome landscapes and overcast days transform into bright green meadows and clear blue skies. The rains wash away the doldrums of winter and nourish the parched ground. New life seems to be represented everywhere. We celebrate Easter. The children celebrate spring break. The animals get friskier. (Cynthia says that I do, too.) But there's another reason I like the spring. It isn't April Fools' Day. It *certainly* isn't April 15. It's not even Mother's Day. It has to do with the warning labels we find on products. You're probably thinking, *Okay, Swindoll has lost it. Warning labels?* Absolutely.

Every spring an internationally known competition called the "Wacky Warning Label Contest" announces its involuntary winner. The point of the contest? It reveals how the fear of lawsuits has driven companies to fork over millions of dollars to place beneath-the-level-of-common-sense warning labels on their products. Everyday people who find these wacky warnings submit their entries to the contest. The 2009 winning label was affixed to a portable toilet seat called "The Off-Road Commode." The seat is designed for outdoorsmen—complete with camouflage padding—and attaches to a vehicle's trailer hitch. Try to picture that! The warning label reads, "Not for use on moving vehicles."[1] (I guess it doesn't come with a seat belt.)

Other warning labels we see are equally ridiculous. A small tractor has a sticker that reads "Danger: Avoid Death." A label on a hair dryer advises, "Do not use while sleeping." An iron-on T-shirt transfer warns, "Do not iron while wearing shirt." On a package of bread pudding the label cautions, "Product will be hot after heating." A sleep aid alerts the insomniac: "Warning: May cause drowsiness." On a child's superhero costume the label reads, "Wearing the garment does not enable you to fly." And—this one is over the top—a Swedish chain saw gives the user a critical reminder: "Do not attempt to stop chain with your hands or genitals." (Okay...yeah, that's always a good idea.) Can you *believe* those warnings?

Sometimes I say to Cynthia, "That is so DUMB it makes me *never* want to buy that product!" More than idiotic, these labels are *insulting* to anyone with half a brain. Do we really need such obvious warnings? Unfortunately, we do. We live in an age when most people don't think for themselves. Slick marketing thinks for us. Advertising lays out our options...wishy-washy feelings guide our decisions...mesmerizing entertainment makes us passive, tolerant, and lazy in our assessments. We now allow the culture to think for us. We have been squeezed into its mold. The warnings are essential.

I lived in Southern California for many years, and I often found myself stunned at the frequent forest fires that ravaged the land. Fortunately, Cynthia and I never experienced loss from these fires, but we knew some who did. Even after moving back to Texas, I always feel a familiar pang when the newscasts report warnings that the California fires have ignited again. Even more tragic are those who ignore the warnings to evacuate. In 2003, more than twenty people lost their lives in a series of fires where the flames moved faster than the residents could flee. When people complained that officials didn't offer enough forewarning, Sergeant Conrad Grayson responded, "We're begging people to leave, and they don't take us seriously. They want to pack some clothes, or fight it in the backyard with a garden hose. They don't seem to understand that this is unlike any fire we've seen. If people don't move fast, they're going to become charcoal briquettes." One resident tried to warn his neighbors to escape, but a number of them responded too casually or ignored him altogether. "They looked like they were packing for a trip," he said. "The ones who listened to me and left the area lived. The ones who didn't, died."[2]

There are times when the most responsible thing you can do is to warn someone of impending danger. You do that because people could be hurt. Danger could be lurking in the shadows. There could even be the potential for death. In sounding the alarm, you are not being cantankerous or neurotic. You're not a naysayer. You're not a doom-and-gloom prophet. You're a *realist*. If you and I see something or know something that has the potential of bringing harm to others, to give a bold, strong warning is our duty! *Not* to do so is neglect.

Warnings We Dare Not Ignore

Much of the first four chapters has centered on looking within the church. Self-examination can be both helpful and healthy as long as we are honest in our evaluation and accurate in our conclusions. In fact, it's essential. Any church that fails to look within may start to drift without knowing it. But we cannot stop with self-examination. If we hope to become, as Jesus commanded, "shrewd as serpents and innocent as doves" (Matt. 10:16), we also need to look around to understand the times in which we live and the culture to which we minister. Not only will this help us become more effective in ministry, it will also bring light to darkened areas of our minds and provide a pathway through the thick jungle of a culture that's lost its way.

The Holy Scriptures issue clear and timeless warnings so applicable to today that you'd swear the ink was still wet on the page. The New Testament includes several passionate warnings to those who are followers of Christ, beginning with the words of the Lord Jesus Himself:

If the world hates you, you know that it has hated Me before it hated you. If you were of the world, the world would love its own; but because you are not of the world, but I chose you out of the world, because of this the world hates you. Remember the words that I said to you, "A slave is not greater than his master." If they persecuted Me, they will also persecute you; if they kept My word, they will keep yours also. But all these things they will do to you for My name's sake, because they do not know the One who sent Me. (John 15:18–21)

These things I have spoken to you so that you may be kept from stumbling. They will make you outcasts from the synagogue, but an hour is coming for everyone who kills you to think that he is offering service to God. These things they will do because they have not known the Father or Me.... These things I have spoken to you, so that in Me you may have peace. In the world you have tribulation, but take courage; I have overcome the world. (John 16:1–3, 33)

Peter offers a warning to his readers from the seasoned voice of experience. He discovered the truth of his words a number of times—both through his own failures and those of others (see Matt. 16:23; Mark 8:33; Luke 22:31; Acts 5:3). His warning is as timeless as it is true:

Be of sober spirit, be on the alert. Your adversary, the devil, prowls around like a roaring lion, seeking someone to devour. But resist him, firm in your faith, knowing that the same experiences of suffering are being accomplished by your brethren who are in the world. (1 Peter 5:8–9)

The apostle John gives godly counsel in the form of a warning to his spiritual children, wisdom gleaned from six decades of faith in Jesus:

Do not love the world nor the things in the world. If anyone loves the world, the love of the Father is not in him. For all that is in the world, the lust of the flesh and the lust of the eyes and the boastful pride of life, is not from the Father, but is from the world. (1 John 2:15–16)

Beloved, do not believe every spirit, but test the spirits to see whether they are from God, because many false prophets have gone out into the world. By this you know the Spirit of God: every spirit that confesses that Jesus Christ has come in the flesh is from God; and every spirit that does not confess Jesus is not from God; this is the spirit of the antichrist, of which you have heard that it is coming, and now it is already in the world.... We know that we are of God, and that the whole world lies in the power of the evil one. (1 John 4:1–3; 5:19)

Clearly, we enter a battle zone—true spiritual warfare—when we claim Christ as Lord and determine to follow Him no matter what. We should not be surprised by conflict. We should expect it! Understand, then, *where* the real war is. The battles should never be fought among Christian brothers and sisters, such as with the worship wars we looked at in chapter 4. The church needs to realize that the *real* battle is spiritual...and to complicate matters, our *real* enemy is invisible.

While I don't see the devil behind every bush, neither do I stick my head in the sand and ignore reality. We need to know there is a conspiracy occurring. There is an insidious war being waged. If we don't see that, we will be hopelessly confused. When John the apostle writes, "Do not love the world nor the things in the world" (1 John 2:15), he understands what our times are like in the last days. Satan heads the world's system. It is a plan that leaves God out, that is hostile to the Holy Scriptures, and that has as its goal to destroy the church that Jesus is building. Under God's permissive will, this world is running a fast-paced course filled with the lust of the flesh and the lust of the eyes and the boastful pride of life. All of this occurs under the watchful eye of God, who allows the adversary to have his way—Satan himself.

Why does the church need such obvious warnings? Because the world wants to do our thinking for us. The enemy of our souls wants to tap into our own sinful natures so that he can drive a wedge between God and us. And that is why we in the church need a strong warning to awaken us to the reality that characterizes our times.

Times in Which We Minister

Nobody addresses the subject of the invisible war better or more often than the apostle Paul. And space hinders me from underscoring all the words he wielded as warnings to us. I'll select only two. As you read these examples, notice the warlike imagery Paul uses:

> Finally, be strong in the Lord and in the strength of His might. Put on the full armor of God, so that you will be able to stand firm against the schemes of the devil. For our struggle is not against flesh and blood, but against the rulers, against the powers, against the world forces of this darkness, against the spiritual forces of wickedness in the heavenly places.... In addition to all, taking up the shield of faith with which you will be able to extinguish all the flaming arrows of the evil one. And take THE HELMET OF SALVATION, and the sword of the Spirit, which is the word of God. With all prayer and petition pray at all times in the Spirit, and with this in view, be on the alert with all perseverance

and petition for all the saints. (Ephesians 6:10–12, 16–18)

Be on guard for yourselves and for all the flock, among which the Holy Spirit has made you overseers, to shepherd the church of God which He purchased with His own blood. I know that after my departure savage wolves will come in among you, not sparing the flock; and from among your own selves men will arise, speaking perverse things, to draw away the disciples after them. Therefore be on the alert, remembering that night and day for a period of three years I did not cease to admonish each one with tears. (Acts 20:28–31)

What's significant about these two sections of Scripture? They are words of warning from Paul, originally directed to the church at Ephesus...to the same church where Timothy would serve as pastor. The closer Paul got to the end of his life, the more pronounced were his warnings to the Ephesian flock.

You'll remember Timothy from chapter 3 where we examined Paul's final letter to this young pastor and discovered some distinctives of a contagious church. As we look again at the book of 2 Timothy, it's helpful to remember that Paul is in a dungeon and about to lose his head, literally. Paul is weary and battle-worn with the years of ministry behind him. Timothy is younger and must take the baton as he continues to run the race. Paul wants him to succeed...but he sees danger lurking. Because Paul's time is short, his words are chosen carefully. The letter of 2 Timothy contains the greatest example of Paul's warnings to the church regarding the times in which we minister.

A General Warning: Difficult Times Ahead

The apostle sets the stage at the beginning of chapter 3 with a simple but sobering statement:

> But realize this, that in the last days difficult times will come. (2 Timothy 3:1)

He begins with intensity: "There's something I want you to know." The verb tense literally reads, "Keep on knowing this." In other words, be aware of this...realize this...stay alert to this...keep this in the creases of your brain. The command is bold, emphatic, and realistic. Eugene Peterson's rendering of this verse is on the mark: "Don't be naive. There are difficult times ahead" (MSG). The only cure for this kind of naïveté is to become a people who learn to think maturely and properly. That alone is a challenge in our day.

The "Wacky Warning Label Contest" I mentioned earlier was developed to reveal America's wacky system of civil justice—what many believe is a major public policy concern. Have you ever read some of the transcripts from courts of our justice system? If you have, then you can understand the concerns. Below you'll see some actual conversations between attorneys and witnesses in the courtroom:

ATTORNEY: What is your date of birth?
WITNESS: July 18.
ATTORNEY: What year?
WITNESS: Every year.

ATTORNEY: What gear were you in the moment of the impact?
WITNESS: Gucci sweats and Reeboks.

ATTORNEY: Is your appearance here this morning pursuant to a deposition notice which I sent to your attorney?

WITNESS: No, this is how I dress when I go to work.

Those are literal statements from the courtroom! But the witnesses on the stand aren't the only ones to laugh at. Keep reading:

ATTORNEY: Now doctor, isn't it true that when a person dies in his sleep he doesn't know about it until the next morning?
WITNESS: Did you actually pass the bar exam?

ATTORNEY: So the date of conception of the baby was August 8?
WITNESS: Yes.
ATTORNEY: And what exactly were you doing at that time?

ATTORNEY: How was your first marriage terminated?
WITNESS: By death.
ATTORNEY: And by whose death was it terminated?

ATTORNEY: Doctor, how many of your autopsies have you performed on dead people?

WITNESS: All my autopsies are performed on dead people.

ATTORNEY: Do you recall the time you examined the body?

WITNESS: The autopsy started around 8:30 p.m.

ATTORNEY: And Mr. Denton was dead at the time?

WITNESS: No, he was sitting on the table wondering why I was doing an autopsy on him.

ATTORNEY: Doctor, before you performed the autopsy, did you check for a pulse?

WITNESS: No.

ATTORNEY: Did you check for blood pressure?

WITNESS: No.

ATTORNEY: Did you check for breathing?

WITNESS: No.

ATTORNEY: So then, it is possible that the patient was alive when you began the autopsy?

WITNESS: No.

ATTORNEY: How can you be so sure, doctor?

WITNESS: Because his brain was sitting in a jar on my desk.

ATTORNEY: But could the patient have still been alive, nevertheless?

WITNESS: Yes, it is possible that he could have been alive practicing law.[3]

That's my favorite line! It's hilarious...but downright tragic. Our culture does all it can to think for us and to squeeze us into its mold. If we watch enough television, our senses are dulled and we become just that stupid. We become passive and disconnected. Our ability to think shrivels. Clear, courageous thinking is now a rarity.

Please hear me! You must continue to absorb the Word of God as you cultivate your mind and form your convictions. What must the church realize? In the words of Paul: "Don't be naive!" Refuse to live in an overly optimistic dream world of make-believe fantasy. We read Peter's words earlier: "Be of sober spirit, be on the alert" (1 Pet. 5:8). Don't think that if you lie low and stay quiet the storm will quickly pass. The Word of God urges us to wake up. Facing reality is how we can survive! The war is real.

The apostle Paul's strong warning is followed by an explanatory statement: "In the last days difficult times will come" (2 Tim. 3:1). Don't misunderstand. The "last days" don't refer to some far-future, prophetic era. Paul isn't holding his breath until a day yet future. He isn't sitting on a rooftop watching clouds form and waiting for a sign from God. These troubles have existed from the time Christ came, lived, died, arose, and ascended...to the present. We are *in* the "last days." Truth be told, we have been since the coming of Christ. The church needs to realize that difficult times will only intensify as we anticipate Christ's return. John R. W. Stott's summary says it well:

Before we study in detail Paul's characterization of these men, we need to absorb his words of introduction. First, we are living in the last days, he says; Christ brought them with Him when He came. Secondly, these days will include seasons of peril and stress. Thirdly, they will be the result of the activities of bad men [and women]. Fourthly, we are to understand this, to be quite clear about it, and so to be prepared.[4]

Let your eyes linger over the word *difficult*. That's a mild translation. The original term, *chalepos,* is used only one other place in the New Testament. The apostle Matthew wrote of two demon-possessed men who were *chalepos,* or "extremely violent" (Matt. 8:28).[5] The term refers to someone inclined to forceful and dangerous activity. The Greek historian Plutarch used the word for an "ugly" wound. I think it helps us gain a better grasp of Paul's counsel to Timothy if we understand *difficult* in those terms. With that in mind, allow me to paraphrase Paul's warning: "Timothy—and my brothers and sisters living in the twenty-first-century church—realize that exceedingly violent and dangerous times are upon us!" Believe those words. Take them to heart. Apply them seriously. If it was difficult in Paul's day, you can imagine how much more intense it is today.

I have been in ministry almost fifty years. But in these recent years I have witnessed harsh and violent things I never saw in my earlier ministry. There were exceptions, of course, but that's the point... they were exceptions. I am more convinced now than ever that when we enter into the Christian life, we enter a battleground, not a playground. Just because everything *appears* peaceful does not mean that everything *is* peaceful. I repeat, the war we fight is an *invisible battle.* We cannot witness the presence of the evil forces in the world, but Scripture assures us that they are there. Don't be naive: the devil and his legions are actively and continually resisting the things of God. That includes you. They are your enemies.

If we could slap a warning label across the times in which we live, it might read "Warning! Difficult times are upon us and they will never go away!" They will only intensify in days to come. The church must realize that. Why? So that we can prepare for it. That's Paul's general warning. Now we shift to a far more specific warning.

A Specific Warning: Difficult People Ahead

Let's return to Eugene Peterson's paraphrase and read the rest of this section of Scripture:

> Don't be naive. There are difficult times ahead. As the end approaches, people are going to be self-absorbed, money-hungry, self-promoting, stuck-up, profane, contemptuous of parents, crude, coarse, dog-eat-dog, unbending, slanderers, impulsively wild, savage, cynical, treacherous, ruthless, bloated windbags, addicted to lust, and allergic to God. They'll make a show of religion, but behind the scenes they're animals. Stay clear of these people. (2 Timothy 3:1–5 MSG)

I'd call that a strong, specific warning! The New American Standard renders a more literal translation:

For men will be lovers of self, lovers of money, boastful, arrogant, revilers, disobedient to parents, ungrateful, unholy, unloving, irreconcilable, malicious gossips, without self-control, brutal, haters of good, treacherous, reckless, conceited, lovers of pleasure rather than lovers of God, holding to a form of godliness, although they have denied its power. (2 Timothy 3:2–5)

Notice the small, three-letter word that begins these verses: *For*...We could understand it as meaning "Because." The general warning to "realize" that difficult times will come is followed by a specific warning that explains *why* they will be difficult. The times are difficult *because* people are difficult. The list of what makes men and women difficult reads like an excerpt from a horror novel. Paul's reference to "men" comes from the Greek term that means *mankind*. He isn't referring just to males in this passage but to people in general. Both men and women alike will be difficult. This, in very specific terms, is what the church must understand. It's the world in which we live and the people to whom we minister.

The list begins by citing three types of "lovers."

Not surprisingly, it starts with self-lovers. They're first because they spawn the rest of the list. When self-love becomes the overwhelming, compulsive, and compelling goal in life, it corrupts *everything* it touches. A "lover of self" is the narcissist at his or her worst. This is a self-lover who also loves money, and along with that, loves pleasure (v. 4). This person chases the material things and the most extreme sensual experiences money will buy. Materialism to the max! This consumerist thinking is summarized by the bumper sticker: "He who dies with the most toys wins." Every time I see that, I think, *No, not really. He who dies with the most toys dies most disillusioned!* God's response is far more eloquent: "You fool! This very night your soul is required of you; and now who will own what you have prepared?" (Luke 12:20).

Paul continues his dirty laundry list by describing these narcissists as *boastful.* It's the word for a braggart who blusters his or her way through a conversation, unconcerned about the conceit that's on display. Paul includes *arrogant* in the list alongside *boastful.* That term literally means "to show oneself above." It describes one who has an exaggerated opinion of himself. With his words he also slanders and insults others. That's why Paul calls them *revilers*, a term that could be rendered "abusive in speech." If you spend enough time with a narcissist, it isn't long before you witness or suffer abuse. You and others mean nothing to this person…except to further his or her agenda. It's all about *them*.

Let me pause and add a technical comment about the next five words. In the original language, each of these five terms begins with the letter *alpha*. When a Greek word begins with that letter, it negates the action or description of what follows. It stresses the *absence* of the qualities one would expect. English has a similar construction with the prefix "un." For example, the meaning of *holy* is changed completely when we add "un" to the front of it. *Godly* reverts to the opposite when we say *ungodly*. And so, these next descriptive words portray the flip side of what God desires…and each falls within a category we could call "family life."

Tragically, the primary circle of influence impacted by the self-loving narcissist is the family. The first description Paul gives reflects the way children often react in an impudent and disrespectful world: "disobedient to parents." When you add "dis" to *obedient*, you get the opposite of what God desires. The phrase describes those who are surly and insolent toward their mothers and fathers. I've never known a time in my seventy-five years on this earth when I've seen more disrespect for parents than now. It is sometimes shocking.

Your parents would be the first to say they are fallen people, so let me offer a blunt suggestion: give them a break. All parents have made bad mistakes. (If you are a parent, that includes you.) Good parents do whatever they can to make it right, and that begins by saying what needs to be said: "I was wrong when I…"; "I am sorry for the times that I…" When you respect your parents, you will forgive them, even when they have not asked for it. Please, as a believer in Jesus Christ, learn to honor those who birthed you and reared you…accept them warts and all. Why? It's a command from God that you never outgrow (see Matt. 15:4–6; 1 Tim. 5:8).

Disobedience often stems from the next term in 2 Timothy 3:2–5: *ungrateful.* See the opposite portrayed by the prefix "un"? It refers to a person devoid even of elementary appreciation. It's a complete failure to see the value of another's sacrifice. There is a deliberate forgetfulness of the past because of the blinding greed of the present. Would it help to have a concrete example? Show up when the will of the deceased is read…or when the siblings have a chance to divide their parents' furniture. The family will fight over the last dollar and dinner plate. They want it exactly equal, unless of course it's slanted in their favor. It's called a spirit of entitlement, and it reeks of basic ingratitude.

How refreshing it is to come across individuals who realize they have their parents to thank for so much of what they have in life. Marian Anderson was one of those individuals. She had a magnificent contralto voice that gave her worldwide acclaim. On one occasion a reporter asked her to name the greatest moment in her life. Those in the room hearing the question wondered what she would say. There were so many great moments, like the night Arturo Toscanini said publicly, "A voice like hers comes once in the century." Or there was that time back in 1955 when she became the first African-American to sing with the Metropolitan Opera Company in New York. Or she could have pointed to the following year when her autobiography, *My Lord, What a Morning*, made the *New York Times* best-seller list. Or when she was selected by the president of the United States to be a delegate to the United Nations. She also had been invited to the White House to sing for the president and the queen of England and her royal husband. In 1963 she was awarded the coveted Presidential Medal of

Freedom. And she would never forget the day she stood in the shadow of the Lincoln statue and sang before seventy-five thousand people in Washington, D.C., including cabinet members, all of the Supreme Court justices, and most of the members of Congress. But she named none of these. Her answer? She smiled and looked at the reporter as she replied, "The greatest moment of my life was the day I went home and told my mother she wouldn't have to take in washing anymore."[6] How great is that? How *rare* is that! She never forgot her roots.

I don't care how high you rise in life...how significant you may believe you are...or how much money you make. Gratitude is what God expects of you. Why? Isaiah puts it this way, rendered so poignantly in the old King James Version:

Look unto the rock whence ye are hewn, and
to the hole of the pit whence ye are digged.
(Isaiah 51:1)

What a vivid expression! Remember the pit from where you came. Every once in a while it's good to drift back to the pit, at least in your mind, and remember. It's amazing the perspective that offers. Remember those who sacrificed for you so you can

251

become who you are now...those who know you and, quite probably, love you more than anyone ever has on this earth. Remember also the grace of God that sustained you from the very beginning. That's the same grace that rescued you from the pit of hell. Gratitude. It's essential at times to remember "the hole of the pit whence ye are digged." Otherwise, you and I can easily become ungrateful and narcissistic...and part of the *problem* in the church rather than part of the *solution*.

The next term, *unholy*, describes those who lack a relationship with God. These are those self-loving individuals whose lives are secular, having nothing to do with the holy things of God. Moreover, they have no desire for them. The word *unloving* also speaks of a lack of desire...but this apathy is for one's own family. This individual does not have even the basic affection for his or her siblings, parents, or children.

The fifth word in the list of these familial terms is *irreconcilable*. It literally means "without a truce." This describes a person unwilling to resolve a conflict or reconcile a relationship. Let me ask you straight: is there someone you need to forgive? If there is, quite likely, it's someone in your family. (Remember, these are familial terms.) Perhaps it's a parent...or a sibling...or even a spouse? What keeps you from taking the initiative and pursuing peace?

May I suggest the reason? *Pride.*

Let's face it: no excuse keeps you from the biblical obligation to forgive that person. No self-justification...no plea of victimization...no "boundaries" veiled behind a bitter spirit. Nothing! Our implacable culture offers endless excuses. Only a narcissist uses someone else's failure as leverage for manipulation...and there's a lot of that going on! There is no place in an arrogant life for forgiveness. At the same time, there is no place in a believer's life for blame and bitterness.

As believers in our glorious Lord Jesus Christ, we are called to a different standard. *His* standard. That's why our forgiveness of others is inseparably linked with God's forgiveness of us. Look closely— and I mean *very carefully*—at the words of both Paul and Jesus:

Be kind to one another, tender-hearted, forgiving each other, just as God in Christ also has forgiven you. (Ephesians 4:32)

"And forgive us our debts, as we also have forgiven our debtors."...For if you forgive others for their transgressions, your heavenly

Father will also forgive you. But if you do not forgive others, then your Father will not forgive your transgressions. (Matthew 6:12, 14–15)

Those are hard statements, but essential. Are you unforgiving toward someone? If so, you may be saved...but according to Jesus, *you are out of fellowship with God.* That is why Christ commanded that you reconcile with others even before you come to worship:

Therefore if you are presenting your offering at the altar, and there remember that your brother has something against you, leave your offering there before the altar and go; first be reconciled to your brother, and then come and present your offering. (Matthew 5:23–24)

If someone has asked you to forgive him, please be big enough to accept the grace of his confession. If that person has not asked you to forgive him or her, remember that God has commanded that you do so anyway. When we cling to a painful memory rather than choose to renew our minds, we will suffer emotionally torturing wounds that are, tragically, self-inflicted (see Matt. 18:34–35).

I urge you to do whatever it takes to reconcile. Go to a pastor or biblical counselor for some assistance. Pray for strength to obey. Humble yourself. Don't go to your grave with that grudge. Don't even go to church with it.

The building blocks of family are those qualities that support whole and healthy relationships. We can find them simply by removing the *alpha* from the terms we just observed, transforming them into positive qualities every family needs: obedience, gratitude, holiness, affection, and forgiveness. But the church must realize that in these last days, when such savage times have come, all five are conspicuous by their absence.

Part of the reason we see this breakdown in our relationships is that we don't give them the time they need to succeed. It gets tough, so we quit. It feels like it will never happen, so we stop. The demands are hard, so we give up. If happiness or "success" (as we define it) doesn't occur immediately, we walk out only to find another set of problems awaiting us. As a Christian, you cannot escape sanctification. If you walk away from one set of problems, the Lord has another set waiting for you. God tailors our trials in order to soften our hard hearts. How should we respond? We must strengthen our determination and hang tough. I know this for a fact. I have experienced it.

I spent the first ten years of my marriage trying to make Cynthia into me. (Can you think of anything worse than a female Chuck?) Finally, she'd had enough. I'll never forget when she said to me, "I don't want you to keep telling people we're 'partners' because we're not partners. I bear your children, and I cook your meals, and I clean the house, but I'm not really your partner." Then she added, "You've never accepted me for who I really am."

"Yes, I have," I shot back.

"No, you haven't."

"*Yes,* I have."

"*No,* you haven't!" As we stood toe-to-toe in our kitchen, I got louder and she got louder until she finally left in tears…and I was left with the dishes. While doing the dishes I finally softened and had to admit to myself, *She's right.* We began a process that took four years to break that habit in me. It involved some serious counseling that we both sought…and it was painful but extremely helpful. It just about wiped me out, though, realizing how true her criticism was. I did very little encouraging back then.

Many years later at a gathering with some friends from our radio ministry, someone asked Cynthia,

"Why don't you share some things about the broadcast?" She walked up and briefly told the history of *Insight for Living*. She closed by saying, "The best part about this is that Chuck and I are in this as partners." At that moment her statement put a big knot in my throat. She hadn't said that word since I heard it as we stood on that cold kitchen floor years earlier. I'll be honest...we almost broke apart those first ten years. We didn't, though, because she stayed with me and stuck it out.

I mentioned in chapter 1 that Stonebriar Community Church celebrated its tenth anniversary in 2008. I can't tell you the times that I was tempted to say, "I'm out of here!" On one such occasion, I lay in bed with tears streaming down both cheeks, and I sighed to Cynthia, "That's it. It's over."

"No, it's not," she replied calmly.

"Yes, it *is*." (I'm sure by now you've picked up on the fact that we've gone to bed more than once with a little argument going on.) "You just don't understand," I told her.

"I *do* understand," she countered. "You're *not* going to quit."

"I am," I said, sobbing. "I'm going in tomorrow...and tell them it's over."

"You have how many people in the congregation?"

she asked me. "They don't even know there's a problem. Don't you dare do that to them."

And I didn't. I owe so much to Cynthia—more than our marriage and our ministry. She has encouraged me by her example to hang in there when things get tough. And as a result, I'm able to look back and see the hand of God. I am able to celebrate more than ten years at our church, more than thirty years at Insight for Living, and more than fifty years of marriage. Those are things I would have missed if I had walked away.

Some of you are on the edge of quitting something when you ought to stay. You're determined to live for Jesus in your marriage, but it's tough sledding. You pray for that child—or that parent—and nothing changes. Or maybe you're not getting the credit you deserve at work, or you're not getting the results you expected. Waiting on the Lord is often the hardest job on the planet. (Just ask Cynthia.) But God does some of His greatest work in the lives of those who wait for Him (see Lam. 3:22–32). I urge you, my friend, hang in there. God is working even though you cannot see it.

I've never regretted the times I did not quit... though at the time it was all I could do to stay. I'm glad I did. You will be, too.

A Subtle Warning: Realize the Danger Outside . . . and Inside

The high school I attended in east Houston was not an innocent, safe place. Fistfights were daily occurrences. It wasn't uncommon to see stabbings. I walked into the boy's restroom on one occasion and a fellow was lying in his own blood with a knife in his chest! *No exaggeration.* I was so scared I didn't know what to do. The guy who had stabbed him was washing the blood off his hands. He yelled at me, "Get out!" Believe me, I set a new record on getting out. It was one dangerous place! Had my parents known how dangerous it was, they would have leveled many more warnings at me than they did.

That's what Paul is doing through his letter to his spiritual son, Timothy. He has warned Timothy about the difficult people who will make difficult times. The apostle's warnings continue with a list of seven more terms that extend beyond the family. In fact, their evil tentacles worm their way into our churches from the roots of society. How? They creep through the cracks of our hearts in unguarded moments. If we don't awaken and realize the seriousness of these warnings, we will fall into deception and our churches will continue to drift toward destruction. There are dangers to realize.

The first of these seven descriptions in 2 Timothy 3:2–5 is understood clearly by people in politics as well as in the church: "malicious gossips." You may be surprised to learn that the original term is the word *diaboloi*...or, literally, "devils."[7] The singular form often refers to the devil himself as one who is the ultimate "slanderer." We've come to expect this kind of smear in politics, especially during an election year. But in the church, it can be downright appalling. How tragic that we, like Satan, can flap our tongues from a motive rooted purely in self-interest (see John 8:44; James 3:15; 1 John 3:10). I appreciate the words of William Barclay:

> There is a sense in which slander is the most cruel of all sins. If a man's goods are stolen, he can...build up his fortunes again; but if his good name is taken away, irreparable damage has been done....Many men and women, who would never dream of stealing, think nothing—even find pleasure— in passing on a story which ruins someone else's good name, without even trying to find out whether or not it is true. There is slander

enough in many a church to make the recording angel weep as he records it.[8]

If we aren't careful, we can all be guilty of gossip. Gossip is giving information we don't have the guts to say in the presence of another person. Part of the motive for talking behind someone's back is that we've exaggerated the facts; another reason is that the information is often hurtful and sometimes confidential. But if we're the people of character we need to be, we won't tittle-tattle behind someone's back. To do so is malicious. The devil operates that way. So does the world. But Christians should not talk like that. The church needs to realize that we have a higher calling.

The next phrase, *without self-control*, goes along with gossip. Not only is this person unable to control his tongue; even worse, he is unable to restrain his whole *self.* The term refers to a lack of control, "particularly in regard to bodily lusts."[9]

Now the picture gets darker, if that were even possible. The next term is a tough one: *brutal.* This is a savagery that is neither sensitive nor sympathetic. It's a term used for untamed beasts that would attack you. Translated "fierce" in some renderings, this is a brutality as ruthless as it is violent.[10]

Need an example? Just watch the news this evening. It's everywhere. Recently I read an interesting book titled *Snakes in Suits*. It sounds humorous until you hear the subtitle: *When Psychopaths Go to Work.*[11] We live in a world where there are many snakes looking awfully slick in suits. This is the individual who gets ahead by tripping others rather than by working hard. Watch out for them. Don't marry one of them. Don't put one of them on your leadership team at your church. Those of you who have done so have learned the hard lesson of what it's like to deal with someone like that. It feels impossible at times. It makes you want to quit.

The words *haters of good* translate a term unique to the New Testament. Paul coined this expression that means literally someone who does "not love" the good.[12] This person's ethical and moral palate has lost its taste. He or she finds it a turnoff even to be around the truly godly individuals.

Used only one other place in the Scriptures, the next term, *treacherous*, is attached to the name of Judas Iscariot—and labels him a traitor (see Luke 6:16). This is the word for an individual who will turn on you.[13] Like Judas, the person can work alongside you for years and appear to be your friend. But suddenly, and without warning, he will surprise you with disloyalty, duplicity, and treachery. I wish there were a way to detect such people. I have been wounded to the core by some of them. You probably have, too. Of course, Jesus knew from the beginning who would betray Him (see John 6:64). It would be helpful if we could know ahead of time, but we don't.

The next two terms go together: *reckless, conceited.* The first refers to someone whose actions are impetuous and irresponsible. They act first and think later (see Acts 19:36).[14] The second sounds initially like a synonym for the words *boastful, arrogant* that we read in 2 Timothy 3:2. But this term rendered *conceited* literally refers to a person so extremely arrogant that he or she is almost insane.[15] The individual presses right on, hell-bent on carrying out his own agenda.

Let's complete this sordid list by reading the end of it again. Paul says that these individuals are

> lovers of pleasure rather than lovers of God, holding to a form of godliness, although they have denied its power. (2 Timothy 3:4–5)

It would be easy for us to shake our heads and cluck our tongues at those on this list. After all, what better description could there be of the world *out there*? Isn't it the *external* danger that causes the need for this warning? Don't the walls of our churches and homes provide a fortress from these influences…a protection from snakes in suits…a sanctuary from the narcissists? I wish! Be careful. Never, ever forget that the far more *subtle* (and powerful) source of danger stems from *within us*…and from within the ranks of our churches. After all, these individuals hold "to a form of godliness." However, they deny its power because they refuse to draw upon it to change their lives. This kind of "holy hypocrisy" creates a spiritual schizophrenia in our homes and in our churches. Children and congregations who grow up in that kind of context become confused as they try to figure out where truth stops and falsehood starts, especially if wthe parents and pastors defend that kind of lifestyle. Thomas Oden offers this insight:

> The troubles Paul envisioned would come primarily from distortions within the worshiping community, not exclusively as external attacks from the state or culture or the economy. … It is sobering when faith realizes that persons may be deliberately unholy and still go to church, covetous and still say morning

prayers, blasphemers and still repeat perfectly the Apostles' Creed; they may be treacherous [that is, betrayers] and still remain on the church board, haters of good and still give lip service to God.[16]

David Wells takes that thought further:

Our world, our resplendent culture, has been turned into a substitute for God. However, this substitute, we quickly discover, offers us no principles by which to live. Furthermore, we also find that the self that has to fill the void at the center of our lives is incapable of fulfilling this function.... If we could see more clearly God in the full blaze of his burning purity, we would not be on easy terms with all the sins that now infect our souls and breed easy compromises with the spirit of the postmodern age.[17]

It is precisely this kind of tolerance for sin that threatens to undo the church of Jesus Christ. If the church does not realize this danger and take a stand against it—first in ourselves personally, and then in our congregations—the church will weaken its standard, it will lose its contagion, and it will continue to drift from the Lord's goals for the church toward a narcissistic obsession to self-satisfaction.

A Personal Warning: Keep Clear of Danger

Secularization theology has taught us to be "tolerant" of the world system—to be more accepting and understanding...and not bigoted. G. K. Chesterton says it well: "Tolerance is the virtue of the man without convictions."[18] It's always easier to claim tolerance and straddle the fence than to choose sides. Tolerance will get you elected. Tolerance keeps you popular with a voting congregation. Tolerance doesn't make waves at the office or across the backyard fence. But tolerance makes no impact for the kingdom of God.

I have to confess, when I get through studying a list of vices like this—full of sins far too familiar to me—I feel like throwing up my arms in frustration. I mean, who *hasn't* been guilty of these things? We all have. But the difference is that *we are concerned* that we have been guilty. It *bothers* us. The Spirit of God brings a healthy conviction and urges us, "You need to come to terms with this." John R. W. Stott says it well once again:

Paul is describing [those who preserve] the outward "form of religion" but were "denying the power of it." They evidently attended the worship services of the church. They sang the hymns, they said the "amen" to the prayers and put their money in the offering-plate. They looked and sounded egregiously pious. But it was *form* without *power*, outward show without inward reality, religion without morals, faith without works. True religion combines form and power. It is not external form without power.... It fosters a worship which is essentially "spiritual," arising from the heart, which expresses itself through public, corporate services, and which also issues in moral behavior. Otherwise, it is not only valueless; it is actually an abomination to the Lord.[19]

You may have heard the old adage from some disgruntled preacher: "Ministry would be great if it weren't for the people." That might be more humorous if it were not so true. When Paul comes to the end of this list, he issues a succinct, strong, and personal warning to Timothy:

Avoid such men as these. (2 Timothy 3:5)

In other words, keep clear of danger! This strong command doesn't mean to avoid sinners in the world around us. (Though we are to avoid their way of thinking.) Jesus Himself sat with publicans and sinners. Paul writes elsewhere, "I did not at all mean [not to associate] with the immoral people of this world...for then you would have to go out of the world" (1 Cor. 5:10, brackets mine). Paul's problem wasn't with the lost person. His problem was with the religious phony. It's the hypocrite that will drive you crazy...and take advantage of his or her position. That's why they are to be avoided. On at least three other occasions Paul issued the same warning to avoid these kinds of individuals (Rom. 16:17; 2 Thess. 3:6; Titus 3:10). Paul also warned Timothy to be careful to watch his own moral character (1 Tim. 4:16). When the church realizes this, it will have a much more realistic perspective and effective ministry.

A Final Warning: Beware of the Deception

We've come upon tough times. I don't mean the economic issues or the natural disasters or the international conflicts. What concerns me most is the insidious nature of our times. Jesus Himself predicted such times. He told us there would be days of tribulation. He said that many would fall away. He warned of betrayal and hatred and murder and vice. He stated that lawlessness would not only occur, it would increase and intensify. He said many false prophets would arise, and most people's love would grow cold. And so, when this is happening, there is no reason we should be surprised.

As Jesus left the earth and turned over the torch of responsibility to His apostles, they picked it up and ran with it. They spoke boldly. They wrote forcefully. They stood firmly. None more so than the apostle Paul. The aged apostle saved some of his boldest warnings and challenges for Timothy. I can't help wondering if Timothy received the news of Paul's beheading before he received the final letter Paul wrote to him. Perhaps the news of Paul's death arrived with the letter. We'll never know. But one thing is certain: Timothy took his words seriously. How often he must have read the last words of the great apostle: "Don't be naive. There are difficult times ahead. There will be those who will attempt to weaken your walk and hurt your ministry. Stay clear of these people!" We must beware of their dangerous deception.

If you ever go to Israel, don't miss the *Yad*

Vashem museum. It stands as an imposing yet mute reminder of the dreadful Holocaust that swept across Europe throughout the late 1930s and into the first half of the 1940s. The building itself is intentionally dull, drab, and gray. It penetrates the Jerusalem skies, as well as the consciences of all who visit. As many times as I've been there, it still moves me to tears. The pathway through the museum winds its way back and forth along painful scenes where you see life-size images of hollow-eyed individuals. Living skeletons, not knowing what kind of future they faced. Piles of children's shoes are stacked on the floor. Video testimonies reveal the savage, inhumane murders committed by the Nazi regime. *Yad Vashem* is the only museum I've ever seen with more exits than entrances. Many people can't make it all the way through. Some stand and stare. A few even collapse. If you're not wiping away tears by the end, you're not getting the message. It is heartrending. No one talks. Everyone shakes his or her head in disbelief.

When you get to the end of the museum, you enter the "Room of Remembrance" and witness notebook after notebook after notebook after notebook after notebook...shelves *filled* with notebooks containing the names of the six million Jews who were killed, all entries done by hand. The museum even preserved the iron sign, written in German, that hung over the entrance of Dachau, which, interpreted, reads "Work Makes You Free." Most victims who passed through the gate were led to believe that lie. But what stood out most to me was a statement printed in one of the official documents distributed to the Nazi guards overseeing the death camps: "The camp's law is that those going to their death should be deceived until the end." Did you catch those last four words? *Deceived until the end.*

We are living in a culture that is politically correct but is ethically, theologically, and morally corrupt. Right down to the core, our culture is totally depraved. We face hardships, conflicts, and trials none of us would have ever imagined. Why? Because we are in a war...an invisible war...a spiritual war. The church must realize this. Every day we encounter our adversary on his turf. Satan's philosophy of mass deception remains alive and well on Planet Earth. Not surprisingly, it is changing the face of our churches. Worshipers are being deceived by the millions.

Everything God's people love, Satan hates. He hates your Christian marriage, and he will do everything he can do destroy it. (After all, it's a picture of Christ and the church.) We're living in a day when the definition of marriage itself hangs in the balance. The adversary hates the family and will do all he can to break families apart. Chances are you are experiencing troubles in your family. Perhaps one of your children is in open rebellion. Why? Our adversary hates harmony in the family. You've likely seen ugly fights in your own church among its leaders or within the ranks of the congregation. Worship wars are common these days. More than likely, the conflicts occurring in your occupation have reached such an intense level you may be thinking, *I don't even know if Christianity works anymore.* It's all part of the enemy's strategy. The devil hates strong minds, secure wills, and stable bodies. He even hates books like this one, because he is being identified for who he really is: a deceiver.

In times like these we will encounter enemy attacks in any number of areas. While we ought not to live in fear of them, we dare not remain ignorant of them either. The enemy *loves* for us to stay ignorant of his schemes...or better yet, to think of him with a shrug. His desire? That people be deceived until the end.

*   *   *

The church must awaken to the fact that we face *difficult times*, as Paul warned. Erosion is taking a terrible toll. The hard news is that our times are going to get a lot worse, especially for those of us who resolve to press on upstream rather than to float along with the culture. The world will lead us directly *away from* the things of God rather than *toward* them. If we do not stay aware of the deception on the loose, we will be led right down that primrose path...to spiritual starvation and to ecclesiastical deception and destruction.

That's what the church must realize. So now... what can we do about it?

That's next.

How Should the Church React?

You cannot pick and choose from the Bible what you want to believe is inspired. The Bible does not present itself that way. Even more, the Bible will have no sustaining power for life if you make yourself the arbiter of what you will and will not believe about it.

—Kent Hughes and Bryan Chapell

How Should the Church React?

For the next few moments, let's travel together to another era. Back in the 1930s, across the Atlantic in Great Britain, you and I are living in England. International tensions are rising, but there is talk of peace in the air. Certainly we deserve it. We fought hard for it. Along with our allies, we won "the war to end all wars," and now we are enjoying the many fruits of that victory. Our own prime minister has made a trip to Germany and has signed a treaty with that strange fellow who wears a silly swastika on his arm, has a funny mustache under his nose, and a goose-stepping army at his disposal. Prime Minister Neville Chamberlain has returned, guaranteeing us that Adolf Hitler will honor the treaty he signed. He has assured us that peace is certain. And we believe it.

But there is one among us who doesn't have such

faith. Standing like a prophet from the Old Testament, this short, balding chap points his stubby finger and warns, "You cannot trust that dictator. He is a brutal man. He is an anti-Semitic murderer. He will invade our shores and take our land. There is no peace as long as he is in power. We must stand against him!"

Though many of us were not ready to hear it at first, as history unfolded, our eyes were opened to the truth of Winston Churchill's warnings. The man had tremendous foresight, discernment, and decisiveness—just like the "sons of Issachar" in the days of David (see 1 Chron. 12:32). Churchill knew what his nation should do, and he ultimately led his people to victory.

Three years after the Second World War, Churchill sat down with pen in hand and wrote his magnum opus. The carefully written six-volume work chronicles the conflict from its subtle beginnings... through its horrific years of bloodshed... to the victorious conclusion and difficult period of reconstruction. These volumes are some of the most treasured collections in my library. This literary tour de force represents Churchill's reflections on events that made better sense in hindsight. His first volume, titled *The Gathering Storm*, covers the events that led up to that great World War. Recently I pulled that book off my shelf and was reminded that each volume has its own theme. The theme of *The Gathering Storm* reveals, in Churchill's own insightful and discerning words: "How the English-speaking peoples through their unwisdom, carelessness and good nature allowed the wicked to rearm."[1] It struck me as I read those words how wise we would be to apply Churchill's hindsight to our own circumstances. Not in regard to geopolitical events... but in regard to the church.

Passionate Warnings We Must Heed

We are living in difficult times. Better stated, *savage* times. One of the greatest difficulties we face, ironically, is getting Christians to *recognize* that fact. Why? Because we do not fight flesh and blood, but the battle is against our adversary the devil and his legions of demons. Furthermore, because our enemy is invisible, we often don't take him seriously. Even when we do think of Satan, most people picture him entirely unlike he really is.

For years I have kept on a shelf in my study

a small, wooden devil. This bright red figurine stands about five inches high, has a bad nose, sinister eyes, and horns. It used to have a tail before it fell off, as well as an arm that held a pitchfork. When you push down on his little head, out pops a sign that says, "Welcome." My sister Luci gave it to me as a "gift" a long time ago. Before she painted over the pop-up sign, it read, "Go to hell." (But that's another story.) As I think about it, her modification is the only thing true about this little caricature. Everything else is nonsense, dim-witted, and ridiculous.

Satan is *not* ugly, horned, and carrying a pitchfork. Rather, he masquerades as an angel of light. He is one of the most beautiful and brilliant creatures God ever created. Satan's beauty is, in fact, what led to his prideful downfall (see Ezek. 28:14–17; 2 Cor. 11:14). Furthermore, the devil is not warning us of going to hell or destruction. Rather, he dangles deceptive salutations in our faces like bait on a hook. He is so winsome that he even lured a third of the angels with him when he fell from heaven (see Rev. 12:4). These have become his demons, supernatural creatures that carry out their insidious, sinister plans against the church of Jesus Christ. Their strategy of mass deception is right on target. They mislead Christians into thinking, *Oh, we're doing so great!* But we are not doing great. Remember? We are living in *difficult times.*

As we saw in the previous chapter, the apostle Paul wrote to a younger pastor, Timothy, about *the last days*, which include the times in which we live. But those words—although powerful—were just warnings that the church needs to realize. Reading those warnings isn't enough. We can do word studies based on the descriptive terms in those verses. We can examine the literary and historical contexts in which they were written. We can even form discussion groups about the sociopolitical implications of the dangers, just as Great Britain must have done in the months leading up to World War II. But merely *hearing* of danger isn't enough. It's incomplete. The church must do more than *realize* the threats. What is missing? The right response.

Some have chosen to remain passive...simply sighing, "We must be in the last days," and looking the other way, hoping things will finally turn the corner. Others in the past have taken a more fanatical approach. They decided to set dates for Christ's return and then sit on rooftops to wait...

and wait...and wait, only to climb down disillusioned, embarrassed, and humiliated. Many Christians believe the best course of action in these difficult times is to vote into office the greatest number of Christians we can—to return to the "spiritual heritage" of America. Others suggest we should take out a full-page ad in *USA Today* or the *Wall Street Journal*, signing our names as the last faithful few standing in the gap for truth (though I'm not sure what that would accomplish). Author and pastor Eugene Peterson offers this perspective:

Eighteen hundred years or so of Hebrew history capped by a full exposition in Jesus Christ tell us that God's revelation of Himself is rejected far more often than it is accepted, is dismissed by far more people than embrace it, and has been either attacked or ignored by every major culture or civilization in which it has given its witness: magnificent Egypt, fierce Assyria, beautiful Babylon, artistic Greece, political Rome, Enlightenment France, Nazi Germany, Renaissance Italy, Marxist Russia, Maoist China, and pursuit-of-happiness America. The community of God's people has survived in all of these cultures and civilizations but always as a minority, always marginal to the main-stream, never statistically significant.[2]

Christians are in the minority, to be sure. God always prefers to do His work through a remnant who face insuperable odds. Babies conceived in aging wombs. Meals for thousands from a meager sack lunch. Every sin atoned for by one Man's death. The world turned upside down by twelve ordinary men who were called as apostles. God specializes in the impossible. In fact, He is greatly glorified in circumstances where human ingenuity, creativity, and ability fall short.

However, shrugging our shoulders and looking the other way is not an option. Staring at the clouds for Jesus is not what He has commanded us to do. Taking out full-page ads won't do that much good—not in the long run. And although having courageous, wise Christians in political office may seem ideal, God has not ordained government to be the transforming agent of salvation or the platform for the proclamation of His truth in the world.

Christ is building His church for that purpose. An awakened church is a powerful and effective influence in a world that's lost its way.

It is time for today's church to awaken to the gathering storm upon us...to realize the invisible war around us...and to apply discernment, decisiveness, and passion for appropriate action.

Scriptural Reactions We Must Follow

The previous chapter wasn't a pretty scene. I offered a raw and realistic warning—straight from the Scriptures—of where we find ourselves today. As we return to the third chapter of Paul's final letter to Timothy, we discover that the great apostle is not just the bearer of bad news. He does not merely warn his spiritual son of the difficult times and then say, "Well, lots o' luck, Timothy." Not Paul. He gives inspired instruction on how the church is to react to a world that's unhinged. In the last five verses of the chapter, we find four practical guidelines worth our attention. The first one comes from Paul's concluding warning in the chapter:

> But evil men and impostors will proceed from bad to worse, deceiving and being deceived. (2 Timothy 3:13)

First, *stay realistic in the appraisal of your times.* Look at the word *evil* in the verse above. Let it say exactly what it says. Don't soften its meaning. Don't alter it or try to take off its edge. For sure, don't ignore it. It means *evil.* Walter Bauer, in his Greek-English lexicon, offers these synonyms: "wicked...bad, base, worthless, vicious, degenerate."[3] All of those terms portray these men as *evil.* Of course, the term *men* refers to mankind and includes women as well. We could translate it "evil people." Hardly an attractive portrait.

The next word, *impostors,* could refer to *sorcerers, conjurers, cheats,* or *swindlers* (be careful how you pronounce that last one). For this context, Bauer suggests these are "persons who veer from correct instruction and lead others into error."[4] Pretty clear, isn't it? We have another descriptive term in English for these individuals: *charlatans.* Watch out for such phonies! Why? Paul adds, "[They] will proceed from bad to worse." Literally it reads, "[They] will advance to the worse"—and their motive, Paul notes, is the same as Satan's: deception. That explains how they can be so effective.

If we in the church of Jesus Christ really believe the truth of verse 13, we will watch the news in a different way. We will see through the facade of much of what we hear in politics. We will discern the lies that appear on our high-definition televisions. And we'll be better able to understand what the enemy is trying to do.

Not surprisingly, both of these groups of people— evil men and impostors—will infiltrate the church. Eugene Peterson, in *The Message,* renders 2 Timothy 3:13 as follows:

> Unscrupulous con men will continue to exploit the faith. They're as deceived as the people they lead astray. As long as they are out there, things can only get worse.

Don't be surprised by the deception. Rather, anticipate it. Assume it. Stay realistic in your appraisal of these days. Thomas Oden says it this way: "Expect a gradual worsening of heretical distortions."[5] There's wisdom in that concise statement. Don't be fooled by *any* of the externals you see: persuasive speech...attractive brochures... celebrity endorsements...big crowds...persuasive logic...appealing personalities...even open Bibles!

I need to talk straight with you. Not everyone who wears a collar and uses a Bible is to be trusted. Just because someone quotes verses doesn't mean his or her message is reliable. (Remember, even Satan quoted Scripture to Jesus.) Not every church that has a huge following is blessed by God. And please, don't equate glitzy entertainment with truth. (Even Satan appears as an angel of light.) There are impostors on the loose—some are preying on churches—some are actually leading them! Watch out. Stay realistic. Pay attention. Apply discernment. Don't be duped by them any more than you are by a little red creature some would call the devil.

Entertaining churches with a shallow, superficial, feel-good message can never prepare you for the doctor's report that reveals cancer. Or the call from the policeman who says your son was in a head-on collision. Or the day your spouse abruptly walks out on your marriage. Suddenly, all of the Christian clichés, clever sermonettes, dazzling performances, and twisted Scriptures offer no help. Why? None of those are realistic. They lack depth. They are papier-mâché facades that crumble under stress.

You need deep truth to cling to. You need a solid foundation to fall back on. You need spiritual muscle to keep going in difficult times. Your soul needs the nourishment of biblical doctrine. That's what Paul wants for Timothy. That's also the kind of strength God wants for you... and for every believer in the church. A proper reaction to our times begins with a realistic appraisal. But it doesn't end there.

Believing the Truth in Difficult Times

How should the church react to such warnings? How do we stay realistic in these difficult days? Paul transitions from describing our treacherous times to instructing us how to react to them:

> You, however, continue in the things you have learned and become convinced of, knowing from whom you have learned them, and that from childhood you have known the sacred writings which are able to give you the wisdom that leads to salvation through faith which is in Christ Jesus. (2 Timothy 3:14–15)

The second guideline tells us how to accomplish the first one: *be convinced of the long-standing truths you have been taught.* The New American Standard translation puts *You* at the front of the sentence. The original language conveys that same emphasis. In other words, Paul tells Timothy, "Evil people and shysters will grow worse.... *You,* however, continue in the truth." The *you* is not only emphatic, it's also singular. It's an *individual* command that applies to each believer in the church. You and I will stay realistic in the appraisal of our times only by continuing in the long-standing truths we have been taught. For Timothy, that learning began at childhood. Earlier in the letter, Paul encourages Timothy:

> For I am mindful of the sincere faith within you, which first dwelt in your grandmother Lois and your mother Eunice, and I am sure that it is in you as well. (2 Timothy 1:5)

As far back as I can remember, my mother was teaching me about Jesus. In fact, I often say with a smile, I can still recall the first prayer that came from my mother's lips: "May God help you if you *ever* do that again!" I can't remember a time my mother wasn't memorizing Scripture. I confess, though, I didn't value it at the time. It used to drive me up a wall! Why? I was just a kid. I wanted to play ball. I preferred to be with my buddies. And my mother wanted to share with me her thoughts from Ezekiel, or wherever she happened to be reading at the time. I didn't see much value in it then.

But now, I appreciate how deeply entrenched she was in the Word of God. She prayed for me and believed in me in spite of my lack of interest and immaturity. She would claim verses for me and share them with me. I didn't know what that meant then (nor did I care), but I do now. It means that from childhood I've known a mother who shared with me "the sacred writings which are able to give you the wisdom that leads to salvation" (3:15). I have been spiritually rescued because of my mother's influence. It was my mother who shared with me the good news of Jesus. She was there when I was born again. I am eternally grateful to her.

This is a great time for you to pause and remember your own roots. Were you raised by parents who loved the Lord? I didn't ask if you were raised by perfect parents. (*None* of us had them...and neither do our children.) But did they love the Lord and tell you about Him? Were they faithful to instill within you an appetite for spiritual things? More and more in these difficult times, how rare is a set of godly parents! Those of us who had them are deeply grateful.

Even if one or both of your parents did not impart the faith to you, God often grants others who will. Lois shows that grandparents can have

an impact on the lives of their grandchildren. I
shared with you in chapter 1 that the most important adult male in my life as I was growing up was
my maternal grandfather. I was closer to him than
I was to my own father.

Sometimes those outside our families can have
the most powerful influence on us for the things
of God. Paul exhorts Timothy to continue in the
truths he has learned, "knowing from whom you
have learned them" (3:14). That includes Paul.
The apostle urges his spiritual son to fall back on
the long-standing bond they share together. If you
look up *Timothy* in a concordance, you will find
his name scattered across two dozen references in
the life and ministry of Paul. The two of them had
been through a lot together. Paul is appealing to the
bond between them so that Timothy will continue
in the virtues and values he saw modeled in Paul.

I have mentors whom I often recall with gratitude—Sunday school teachers and high school
instructors who looked past the nonsense in my life
and saw some jewels in the midst of the trash. I met
a man when I was overseas in the Marine Corps
who took me under his wing for sixteen months as
we learned the Scriptures together. How grateful I
am for him. When I enrolled at Dallas Theological

Seminary, I encountered men who had walked with Jesus forever, it seemed. I had never been around such godly men. They weren't perfect, but they helped deepen my life, and I love Jesus more today because of them.

Do you have mentors or those who have invested in your walk with Christ? Do you occasionally write them a letter of thanks? Every once in a while, pick up the phone and say, "I want to tell you how much you meant to me back when...," and then mention a few of the things they taught you. You have no idea how much that will encourage them. Stay in touch with those who influenced you. Hold them close in your heart. Retain their names in your memory. Review those notes you took from their years of distilled wisdom. Pray for them. Thank God for their investment in your beliefs and convictions. Your life was refracted through the personal experience you had with that good witness. Go there often.

Every once in a while I find myself wanting to pick up the phone and call my old mentor Ray Stedman, a man with whom I served as a young pastoral intern. Because of that relationship, I'm more discerning...my thinking is keener...I'm more relaxed...my life is better. Ray has been with the Lord for years now, and I miss him. What a fine model to pattern my life after. I want to stand true to the Scriptures, "knowing from whom [I] have learned them."

As the apostle Paul anticipates his own imminent death, he motivates Timothy to remember their bond and to be convinced of the long-standing truths he has been taught. Sometimes the most compelling incentive to stand firm in the faith is the memory of the life of a faithful mentor (see 1 Cor. 4:16; 11:1; 2 Pet. 1:15).

The simple Scriptures that can lead a child to salvation are also inexhaustible enough to take us deeper and deeper in our walk with God as adults. David Wells expresses it this way:

In its biblical setting...the gospel does not give us a choice between its simplicity and its profundity. It is both. It is both so simple that everyone can understand it and so profound that none can fully plumb its depths. It is this matchless combination of simplicity and profundity that has to be preserved if Christian faith in its biblical fullness is to be preserved. Those evangelicals who took its simplicity and abandoned its profundity are now finding that Christian faith itself is beginning to crumble in their hands.[6]

In other words, there's no reason to abandon reliable information just because it's been around for a long time. We never outgrow the truth. On the contrary, we are instructed to continue in it... we must abide in those long-standing truths... we must remain convinced of them. That is how the church must react in such difficult times. John Calvin expressed centuries ago what remains true to this day:

> Nothing is more inconsistent with the nature of faith than light [uncertain] evidence which allows us to embrace everything indiscriminately, whatever it may be.[7]

What a great statement. In other words, resist the temptation to grab hold of the "new and improved." That's marketing slang for a consumerist culture. You cannot improve on the long-standing, orthodox truth. Hold fast to it.

At the same time, let me say that there is no reason to reject what is new and fresh (read this carefully) *if it is in keeping with the long-standing truths set forth in the Scriptures.* Nothing is necessarily wrong with innovation unless it drifts from orthodox Christianity. We can—and must—communicate clearly to a contemporary audience. There is everything right about that. Every time I speak, my task is to make sure that my words are relevant to and easily grasped by twenty-first-century people. But in no way are my efforts at relevancy to take away from the impact of the truth. When we sacrifice truth on the altar of relevance, our words are no longer relevant. John R. W. Stott expresses it this way:

> To be sure, the church of every generation must seek to translate the faith into the contemporary idiom, to relate the unchanging Word to a changing world. But a translation is a rendering of the same message into another language; it is not a fresh composition. Yet this is what some modern radicals are doing, setting forth concepts of God and of Christ which Jesus and his apostles would not have recognized as their own.... The apostles themselves constantly warned their readers of newfangled ideas and called them back to the original apostolic message....

Here Paul enjoins Timothy to *abide* in what he has learned.[8]

Don't see the truth as out of date just because it goes back to your childhood and centuries beyond that! Truth then is truth now. Reliable information is timeless information. Don't try to improve on the long-standing truths of the Word of God. Rather, be convinced of them.

Leaning on the Truth in Difficult Times

One of the most strategic attacks the adversary wages against the church has to do with the inspiration of Scripture. It is *the* watershed issue of every new generation. The same tactic the serpent used against Eve in the Garden of Eden is the method he employs today in the church (see Gen. 3:1–5; 2 Cor. 11:3). If Satan can get us to doubt the truth of God's Word, then we have no standard by which to live, no clear message of salvation, and no guidelines for the oversight and advancement of Christ's church. If the truth of the Bible is muddled or cloudy in our minds, we have nothing to guide us but our own wits. And they are not enough! As my mentor Howie Hendricks often says, "A mist in the pulpit puts a fog in the pew."

Our third guideline can be expressed this way: *stand firm on the inspired Word of God.* We have a very good reason to be convinced of the long-standing truths we have been taught.... *They are inspired!* Paul reveals to Timothy this marvelous fact:

All Scripture is inspired by God. (2 Timothy 3:16)

This may be familiar territory for you. But believe me, the words *inspired by God* sound eccentric to postmodern ears. Most people have never been taught about the inspiration of Scripture, and many who have been exposed to the biblical doctrine also have been instructed to disbelieve it. It wasn't always that way.

There was a time when theological thinking, biblical understanding, and doctrinal truth were our guides for living. Even in my lifetime, I can remember the general opinion that if the Scripture said it, that was our guide. If the Bible addressed it, we didn't drift from the standard. If the Word of God declared it, that's what we believed. Sounds terribly narrow and naive today, I know. But I can remember when politicians, as well as educators, cited the Scriptures frequently. Prayer was a part of every classroom in my elementary school years. No one even *thought* of it as being inappropriate. (Being "politically correct" was unheard of.) Presidents often quoted from the Bible (no, that's not a misprint). Pastors stood and spoke fervently in favor of the Holy Scriptures... they took the Scriptures literally...they taught the Bible with confidence and authority. Evangelical pulpits were known for strong doctrine and a commitment to biblical exposition. Why? Because the Bible was viewed as inspired of God.

No longer. Today God has been reduced to a national mascot where *God* can mean anything to anybody. Politicians frequently gush the politically correct, "God bless America," but none of them dare use the politically incorrect *J* word. Prayer in school is now the stuff of lawsuits, and no president has openly quoted the Bible in decades. Ministers who view the Word of God as inspired are dwindling each year. And many churches have become entertainment centers where people are made to *feel* good about themselves, rather than to repent of their sins. Author and law professor Stephen Carter writes,

My date book contains cartoons first published in *The New Yorker*. One shows a young boy in front of his class, doing arithmetic at the blackboard. He has just written "7 × 5 = 75" and says to his astonished teacher, "It may be wrong, but it's how I feel." There, in a nutshell, is the problem with the post-secular university. Faith is dead, reason is dying, but "how I feel" is going strong.[9]

If the Bible is not inspired, then it is not authoritative. And if it is not authoritative, then its commands are mere suggestions on par with every other book of morals. Furthermore, what it says about God is only as valid as any other religion's so-called holy writings. See the problem? With no inspired text, our guide then becomes our feelings. It's the same slick lie Satan whispered in Eve's ear in the garden. And that deception destroyed the spiritual lives of the whole human race. Our times are "difficult" because of it.

When Billy Graham released his autobiography, *Just as I Am*, I devoured the 760-page volume in a matter of weeks. One of the many parts of Billy's life that intrigued me occurred at the beginning of his ministry. Having been challenged by a friend named Chuck Templeton that "people no longer accept the Bible as inspired," Billy began to wrestle with the doctrine of inspiration. He finally came to a spiritual and emotional impasse. While on a walk alone in the woods one night, Billy opened his Bible on an old tree stump, knelt down, and began to pray. He writes,

The exact wording of my prayer is beyond recall, but it must have echoed my thoughts: "O God! There are many things in this book I do not understand. There are many problems with it for which I have no solution. There are seeming contradictions. There are some areas in it that do not seem to correlate with modern science. I can't answer some of the philosophical and psychological questions Chuck and others are raising." I was trying to be on the level with God, but something remained unspoken. At last the Holy Spirit freed me to say it. "Father, I am going to accept this as Thy Word—by *faith!* I'm going to allow faith to go beyond my intellectual questions and doubts, and I will believe this to be Your inspired Word."[10]

The difficult times in which we live will try everything possible to persuade us to doubt God's Word. Science, philosophy, psychology, and sometimes even shades of theology will be held out as proof that "people no longer accept the Bible as inspired." But they do. Paul did. So did Jesus. So does Billy. Many of us still do.

While there are numerous objective facts that support, and some would even argue *prove*, that the Bible is inspired, in the end we each find ourselves kneeling by a stump and trusting the wisdom of our infinite God over the limitations of human intellect. David Wells reminds us: "Christianity is not just an experience, we need to remember, but it is about truth."[11] Without apology, without embarrassment, and without committing intellectual suicide, we believe by faith that God's Word is what it says it is. An awakened church stands firm on the inspired Word of God.

The Bible declares its inspiration: "All Scripture is inspired by God" (2 Tim. 3:16). The words *all Scripture* literally mean "every individual writing." That's every word in the original Hebrew, Aramaic, and Greek. And to the degree that our modern translations accurately render the original text, they, too, are authoritative. *All Scripture.* That means that *all* parts are equally inspired. If you carry a red-letter edition, the text in red isn't more inspired than the black print surrounding it. The red letters represent the words of Jesus, but they are no more inspired than the Epistles of Paul, the writings of Moses, or the book of Revelation. The written Word of God comprises *all* Scripture. That includes the Old Testament, by the way. Just because you're a Christian doesn't mean that the Gospel of Luke is more inspired than the book of Leviticus. You may have to work harder to glean the timeless truths from Leviticus, but they are just as relevant for you. Why? Because Leviticus—and *all* Scripture—is "inspired by God."

The word *inspired* comes from a unique term that appears only once in the New Testament. The Greek adjective *theopneustos* is a compound word from *theos,* meaning "God," and *pneustos,* meaning "spirit" or "breath."[12] The New International Version renders the inimitable term literally: "All Scripture is *God-breathed.*"

The Scriptures are the God-breathed message from God to humankind. That means God superintended the human authors so that they used their individual personalities to compose and record Holy Scripture without error—right down to the very words themselves. This was not mindless dictation but the writing of various authors who were carried along in the process by the supernatural power of the Holy Spirit (see 2 Pet. 1:21). The result? The Bible you have—all sixty-six books—represents the very Word of God.

Let me define and explain three terms that are often confused:

- *Revelation*—God's *giving* of His truth
- *Inspiration*—Men's *writing* of God's truth
- *Illumination*—Our *being enlightened* by that same truth

The word *revelation* refers to God's giving of His Word to humankind—either in spoken or written form. That has ceased. There is no longer revelation given from God now that the Holy Scriptures are complete. After John wrote the last "Amen" in Revelation 22:21, we had all the revelation we need for life and godliness found in the Bible (see 2 Pet. 1:3–4). The word *inspiration* refers to the process of human writers recording, without error, the very words and mind of God.

That's what "God-breathed" is all about. The work of inspiration has also ceased. The third term, *illumination,* refers to the understanding or insight the Holy Spirit gives one who reads or hears the written Word of God. Revelation has ceased. Inspiration has ceased. But illumination continues on; it occurs every day. It could even be occurring as you read the Scripture from this chapter.

Practically speaking, *illumination* plays a part in how the church should react to its difficult times. If you need direction in life, you don't need to look for Jesus' face in a burrito, or try to interpret the clouds in the sky for a sign from God, or rely on the advice of a professor with three PhDs. When you're not sure which direction to go, *read your Bible.* Seek the Scriptures and pray to your God. Ask the Lord for guidance and for Him to illuminate His Word as you observe the text, interpret its literal meaning, and apply its truths. You can also ask your Bible-believing pastor or a godly mentor or Christian counselor for guidance *from the Scriptures.* The Word of God is like a light that illumines our dark paths (see Ps. 119:105; 2 Pet. 1:19). It guides us. It provides direction. It gives us insight we would never have otherwise. Stand firm on the inspired Word of God.

Living the Truth in Difficult Times

If God's Word *is* inspired, then it *has* authority and exceeding benefit to our lives. Paul explains to Timothy the benefits of inspiration:

> All Scripture is inspired by God and profitable for teaching, for reproof, for correction, for training in righteousness; so that the man of God may be adequate, equipped for every good work. (2 Timothy 3:16–17)

Scripture, *because* it is inspired, is also *profitable*. Walter Bauer states that the term *profitable* can mean "to be successful in accomplishing some objective."[13] That definition reminds me of the beautiful words of the Lord, recorded by inspiration through the prophet Isaiah:

> *For as the rain and the snow come down from
>   heaven,
> And do not return there without watering the
>   earth
> And making it bear and sprout,
> And furnishing seed to the sower and bread to
>   the eater;*

*So will My word be which goes forth from My
   mouth;
It will not return to Me empty,
Without accomplishing what I desire,
And without succeeding in the matter for which
   I sent it.* (Isaiah 55:10–11)

God's Word is always successful in accomplishing its objective. And what objective is that? Very
simply, it's the transformation of our lives…and
the building up of Jesus' church. A fourth guideline challenges us to cooperate with Scripture's
inspired objective: *allow the truth to fulfill its purpose in your everyday life.* The church should react
to its times, not by simply reading the Bible for
insightful *information*, but by allowing its truths to
bring about inner *transformation*. For the church,
life change should be a normal response from
exposure to truth, just as crops grow as a natural
result of falling rain. Our belief affects our behavior…our creed shapes our conduct…our doctrine
determines our duty. God designed it that way.

The benefits of the church's having an inspired
text relate to four primary areas. First, Paul says, the
Scriptures are *profitable for teaching* (2 Tim. 3:16).
That means our source for truth comes directly

from God through the pages of Holy Scripture. The foundation of our faith is in the Bible...and in the Bible alone.

The Word of God is also profitable *for reproof* (3:16). According to Greek scholars Louw and Nida, the term means "to state that someone has done wrong, with the implication that there is adequate proof of such wrongdoing."[14] Without the Word of God, we have no standard of morality—no "proof" of truth. But with God's Word, we have an objective standard that enables us to distinguish right from wrong. We can call a spade a spade because the Bible allows for no subjective truth. The value of having God's Word—and even better, of knowing its truths—is beyond measure when it comes to discerning and coping with our times.

The third benefit of Scripture is *for correction* (3:16). The term carries the meaning "to set up straight." The New Living Translation says, "It straightens us out." What a great way to express it. When we expose our minds to the truth of God's Word, our crooked thinking is straightened. Our minds are renewed...the world's mold is broken... we are reshaped into the image of Christ...and our passion for Jesus' church grows. Rather than the church adjusting the Bible to fit its agenda, "correction" allows just the opposite to occur.

Paul lists a fourth advantage of having an inspired text: "for training in righteousness" (3:16). We get our word *pedagogy* from the Greek term for "training."[15] It implies a process of growth that occurs as we submit ourselves to the scrutiny of the Scriptures. One of the typical characteristics of adolescence is the mind-set of *It's all about me.* That's why a teenager's favorite place is in front of a mirror. Every pimple is a life-changing issue. Every hair out of place requires immediate attention. But as we grow older, we realize that maturity has different priorities. Adults take care of *others*—often their own children. That analogy applies to the spiritual life as well.

When we're young in the faith, we need to learn appropriate life skills: how to relate, how to forgive, the importance of accepting others, the necessity of extending grace and mercy, the value of being compassionate, the necessity of prayer, and much more. Those skills take training—a lifetime of training!

Paul reminds Timothy that these four benefits of Scripture have one goal: "so that the man of God may be adequate, equipped for every good work" (3:17). Not only does the Bible reveal what's wrong with our lives, it also trains us to develop as believers so that we become equipped to serve others. That's a mark of maturity.

With benefits like that, it's no wonder that Satan's first line of attack is against the Word of God! Once the inspiration of Scripture is called into question, and the lines are blurred between right and wrong, then the doctrinal dominoes begin to fall one by one. The church has no basis of truth... no standard that proclaims salvation... no authority to call the world to repentance... and none of the essential benefits that produce spiritual maturity. With inspiration in the balance, humanity is left as we were in the Garden of Eden—helpless and hopeless. Satan's old lie still works, and its results still kill.

We live in an age that has drifted from a wholesome standard of morality to a wholesale and undiscerning emphasis on tolerance. Biblical standards are being replaced with political correctness. Criminals are being defended more passionately than victims. If we claim something is immoral, we are marked as bigoted, prejudiced, and out of touch. If we stand against same-sex marriage, we are branded as intolerant, homophobic, and guilty of "hate speech." If we are pro-life, we are seen as antiwomen, narrow-minded, and lacking compassion. If we promote abstinence as the best method for birth control, as well as for preparation for a healthy marriage, we become a laughingstock, and we're told we don't live in the real world.

Even though Scripture clearly states what is right and wrong, we have no hearing in the world's ears. Why? Because Scripture is not viewed as God's Word. There is a blurring of the line between right and wrong. That's the world, and it shouldn't surprise us. That will *always* be true of the world's system, as long as it's headed by Satan.

But *that should never describe the church*, headed by Jesus Christ. Unfortunately, it often does.

So how should the awakened church react in such difficult times? How can we avoid the drift that has occurred in society from infecting and destroying our churches? How can we renew our passion for what Jesus is building? Let's review the four guidelines:

- Stay realistic in the appraisal of your times.
- Be convinced of the long-standing truths you have been taught.

- Stand firm on the inspired Word of God.
- Allow the truth of God's Word to fulfill its purpose in your everyday life.

Practical Principles We Must Remember

Remember Jay Leno taking his microphone to the streets and exposing the laughable ignorance the general public has about the Bible? I wish the laughs were only *outside* the church. Unfortunately, a growing number of our new generation of Christians reveals a poor understanding of the Book they believe to be inspired.

Larry Fowler, executive director of global training for Awana, noted a deficiency in the biblical knowledge of incoming college freshmen. Read his own words as recorded in his book, *Raising a Modern-Day Joseph*:

I asked Pat Blewett, Dean of the College at Columbia International University, how he viewed the Bible knowledge of incoming college freshmen. He said that ten to fifteen years ago, the average score for freshmen on the college's Bible knowledge test was about 60 percent; now it's less than 40 percent.

Perhaps the greater tragedy is the number of Christian colleges and universities who are no longer concerned enough about biblical knowledge even to test students on it. Instead, many now test for spiritual formation without any concern for the biblical foundation on which true maturity comes. In late 2005, Awana asked two questions of a hundred Bible colleges and seminaries: (1) "Do you measure the Bible knowledge of incoming freshmen?" (2) "If so, have you seen a trend in their scores over the past ten years?" Fifty-eight schools responded. A number of responses included comments such as these:

> The general consensus of the Bible and theology faculty is that there has been a marked decrease in the level of Bible knowledge in recent years. It seems that even students who have gone to church all their lives are not as biblically literate as students in years gone by. (David Reese, Toccoa Falls College)

> I have been teaching at Puget Sound Christian College for 23 years in the Bible department.

The level of Bible knowledge for incoming students has decreased dramatically over this period. Our assumption now is that incoming freshmen know nothing about the Bible, and that we must start at the most basic level. (Mark S. Krause, Dean, Puget Sound Christian College)[16]

Shocking results, aren't they? Those disturbing facts represent incoming freshmen at Christian schools. Let me be more specific: *that represents our children and grandchildren.* It may even represent you. Unless you are unusual, you probably know less about the Bible than your grandparents knew. The biblical ignorance is, at times, heartbreaking. Why? Because, practically speaking, even if you believe the Bible *is* the Word of God, it does you no good if you don't read it. You cannot apply what you do not know.

Let me conclude this chapter with two practical principles I'd like you to remember. First, *without the Bible we would never find our way.* In other words, if we didn't have the Word of God, we would be hopelessly lost in life and in eternity. I love the story Kent Hughes tells in his book *To Guard the Deposit*:

Dr. William Evans, who pastored the College Church [in Wheaton, Illinois] from 1906–1909, was an unusually accomplished man. He had the entire *King James Version* of the Bible memorized as well as the New Testament of the *American Standard Version*. Dr. Evans also authored over fifty books. His son, Louis, became one of the best-known preachers in America and for many years pastored the eminent First Presbyterian Church, Hollywood. When Dr. William Evans retired, he moved to Hollywood to be near his son, and when Louis was away he would substitute for him [in the pulpit].

One unforgettable Sunday Dr. William, as he was affectionately called, spoke on the virgin birth. All were amazed when he raised his Bible and tore out the pages that narrate the birth of the Lord. As the tattered scraps floated down toward the congregation, he shouted, "If we can't believe in the virgin birth, let's tear it out of the Bible!" And then as he drove home his point, he tore out the resurrection chapters, then the miracle narratives, then anything conveying the supernatural. The floor was littered with mutilated pages.

Finally, with immense drama he held up the only remaining portion and said, "And this is all we have left—the Sermon on the Mount. And that has no authority for me if a divine Christ didn't preach it." After a few more words, he asked his listeners to bow for the benediction. But before he could pray, a man in that vast and sedate congregation stood up and cried, "No, no! Go on! We want more!" Several others joined in. So Dr. Evans preached for another fifty minutes.

Dr. Evans was right. You cannot pick and choose from the Bible what you want to believe is inspired. The Bible does not present itself that way. Even more, the Bible will have no sustaining power for life if you make yourself the arbiter of what you will and will not believe about it.[17]

Let's imagine that you and I are exploring the jungles of Africa. We get into a deep, dense area of the jungle, so thick it's almost dark. It isn't long before we have lost our way. If our lives depended on it, we couldn't tell if we were going north or south. There is no sun, no stars, and no trail or river to follow. (Let's throw in a few nasty mosquitoes for good measure.) Got the picture? We are *hopelessly* lost. Suddenly, a twig snaps behind us...and we hear footsteps approaching. But we're relieved when someone calls our names and walks into the clearing. "I'm glad I found you," he says. "I have a map and a compass I thought you might need. Would you like them?" Now, pause for a moment. How many of us would answer, "Are you kidding? That map of Africa is really old. I'm not sure I can trust it. I mean, look how wrinkled and worn it is! And that compass...it may or *may not* be pointing north...how can I know for sure? No thanks; I think we'll stay on our own." We would be thickheaded if we said that! (And we would die in the jungle.)

The Bible is God's map and compass given to us. The compass *always* points north. The map *always* guides correctly—in spite of our feelings and regardless of the valleys it leads us through. The problem occurs when we doubt that this is true. Without the Bible we would never find our way.

The same is true of the Global Positioning Systems (GPSs) in our cars. I love the GPS in my truck. I've come to depend on it. I just punch in the address where I want to go...and *presto!* The whole route is laid out for me. As I drive along, the system even talks to me: "At the next corner, turn right." Sometimes I expect it to say: "You're lost, you dummy! I've told you four times not to go that far." But instead it responds with a kind but clear "Recalculating" and determines another route to get me there.

The Bible is our spiritual GPS—we could call it "God's Positioning System." You'll be going along in life and a passage of Scripture will come to mind that stops you in your tracks. It's almost as if God is saying, "Hey, I'm trying to get your attention. Turn here. Change your direction. I want you to follow My lead." Ever had that happen? I certainly have. Truth be told, God has done a lot of "recalculating" in my life! But I've found it true that I've never gotten lost when I have followed His Word. I may have *felt* lost... but I've never *been* lost. Not once.

That brings us to the second principle to remember: *with the Bible, we should never lose our way.* That sounds similar to the first principle, but it's different. The better we get to know the Scriptures, the more intimately we will know the Lord of the Scriptures—and we will *never* lose our way. Those aren't just words... those are carefully chosen terms.

May I urge you to become a better student of your Bible? Familiarize yourself with its contents. Filter today's "difficult times" through its grid. The better you know the Word of God, the better you will recognize the trail signs to help you find your way through the jungle. Otherwise, you'll wander and follow every stray sound. Your whole life will be "recalculating." There's no need for that.

And let me warn you, just because you follow the map and trust the compass, it doesn't mean the road is always straight, smooth, and without potholes. God's plan for our lives includes the journey as well as the destination. Chances are good you'll feel lonely at times when others around you aren't lonely. It's very possible that you'll experience attacks from the enemy that others aren't experiencing. In fact, you will *know* the enemy is working against you because you're walking in obedience to the revealed Word of God. That's okay. I urge you to value God's Word...to study all of it...to see all Scripture as equally inspired...and to follow it tenaciously.

In light of such treacherous times, we can't pull the covers up over our heads and hope that tomorrow morning will be better. An awakened church remains realistic in its appraisal of the world. We cannot live with, as Churchill wrote, "unwisdom, carelessness, and naive good nature." That type of Pollyanna only allows the enemy to rearm.

Without a firm belief in the inspired Word of God, our churches will not endure. Don't misunderstand, Jesus *is* building His church, and the gates of Hades *will not* prevail against it. But our local churches may or may not be part of that grand plan. Our participation is a privilege, not a prerogative. Our churches must believe the Word, teach the Word, and hold believers accountable to the truths of the Word. Otherwise, we're playing religious games.

Some in the church, thankfully, are realizing what is happening... they are awakening and reacting appropriately.

*   *   *

While greeting various people following one of our morning worship services at Stonebriar Community Church, I noticed an older couple waiting patiently until all others had left. Both of them took my hand in theirs and struggled to say what was on their hearts. I knew they felt something deeply because their eyes were red from weeping. The husband was so moved, he could only repeat the words, "We're starving... we're starving." His wife explained that they were visiting, that they had been searching for a church where the worship was meaningful, where the music ministered to their souls, and where God's Word was faithfully proclaimed.

Her husband interrupted. "We're starving. We've not been fed like this for years. Our pastor no longer stands strong in the Scriptures...we're on a long drift...and our souls are parched." It was obvious that God had spoken to them, that our music had brought them hope and comfort, and that the preaching of the Word had nourished their souls. They have ached as the church they have been a part of most of their lives has long since left its roots and is now only a shell of what it once was.

They left, assuring me, "We'll be back, and we plan to bring our friends. All of them are also starving!"

It may sound simplistic that my counsel to the church in such difficult times is to recommit itself to the inspired Word of God. I mean...*that's it?* Why not offer ten points for rapid church growth, or seven surefire principles for leadership, or twenty-five ways to—*wait a minute!* That's marketing talk...that's consumer lingo...that's turning the church into a business with a cross stuck on top. That's not what Jesus is building.

The best counsel I can offer the church is for us to recommit ourselves individually, as well as corporately, to believing and living the inspired Word of God. It's all right there. Read again Paul's words to Timothy—aloud, if possible—as if they are his words to your church... *and to you personally*:

> All Scripture is inspired by God and profitable for teaching, for reproof, for correction, for training in righteousness; so that the man of God may be adequate, equipped for every good work. (2 Timothy 3:16–17)

Indeed, what we believe about the Bible will determine how we live. But let me add that a deep commitment to biblical doctrine and a dedication to every good work—from local ministry to missions—is not enough. A local body of believers can *still* drift away from Jesus' plan for His church... even with solid doctrine and genuine deeds.

As strange as that may sound, there is still something missing.

The Church on a Long Drift

*Much of our spiritual activity
is nothing more than a cheap
anesthetic to deaden the pain
of an empty life.*

—Lewis Sperry Chafer

The Church on a Long Drift

I don't remember much about high school chemistry. Truth be told, most of it was Dullsville to me. Downright boring. But one experiment I'll never forget.

We boiled a frog.

My chemistry teacher gathered the class around an oversize beaker half full of water. We took this little frog and dropped him in. We didn't even put a lid on the glass. The frog kicked around and swam from side to side, completely comfortable with his surroundings. Our teacher slid a Bunsen burner underneath the beaker, lit the flame, and kicked up the temperature about .017 degrees Fahrenheit per minute. Then we waited and watched in silence. (It was the only time I remember every one of us in that class paying attention.) The water started getting warmer...and warmer...and a little warmer... and, finally, tiny bubbles started to rise. The little frog by now had slowed his kicking, eventually stiffened, and, ultimately, boiled to death. Most of the guys in the class thought it was great! If I remember correctly, the thing turned white at the end. Pretty gross.

My teacher told us that if we had dropped that amphibian into boiling water to begin with, it would have hopped right out. But by putting it in nice, comfortable, tepid water and slowly turning up the heat... the frog eventually stewed in its own grease. I have no idea how that related to chemistry. But its implications for the church are permanently burned into my brain.

If we took most evangelical believers from the 1930s and dropped them into a mainstream, twenty-first-century church, it would be a complete shock to their systems. They would scramble to get out immediately! How did such a difference come about over the years? Many local churches tolerated a rise in our secular temperature, and in the passing of decades, the church in general has drifted from its biblical convictions. Never with a formal announcement, and often without many people even knowing it was happening, postmodern thinking has progressively replaced biblical beliefs. The church has been on a long drift, which has now reached epidemic proportions. What occurred? In a word: *erosion.*

Like that Russian church that disappeared brick by brick...like the edge of the cliff beside my grandfather's bay cottage...and like that white frog bobbing in the beaker, erosion has taken its toll. Put bluntly, today's church is in hot water!

Toward the end of the eighteenth century, historian Edward Gibbon spent almost twenty years writing his six-volume masterpiece, *The History of the Decline and Fall of the Roman Empire.* Rome represents a prime example of the *process* and *results* of erosion—as observed in its "decline" and "fall." I have read that the average age of the world's greatest nations is only about two hundred years. Those nations always followed a predictable cycle. Picture it as a large circle, and start the clockwise cycle from the bottom. The nation goes from bondage to spiritual faith...to great courage... to liberty...to abundance...to complacency... to apathy...to dependence...back into bondage. The cycle represents erosion.

As I think of the spiritual apathy of the church in America, I shudder to think of what lies ahead for us in the life cycle of our once-great nation.

Let's Consider a Twenty-First-Century Example

For more than twenty years, Cynthia and I have enjoyed a friendship with a wonderful Christian couple who live in another state. They are bright, balanced, and clear-thinking people...but they are also brokenhearted. The husband, who is a physician, recently sent me a letter. I have asked for permission to reproduce some of what he wrote me below. (I have omitted names for obvious reasons.) He writes,

> *Chuck,*
> *I just finished listening to your sermon called, "Worship: A Commitment...Not a War." It hit me like a cup of cold water on a lost man wandering in the desert. I believe this is the most important message to the church I've listened to in the last twenty years.*
> *Absolutely everything you talked about has been happening in our church gradually [that's an* erosion *word] over these last twenty years. I joined our church twenty-six years ago in the most fruitful days of our former pastor's ministry. It was an exciting time of church growth*

and personal, spiritual growth fueled by his expository preaching.

But toward the end of the 1980s I started to notice a change. We began to take our cues from other large churches. We sent delegations of our pastors to study their methods and our emphasis changed from preaching to believers to talking to "seekers." The unapologetic preaching style of our pastor that convicted me of many failings in my spiritual life now gave way to a watered-down style tailored to the needs of "seekers." I'm very grateful for the truth from God's Word that he taught me, but near the end of his ministry I looked forward to his replacement. I was eager to digest more substantial spiritual teaching. I anticipated a new pastor would have the same fire in his belly our pastor had when I first joined the church. I believed the church would benefit from that change.

It has been three years now since our new pastor arrived. Although he is an accomplished public speaker, and I'm sure he has a heart for God, unfortunately I feel as though he's taken us even further down the path *[those are* erosion *words] of modern [weak] worship that you described in your message. Gone is expository preaching. "Sermonettes," as you described, are all too common here. (Today's sermon lasted twelve minutes.) The music grows more and more [erosion words] superficial.*

With your permission, I would like to send a copy of the sermon you preached on worship to our present pastor. Perhaps you could also send about five copies of the CDs because there are others I know who need to hear this. God bless you for your courage and faithfulness in preaching the Word.

Did you notice the ominous terms of erosion in his letter? Tragically, this story is far from an isolated or rare situation.

I had the privilege recently to address about eighty pastors and wives during an Insight for Living Bible conference. We gathered in a small room, and I listened to story after tragic story of the fallout occurring in their churches because of erosion. As they candidly shared with me, I did my best to encourage them. My great hope for those men and women was that they might come to experience the joy that is mine week after week. Without wanting to sound self-serving in any way, I told them about the privilege I have of engaging in a serious study of the Scriptures and preaching to a congregation who loves strong, biblical exhortation and practical application. Some of the pastors who sat before me had longing in their eyes. I think I could have expanded our church staff by at least forty men that day!

But I quickly added that our church's blessings haven't come easily. There was a price to be paid. I told the group the story of the erosion of our eleven-year-old church and the extremely painful journey we traveled to get back on course (much of what I wrote about in chapter 1). Using our church as an example of what can happen—both negatively and positively—I spoke forcefully and unapologetically, knowing that no church is immune to the slow, silent, and subtle presence of erosion.

Please understand, I don't want to give the impression that I believe Stonebriar Community Church is the only place that has it right. Absolutely not. That would be pride beyond description. By the grace of God we are able to do what we do...and also to keep doing it for His glory. (And we still have much to learn.) But we are not alone in the struggle against the long drift. Truth be told, many churches have awakened to the threat of erosion. They have remained on guard. They have stayed alert. They are continuing to preach God's Word. But their battle is not over. It never will be.

Without constant, ceaseless effort, erosion will take its toll on *any* ministry. You may be surprised to know that it even happened to a church founded by the apostle Paul back in the first century.

Let's Return to a First-Century Setting

I can always tell when my truck's tires need balancing and rotating. When I lift my hands off the steering wheel, the vehicle slowly drifts to one side. The thought struck me one day that this is what the church's ministry is like. The world, the flesh, and the devil have irreparably thrown our churches off balance. We cannot for one moment take our hands off the wheel or our eyes off the road. If we do, it's just a matter of time until we drift off into the ditch of destruction. Only with our hands on the Scriptures and our eyes on the Lord can we restrain the drift.

The church has been on a long drift that goes as far back as the first century. One of the clearest examples of erosion occurred at the church in the ancient city of Ephesus. Paul founded that church—along with his traveling companions, Priscilla and Aquila—at the end of his second missionary journey. After Paul shared the Word of God with the Jews in the synagogue, they asked him to stay longer in Ephesus. But he refused, saying, "I will return to you again if God wills" (Acts 18:21). Indeed, God was willing.

Ephesus: A Church Founded on Solid Biblical Teaching

When Paul returned to Ephesus on his third missionary journey, he found some disciples there and baptized them. In addition, as he had done before,

> he entered the synagogue and continued speaking out boldly for three months, reasoning and persuading them about the kingdom of God. But when some were becoming hardened and disobedient, speaking evil of the Way before the people, he withdrew from them and took away the disciples, reasoning daily in the school of Tyrannus. (Acts 19:8–9)

I always smile when I read that last verse. The Greek name Tyrannus is from the same root as our word *tyrant.* I wonder if his mother named him that or if his name came from former students of his school! The Ephesian church got its start in a school—as some churches do today. Paul enjoyed the freedom to teach daily, which included declaring the great news of the gospel of Jesus Christ. And notice this:

> This took place for two years, so that all who lived in Asia heard the word of the Lord, both Jews and Greeks. (Acts 19:10)

No demographic study underpinned the founding of this church. No secular marketing, neighborhood canvassing, or fleshly methods for enlarging the numbers occurred. There was no manipulative technique to induce people to give more of their money. There was none of that! Paul simply taught the Word of God for more than two years...and God validated His Word with miracles (see Acts 19:11–12). Paul was consistently faithful to preach with accuracy and clarity and practicality...and as a result, the message spread as the congregation grew deeper and larger.

Understand, there's nothing wrong with creatively communicating to our neighborhoods about our churches. But when promotion receives more emphasis than the essentials—the apostles' teaching, fellowship, the breaking of bread, and prayer (see Acts 2:42)—then the tail is wagging the dog. The church starts drifting off course. Erosion sets in. On the other hand, when we commit ourselves to the essentials, our churches will be contagious for the right reasons. And in Ephesus, that is exactly what was occurring: "all who lived in Asia heard the word of the Lord, both Jews and Greeks" (19:10). Word of mouth has always been God's preferred method of getting the message out.

When we read of God's blessing on Ephesus, we might be tempted to think, *How wonderful! With Paul in leadership and God's Word being taught, it must have been an easy, downhill slide from this point.* Not at all. On the contrary, behind the scenes a price was being paid.

Growth: A Body Tested in Many Different Ways

The Ephesian church was expanding, to be sure, but there was also great testing. Never doubt this fact: wherever we experience the bold and uncompromising declaration of God's truth, we will encounter the test of spiritual warfare. Satan hates it when

God's Word is declared, believed, and obeyed. It is always when believers are in close harmony with one another…when the body of Christ is being taught…when Jesus is building His church that the attacks kick in. The gates of Hades will pull out all the stops in hopes of hindering the ministry. But look at the power the Lord provided in the midst of the battle:

> God was performing extraordinary miracles by the hands of Paul, so that handkerchiefs or aprons were even carried from his body to the sick, and the diseases left them and the evil spirits went out. (Acts 19:11–12)

God was at work in Ephesus. Not only were healings occurring, but also spiritual victories took place as evil spirits departed. When the teaching of the Scriptures occurs, when the name of the Lord Jesus Christ is lifted up, when God's people remain faithful to His truth, the impact is absolutely remarkable. Read the following account and imagine the original scene:

> Fear fell upon them all and the name of the Lord Jesus was being magnified. Many also

of those who had believed kept coming, confessing and disclosing their practices. And many of those who practiced magic brought their books together and began burning them in the sight of everyone; and they counted up the price of them and found it fifty thousand pieces of silver. So the word of the Lord was growing mightily and prevailing. (Acts 19:17–20)

How marvelous! Lives are changing and Christ is honored... diseases are healed and evil spirits are sent packing... God's Word is making an impact and the church is growing and staying healthy. Finally, the tests are over! Wrong.

Just as we saw in chapter 2 of this book, the church is *never* free of attacks, even in times of peace. When we believe we are safe, and when we relax, become indifferent, and let down our guard, the church begins to erode. Attacks come at the church from every direction. Ephesus was no exception:

About that time there occurred no small disturbance concerning the Way. For a man named Demetrius, a silversmith, who made silver shrines of Artemis, was bringing no little business to the craftsmen; these he gathered together with the workmen of similar trades, and said, "Men, you know that our prosperity depends upon this business. You see and hear that not only in Ephesus, but in almost all of Asia, this Paul has persuaded and turned away a considerable number of people, saying that gods made with hands are no gods at all. Not only is there danger that this trade of ours fall into disrepute, but also that the temple of the great goddess Artemis be regarded as worthless and that she whom all of Asia and the world worship will even be dethroned from her magnificence." (Acts 19:23–27)

The temple of the Greek goddess Artemis stood in Ephesus as one of the seven wonders of the ancient world. Thousands of people came from great distances to worship there. The local craftsmen enjoyed a lucrative trade by hawking miniature silver shrines of Artemis to the tourists and pilgrims. A silversmith named Demetrius recognizes that Paul's message of Jesus Christ is receiving an ever-enlarging acceptance. As a result, fewer and fewer people are buying the little idolatrous silver shrines. So what does Demetrius do? He stirs the pot! He brands Paul and the Christians as troublemakers, and he ignites an all-city riot that targets the ministry at Ephesus. As the adversary fuels the fiery words of Demetrius, they achieve their purpose. His fellow hucksters react accordingly:

> When they heard this and were filled with rage, they began crying out, saying, "Great is Artemis of the Ephesians!" The city was filled with the confusion, and they rushed with one accord into the theater, dragging along Gaius and Aristarchus, Paul's traveling companions from Macedonia. (Acts 19:28–29)

A few years ago, Cynthia and I journeyed to the ruins of Ephesus with a group of Christian friends. It is impossible to describe the exhilaration of walking on the same first-century stone streets where Paul walked...of seeing the same hills that surrounded Ephesus in his day...and of touching many of the archaeological remains the great apostle would have seen on a daily basis. But the most stirring moment occurred as we entered the vast theater, the very place spoken of in this passage. If you ever visit Ephesus, you will not miss it.

The theater is a magnificent archaeological discovery, so large that it could accommodate twenty-five thousand spectators in Paul's day.

As I stood in the theater, with the high, stone seating wrapping around me, I imagined the first-century scene that took place as the city "rushed with one accord into the theater." Enraged at the financial ramifications of Paul's message, the craftsmen rouse the city under a pretext of religious concern until "a single outcry arose from them all as they shouted for about two hours, 'Great is Artemis of the Ephesians!'" (Acts 19:34). Pause and let that sink in: *twenty-five thousand people shouting the same line over and over and over... for two hours!* The sound was deafening—far worse than a European soccer game. (It was even worse than a Dallas Cowboys football game!)

The passionate apostle wanted to walk out into the theater and address the crowd. But the disciples restrained him. The crowd would listen to no one associated with Paul or the Christian ministry. The pagan culture had risen up against what Jesus was building in Ephesus. It seems a hopeless cause... until God steps in.

Of all people, the town clerk speaks up and offers a rational rebuke of the needless riot. His motive has nothing to do with the defense of the church. But his wise words quiet the crowd, defuse the explosive situation, and dismiss the assembly in peace (see vv. 35–41). Never forget, God can use anyone to further His purposes, even someone who isn't a part of the church. Remember the promise? The gates of Hades will not prevail.

Impossible situations are never without a solution to our all-powerful Lord. But they often come suddenly upon a faithful, growing church—to test its dependence on God. Overt and bold attacks are normal. It's the silent, slow, and subtle attacks of erosion of which we must remain particularly aware. Paul knew that well…and would shortly remind the Ephesian church of it.

After the apostle left Ephesus, he made his way throughout Macedonia and Greece, evangelizing, ministering, and building up the churches in those areas. He wanted to journey to Jerusalem in time for the Feast of Pentecost that year, so he bypassed Ephesus on his way to Israel. Instead, he sent for the Ephesian church's elders to meet him on the Aegean coast at Miletus (see Acts 20:1–17). As they came together, it must have been quite a reunion. With the pristine blue Aegean Sea in the background, Paul sat with the men, cautioning the elders about their future. The subject of his warning? *Erosion*. Please, read his words very carefully:

> Be on guard for yourselves and for all the flock, among which the Holy Spirit has made you overseers, to shepherd the church of God which He purchased with His own blood. I know that after my departure savage wolves will come in among you, not sparing the flock; and from among your own selves men will arise, speaking perverse things, to draw away the disciples after them. Therefore be on the alert, remembering that night and day for a period of three years I did not cease to admonish each one with tears. (Acts 20:28–31)

The first three words sum up Paul's charge to the Ephesian church: *Be on guard*. This phrase translates a single Greek term that means "to be in a continuous state of readiness to learn of any future danger, need, or error, and to respond appropriately."[1] This vigilant state of mind required that the elders, first, "be on guard for yourselves." That's an awareness of *personal erosion*. Paul predicts the painful truth that "from among your own selves men will arise, speaking perverse things." Only by staying on guard will the leaders keep from drifting personally. They must also "Be on guard...for all the flock." That's an awareness of *corporate erosion*. Savage wolves, Paul warns, will come in and pick off the sheep. Protect them!

Paul then repeats the command to "be on guard," but in different words: "Be on the alert," he warns. The original term for this phrase occurs many times in the New Testament. Interestingly, Paul had written the identical command, while living in Ephesus, to the church at Corinth:

> But I will remain in Ephesus until Pentecost; for a wide door for effective service has opened to me, and there are many adversaries....*Be on the alert*, stand firm in the faith, act like men, be strong. (1 Corinthians 16:8–9, 13, emphasis added)

On the night the Lord Jesus was betrayed by Judas, denied by Peter, and deserted by all His disciples, Christ used this same command to urge Simon Peter to remain alert against fierce temptation:

Simon, are you asleep? Could you not *keep watch* for one hour? *Keep watching* and praying that you may not come into temptation; the spirit is willing, but the flesh is weak. (Mark 14:37–38, emphasis added)

A restored Peter later used the very same command he heard from Jesus to exhort fellow believers to stay on guard:

Be of sober spirit, *be on the alert*. Your adversary, the devil, prowls around like a roaring lion, seeking someone to devour. (1 Peter 5:8, emphasis added)

Ultimately, all attacks from Satan against the church are assaults against God's people—first personally, then corporately. Erosion works its way out in concentric circles like ripples in a pond. The apostle Paul knew that staying aware of the *process* and *results* of erosion would be essential to help prevent the Ephesian church from its own tragic "decline and fall." This commitment to a continuous state of readiness required an example to recall, which Paul provided in himself: "remembering that night and day for a period of three years I did not cease to admonish each one with tears" (Acts 20:31). And with a tender good-bye, Paul boarded the ship at Miletus. His words rang in their ears as they watched the old sailing vessel slip over the horizon.

So...what happened at Ephesus after they said their good-byes?

Counsel: A Mentor Urging and Encouraging His Timid Colleague

It isn't clear whether Paul ever returned to Ephesus, but he certainly wanted to. After his journey to Jerusalem, and subsequent arrest there, Paul eventually found himself a prisoner in Rome...where he wrote the Ephesian church a letter—we know it as the six-chapter letter to the Ephesians. Some time later, after Paul was released from prison, he traveled about freely. It was at this time he may have visited Ephesus again, because he left Timothy there. His first letter to Timothy tells us why:

As I urged you upon my departure for Macedonia, remain on at Ephesus so that you may instruct certain men not to teach strange doctrines. (1 Timothy 1:3)

Those "savage wolves" (Acts 20:29) of which Paul warned the Ephesian elders no doubt had begun to infiltrate the church. So Paul urged Timothy to remain in Ephesus to help prevent any *corporate erosion* from infecting the flock. Paul also warned Timothy, just as he had the elders, to be on guard against *personal erosion*:

> Let no one look down on your youthfulness, but rather in speech, conduct, love, faith and purity, show yourself an example of those who believe. Until I come, give attention to the public reading of Scripture, to exhortation and teaching. Do not neglect the spiritual gift within you, which was bestowed on you through prophetic utterance with the laying on of hands by the presbytery. Take pains with these things; be absorbed in them, so that your progress will be evident to all. Pay close attention to yourself and to your teaching; persevere in these things, for as you do this you will ensure salvation both for yourself and for those who hear you. (1 Timothy 4:12–16)

Timothy was his own man...and very different from Paul in a number of ways. First of all,

Timothy was younger, probably between thirty-five and forty years old. Paul calls this "youthfulness." Timothy's youth suggests several things: he doesn't have Paul's experience...or Paul's seasoning...or Paul's wisdom...or Paul's courage.

In a recent elder meeting at our church, I asked Stan Toussaint (a man in his eighties) to "tell us what stands out in your mind regarding elders." I expected some profound, theological answer from the Greek text, but instead Stan answered simply: "I've learned that an elder needs to be older." (I told him he had a great grasp for the obvious!) But he was spot on. Many contemporary ministries suppose that what we need in order to reach a new generation are "younger elders." Talk about an oxymoron! As Dr. Toussaint pointed out, elders are older. Why else are they called elders? True, you *can* be wise at forty years old, but if you are, you are rare. There's nothing wrong with youthfulness in church leadership, as long as the individual shows himself "an example of those who believe." Timothy must have been an exceptional young man. But even an excellent and disciplined individual can erode. Paul warned Timothy of that.

I'm sure Timothy felt intimidated. Can you imagine pastoring the church in Ephesus, living in the shadow of the great apostle Paul? In addition to being young, Timothy also had "frequent ailments" and probably suffered from a timid personality (see 1 Tim. 5:23; 2 Tim. 1:6–7). When you're younger *and* sickly *and*, on top of that, timid, you have your work cut out for you if you're a senior pastor. That combination opens the gate for erosion if not checked regularly. Paul's two letters to Timothy show tremendous passion in repeatedly reminding the young pastor to stand firm, to stay on guard against personal and corporate erosion, and to preach the Word consistently and with enthusiasm.

With Paul's last letter to Timothy completed, the Word of God is silent on Ephesus for decades. We don't know how things went for Timothy. We're unsure of the church's condition long-term. Our great hope is that they took Paul's words to heart.

Fast-forward thirty years...and get ready for a disappointment.

Erosion: An Appraisal... Thirty Years Later

By the end of the first century, the beloved disciple John was the only apostle still drawing a breath. John's brother James was the first to go...Peter was also gone...Paul had been dead for decades...and

348

all the other apostles had been martyred for their faith in Jesus. Only John remained. He found himself exiled as a Roman prisoner on a scrubby island on the southern part of the Aegean Sea.

The Lord Jesus appeared to John on the Island of Patmos and told him to write letters on His behalf to seven churches. Guess which church was first on the Lord's list? You got it: Ephesus.

> To the angel of the church in Ephesus write: The One who holds the seven stars in His right hand, the One who walks among the seven golden lampstands, says this:... (Revelation 2:1)

Finally! Now we shall see how the Ephesian church fared over the last thirty years. The Lord wastes no time in His evaluation of these believers:

> I know your deeds and your toil and perseverance, and that you cannot tolerate evil men, and you put to the test those who call themselves apostles, and they are not, and you found them to be false; and you have perseverance and have endured for My name's sake, and have not grown weary. (Revelation 2:2–3)

What a great report! The Ephesian church had taken Paul's words to heart and remained on guard against the "savage wolves" who tried to lure away the flock with deceptive words. They had persevered in strong doctrine and in doing good deeds for the name of the Lord Jesus. Who among us would not want to hear such a commendation from Christ? Yet, the Lord has more to tell them:

But I have this against you.... (Revelation 2:4)

Whoa...wait a minute! *But?* The Lord's appraisal of the church at Ephesus was stellar! They were busy...they were faithful...and they were orthodox. So where does the *but* fit in the picture? There are several Greek terms that could be translated "but," yet Jesus chose the strongest contrasting conjunction available. It was very emphatic.

This is the kind of *but* that occurs when your doctor tells you, "Well, you did pretty well on the treadmill, your heartbeat looks normal, and your blood pressure is okay... *but* something concerns me." At that point, all the good news is eclipsed behind that three-letter word. Suddenly, that emphatic negative particle makes your stomach turn. There are a number of times in the Scriptures that this particular *but* announces a dramatic turn. (Some examples are Rom. 8:37; 12:2; 1 Cor. 1:27; 6:11; 1 Thess. 4:7; 5:9.) (I've always wanted to write a book called *Great "Buts" of the Bible*, but I'm not sure I could find a publisher.) As John writes of Jesus' appraisal of the Ephesian church, his use of the term represents one of those dramatic turns.

Ephesus had stood strong for years... they had solid doctrine... they had performed good deeds... they had held the heretics at bay as they stayed true to the name of the Lord... so what could possibly be lacking? Jesus tells them:

But I have this against you, that you have left your first love. (Revelation 2:4)

Not only is the *but* emphatic, so is the weight given to the order of words in the original language. We could translate the phrase this way: *"Your first love you have left."* Those few words were hard to hear. They were strong in their deeds and solid in their doctrines, but their devotion had cooled and become weak. How is that possible?

Remember when you were first married? Every evening was made for romance... every song was a love song...every drive was an occasion to hold hands...every part of life was about joy and intimacy and fun and passion. But as the years began to stack up, something happened. Your life began to focus on your career, and the kids, and those pesky deadlines, and never-ending church work, and all manner of busyness. The results? You're no longer as vulnerable with each other...your enthusiasm has waned...and before you know it, an intimate relationship is replaced with perfunctory obligations. You have left your first love. Your affection has cooled. It was never on purpose...it just, well, happened. There is no clearer picture of erosion.

What had eroded in the Ephesian church? Not their doctrine...not even their deeds...but their *devotion* to Jesus. They had remained on guard against heresy and passivity. But love? Well, that was assumed. John F. Walvoord offers this practical insight:

This rebuke contrasts with what Paul wrote the Ephesians 35 years earlier, that he never stopped giving thanks for them because of their faith in Christ and their love for the saints (Eph. 1:15–16). Most of the Ephesian Christians were now second-generation believers, and though they had retained purity of doctrine and life and had maintained a high level of service, they were lacking in deep devotion to Christ. How the church today needs to heed this same warning, that orthodoxy and service are not enough. Christ wants believers' hearts as well as their hands and heads.[2]

Maybe Paul's portrait hung in the narthex of the Ephesian church sanctuary. Maybe the church had a room of sweet memories that included a few of Paul's writings. Perhaps a few white-haired men and stooping older ladies talked respectfully of Paul. But there was now a cool formality...in simple terms, they didn't love Christ as they used to.

One of my friends and his wife journeyed with Cynthia and me and our group when we traveled to Ephesus years ago. I like what he writes in reflection of his experience there:

What I had found most fascinating about Ephesus was at the end of the road that began just outside the theater. Called the Arcadian Way, this street served as the main thoroughfare from the harbor to the city; Ephesus lay along major caravan routes from the east and its harbor provided shipping routes to the west. I paced down the street toward the ancient harbor, past the usual right turn toward the exit, and walked as far as the street would allow. I looked in every direction… but no sea. Centuries of silt from the Cayster River had accumulated in the harbor and gradually pushed the waterfront away from the city. The citizens had tried to restrain the silting, but they eventually had given up. Today the ruins of Ephesus sit about *five miles* from the Aegean Sea! Grain after grain of silt, year after year of deposits, finally reduced a city of great influence to insignificance.… I began to relate that silting to the spiritual life—the silting of the heart, not the harbor. Grain after grain of busyness, year after year of neglected devotion to Jesus, had finally reduced a church of such doctrinal strength to devotional attrition. The Ephesian Christians had lost their first love by allowing the silt of spiritual indifference to accumulate over the years. It can happen to anyone. Even to you and me.…As believers, we never outgrow the basics. We either build on them or abandon them. We can wake up after a number of years and discover that our lack of passion for Jesus has gradually silted Him five miles away from our hearts. We then find ourselves living in the ruins of once-vibrant spiritual lives.[3]

What happened in the century-one church at Ephesus? The church had a solid beginning...great teaching from godly men...stronghearted convictions and discerning leaders...but slowly, almost imperceptibly, they left their first love. I ask you: how on earth could that have possibly occurred? *Erosion.*

That leads me to ask two questions—both worth pondering: First, what's to keep the same erosion from occurring in *my* church? Second, how can I fight that kind of erosion in my own life?

Let's Learn Some Never-to-Be-Forgotten Lessons

Let me take up my prophetic pen for a moment and list four lessons to remember:

1. Erosion *is happening* in many once-strong churches. (The letter from my friend is just the tip of the iceberg.)

355

2. Erosion *can happen* without a church's real-izing it. (Why? It is slow…silent…and subtle.)
3. Erosion *will happen* in churches that fail to heed the warnings. (Ephesus proves that.)
4. Erosion *could happen* in your church. (How do I know? It happened in mine.)

In the final analysis, churches don't erode, people do. Churches merely reflect the lives and convictions of those individuals who make up the body of Christ. We can stem the tide of erosion only one life at a time—beginning with our own.

C. S. Lewis once made the statement "The true Christian's nostril is to be continually attentive to the inner cesspool."[4] If I may write it far less eloquently, "We need to smell our own stink." Why? Because we are *all* depraved…*all* given to selfishness…*all* drawn to embrace what the world tempts us to crave.

One of the most difficult thirty-six-hour periods of my life occurred in the early 1980s. It was my unhappy task to confront a well-known Christian with the truth of the hypocrisy that was occurring in his life. To the shock of us all, he had been carrying on a four-year affair with another woman. He had hidden it behind a veneer of spiritual activities in which he had taught the Scriptures...had held an important position in a local church...and had served as a leader among his faculty. Through a series of events that came to my attention from someone who had proof—in fact, pictures—it was my unenviable task to face this individual with the truth. I wish I could say this was the only time since then I have had to deal with such a tragedy.

The results of that very painful and serious time forced me to come to terms with the process of erosion that led the man down that trail. As F. B. Meyer puts it, "No one suddenly becomes base."[5] The principle here is universal. No tree suddenly rots and falls. No marriage suddenly ends in divorce. No school suddenly collapses. No church suddenly splits. It's a process of deterioration and inner drifting that often continues unnoticed or, worse, ignored.

One of our problems as evangelical Christians—especially those of us in America—is that we often insulate ourselves in a Christian hothouse. By that I mean the world we live in is surrounded with all things Christian: Christian lingo, Christian friends, Christian books, Christian activities, Christian coffeehouses, Christian clichés, Christian music, Christian stores, Christian bumper stickers. What's next? Putting Christian gasoline in our cars?! (Well, we would if we could.) *Everything* in our world is Christian. The danger? Before long we can begin to lose our edge—to develop a perfunctory spirit toward spiritual things. We begin going through the motions of religious activity, and all the while we're trafficking in unlived truth. When that occurs, we have stopped taking God seriously. Erosion has begun. We have "left our first love."

Trust me, churches that keep you always busy are predisposed to erosion. Join this program... enroll in this study...go on this trip...come to this concert...teach this class...serve here...meet there...be hardworking...stay productive... count those heads...keep busy! Sadly, many of those same churches fail to encourage personal reflection, growth, and analysis. Their focus? The bottom line. Busyness equates to success. Lewis Sperry Chafer summed it up this way: "Much of our spiritual activity is nothing more than a cheap anesthetic to deaden the pain of an empty life."[6]

Is it really possible for a Christian to become overexposed to spiritual things? Yes, *if having blessings from God in such abundance makes us hardened to them.* It can happen when we become the benefactors of a great number of God's blessings. Our business goes well. Our health is good. Our children are fine. Our marriage is strong. Our church is good. The music is great. Our pastor is solid. Our home is lovely. Our ministry is bearing fruit. Our cars are new. Our neighborhood is clean. Our schools are safe. We've made good decisions in life. Blessing after blessing after blessing...

"*But!*" Jesus interrupts. "I have this against you, that you have left your first love."

How does this kind of personal erosion occur? Nobody ever picks up a phone, calls a friend, and says, "Hey, today I feel like ruining my life." We don't do that. But we do, on occasion, entertain thoughts like, *I don't want the lordship of Christ to touch this area of my life. This is mine! After all, look at what's happened as a result. It's not that bad. I can handle it.* And we allow a subtle but destructive drift—the dethroning of His authority and an enthroning of our own. It happens because we've gotten bored in the Christian hothouse.

A believer who wades through God's favor and God's blessing and God's bounty day after day, week after week, year after year can begin to court the dangers of erosion. How? Things get to be predictable. They become routine. You grow cynical.

And before you know it, you can be lusting while you're singing a gospel song. You can be thanking God for His forgiveness of your sins while you harbor bitterness toward your brother or sister in Christ. What you're doing is just another religious duty. A. W. Tozer writes,

> Familiarity may breed contempt even at the very altar of God. How frightful a thing it is for the preacher when he becomes accustomed to his work, when his sense of wonder departs, when he gets used to the unusual, when he loses his solemn fear in the presence of the High and Holy One; when, to put it bluntly, he gets a little bored with God and heavenly things.[7]

What's true in the pulpit is true in the pew. Something is wrong if you can turn to the words of Jack Hayford's song and sing: "Majesty, worship His majesty!"[8] and your soul isn't stirring deep within you. Something has drifted far off course if, when you worship, there isn't a sense of awe and respect for your heavenly Father and the Lord Jesus Christ. That's what concerned Jesus so much about the first-century Ephesian church—their perfunctory, ho-hum, business-as-usual attitude about life and ministry. By the way, Jesus has that same concern for us in the twenty-first century.

Two Very Real Objections

As I write this chapter, I anticipate two common objections. The first goes something like this: "My life has already eroded so badly, there's no sense in turning back." Let me remind you of Paul's words, written while he was in Ephesus:

> No temptation has overtaken you but such as is common to man; and God is faithful, who will not allow you to be tempted beyond what you are able, but with the temptation will provide the way of escape also, so that you will be able to endure it. (1 Corinthians 10:13)

You know the tragedy of this verse? Its familiarity. Our acquaintance with it often keeps us from relying on its promise or applying its truths. Read it again as Eugene Peterson paraphrases it:

> No test or temptation that comes your way is beyond the course of what others have had to

face. All you need to remember is that God will never let you down; he'll never let you be pushed past your limit; he'll always be there to help you come through it. (1 Corinthians 10:13 MSG)

Nothing is too far gone for the Lord to turn it around. It is never too late to start doing what is right. Erosion may have occurred in your life, but Jesus is there with His arms wide open. He is waiting for you to return to your first love. God longs for you to begin again with Him.

The second objection I anticipate comes in these words: "The erosion you have described, I fully understand... but it will *never* happen to me." If that represents your outlook, I point you to the verse Paul penned just prior to the one above:

Therefore let him who thinks he stands take heed that he does not fall. (1 Corinthians 10:12)

I like the way *The Living Bible* renders this verse: "Oh, I would never behave like that." It's the voice of a novice... it's the attitude of the naive... and I'll just shoot straight with you: *it stinks of pride.* Don't kid yourself. Look at what happened to the Ephesian believers, and Paul had taught them! It *can* happen to you, my friend. And it can happen to *me*. If you really see yourself as impervious to erosion, then, ironically, the process of erosion *has already started*. The concentric circles of peril have begun.

> Don't be so naive and self-confident. You're not exempt. You could fall flat on your face as easily as anyone else. Forget about self-confidence; it's useless. Cultivate God-confidence. (1 Corinthians 10:12 MSG)

Like the Christians in Ephesus, have you left your first love? Have you lost the delight of your walk with God? Has it become "business as usual"?

Maybe you are busy in the Lord's work, but you now realize you have lost the awe of it all. The joy of ministry has fled away; now you're simply maintaining a schedule. I urge you to take a moment right now and examine your motive: why do you choose to say yes so often to those who make requests of you? I'm not referring to decisions between *the good* and *the bad*, but to choices between *the good* and *the better*. Realize that when you say yes to something, you are saying no to something else.

Often, by saying no to the good things, you allow yourself room to say yes to far more important priorities.

If you're not taking God seriously as much as you used to, can you detect an area of erosion that has begun to occur? Would you be honest enough to call it by name, painful as it may be? If you neglect to take time to evaluate yourself, you will never notice your own drifting. The change is too slow, too silent, and too subtle...not unlike that frog boiling in a beaker.

*   *   *

Before this day is over, I urge you to find a quiet place and ask yourself these two questions:

- Is Jesus really the first love of my life?
- Does He truly make a difference in how I live my life?

God's mercy is here, and He will help you through it. Honestly acknowledge where you are. He won't rebuke you for coming with that kind of honesty. On the contrary, He welcomes you. Look at the beautiful prayer King David expressed after experiencing a miserable bout with erosion:

364

The sacrifices of God are a broken spirit;
A broken and a contrite heart, O God, You will
not despise. (Psalm 51:17)

That's called repentance. It's the only cure for the long drift.

CHAPTER 8

It's Time to "Restore the Years"

In a strange twist, the preaching of the cross is now foolishness, not only to the world but also to the contemporary church.

—Steven J. Lawson

It's Time to "Restore the Years"

M y wife called you, didn't she?"

I heard the question after a morning worship service. So I turned and saw a man with a severe look on his face, glaring at me. I offered a handshake to the gentleman and responded with a smile, "Excuse me?"

"My wife," he repeated, without shaking my hand, "she called you, didn't she?"

"Uh, I'm sorry, but...I don't know who your wife is."

"No, no, no," he demanded. "Don't jerk me around, Preacher. She called you this week, didn't she?"

Smile gone. "No, I haven't talked to—"

"She didn't call and tell you about what happened between us this week?"

"No."

"I thought that when you were preaching you wanted me to hear it because she had talked to you."

"Sir, I don't even know your name."

Believe it or not, this conversation has happened to me more than a few times. In fact, it occurs with many pastors. The convicting power of the Word of God penetrates the secret places of the heart. It's amazing how the Spirit of God ignites the Scriptures in the mouth of the preacher and personally applies it to each individual listener. Like the man that morning, numerous individuals throughout the years have been convinced that I have been reading their mail or talked with their spouses during the week. I always assure them that I haven't... but God has.

The Word of God is penetrating... and poignant... and convicting... and comforting—all at the same time. The exposition of the Scriptures exposes hypocrisy, offends the self-righteous, and at the same time encourages the weary and wounded. Nothing else can pierce the thick veneer of our facades like the Bible. As the author of the book of Hebrews reminds us:

For the word of God is living and active and sharper than any two-edged sword, and piercing as far as the division of soul and spirit, of both joints and marrow, and able to judge the thoughts and intentions of the heart. (Hebrews 4:12)

That is why the church must include the bold delivery of the Word of God. Its proclamation is essential for life and godliness. We won't receive truth to live by from our culture. We don't get any insight into eternity from these savage times. Even our educational institutions, while they train us to make a living, do nothing to prepare us to make a life. Only the Word of God does that. Unfortunately, in far too many churches where the Bible should be proclaimed with consistency and conviction, people find little help.

I'll never forget the week I spent with starvation victims. You couldn't tell their condition by looking at them. Everyone wore nice clothes. They appeared well-fed. They drove fine automobiles. Most were highly educated. All the marks of affluence were present, but they were starving nonetheless. When I stood up to speak to them, the thought kept coming to my mind that a famine had taken its toll. Not a lack of bread or a craving for water, but there was a famine in that place of hearing the

Word of the Lord. Even when I addressed the most basic scriptural principles, they gobbled it up. They were so hungry for truth, I saw some taking notes even when I wasn't speaking!

We are not suffering from a famine of churches. We have them by the dozens. Some metropolitan areas have literally hundreds of churches within their city limits. We have churches and cathedrals and chapels by the thousands in these United States. So why is there such a famine? The answer, quite simply, is that God's Word has been replaced with artificial food. The wolves of postmodernism have invaded the pantry, and now houses of worship that once were places of feasting have become places of famine. The dinner bells ring each Sunday...and beautiful tables are set with fine china and silverware and fabulous decor—but there is no solid food served, only junk food. Everyone leaves hungry.

If Rip van Winkle were a Christian, and if he had fallen asleep fifty years ago, then awakened last week, he would be stunned. He would never have *dreamed* that the church would have changed so much. The contemporary church offers very little by way of nourishment to hungry worshipers. So it shouldn't surprise us that there's a famine in the land. What caused the church to drift from God's Word while ol' Rip took his nap? Pastor Steven J. Lawson explains:

> As the church advances into the twenty-first century, the stress to produce booming ministries has never been greater. Influenced by corporate mergers, towering skyscrapers, and expanding economies, bigger is perceived as better, and nowhere is this "Wall Street" mentality more evident than in the church. Sad to say, pressure to produce bottomline results has led many ministries to sacrifice the centrality of biblical preaching on the altar of man-centered pragmatism.
>
> A new way of "doing" church is emerging. In this radical paradigm shift, exposition is being replaced with entertainment, preaching with performances, doctrine with drama, and theology with theatrics. The pulpit, once the focal point of the church, is now being overshadowed by a variety of church-growth techniques, everything from trendy worship styles to glitzy presentations to vaudeville-like pageantries. In seeking to capture the upper hand in church growth, a new wave of

pastors is reinventing the church and repackaging the gospel into a product to be sold to "consumers."

Whatever reportedly works in one church is being franchised out to various "markets" abroad. As when gold was discovered in the foothills of California, so ministers are beating a path to the doorsteps of exploding churches and super-hyped conferences where the latest "strike" has been reported. Unfortunately the newly panned gold often turns out to be "fool's gold." Not all that glitters is actually gold.

Admittedly pastors can learn from growing churches and successful ministries. Yet God's work must be done God's way if it is to know God's blessing. He provides the power and He alone receives the glory only as His divinely prescribed plan for ministry is followed. When man-centered schemes are followed, often imitating the world's schemes, the flesh provides the energy and man receives the glory. . . . In a strange twist, the preaching of the cross is now foolishness, not only to the world but also to the contemporary church.[1]

I find those terms fascinating: *bottomline results...consumers...markets.* You'd think Lawson was describing a business plan for more Starbucks coffee shops!

Jesus predicted that "the gates of Hades will not prevail against" the church (Matt. 16:18 NRSV). But that's not to say that the adversary won't attack it any way he can. One of the most devastating causes of erosion in the church has been the drift of pastors from the bold proclamation of God's Word. Many who step into pulpits today do so reluctantly, sometimes even apologetically. It is as if they are ashamed of their calling. The ground of conviction has slipped from beneath their feet. As a result, their congregations remain famished.

Let's Hear the Complaint of a Lonely Pastor

While serving as pastor of Christ Our King Presbyterian Church in Bel Air, Maryland, Eugene Peterson lamented,

American pastors are abandoning their posts, left and right, and at an alarming rate. They are not leaving their churches and getting other jobs. Congregations still pay their salaries. Their names remain on the church stationery and they continue to appear in pulpits on Sundays. But they are abandoning their posts, their *calling*. They have gone whoring after other gods. What they do with their time under the guise of pastoral ministry hasn't the remotest connection with what the church's pastors have done for most of twenty centuries....

The pastors of America have metamorphosed into a company of shopkeepers, and the shops they keep are churches. They are preoccupied with shopkeeper's concerns—how to keep the customers happy, how to lure customers away from competitors down the street, how to package the goods so that the customers will lay out more money.

Some of them are very good shopkeepers. They attract a lot of customers, pull in great sums of money, develop splendid reputations. Yet it's still shopkeeping; religious shopkeeping, to be sure, but shopkeeping all the same. The marketing strategies of the fast-food franchise occupy the waking minds of these entrepreneurs....

The biblical fact is there are no successful churches. There are, instead, communities of sinners, gathered before God week
after week in towns and villages all over the
world. The Holy Spirit gathers them and
does his work in them. In these communities
of sinners, one of the sinners is called pastor
and given a designated responsibility in the
community. The pastor's responsibility is to
keep the community attentive to God. It is
his responsibility that is being abandoned in
spades.[2]

I confess that there are days I feel much the
same! Where have all the stronghearted expositors
gone? When I look back over the past few decades,
I find *many* solid voices of men who filled pulpits.
Not wild-eyed, out-of-balance fanatics, but intelligent, well-read, careful and keen students of
Holy Scripture. These pastors faithfully comforted
the afflicted and afflicted the comfortable. Most
important, they spoke for God...they stood for
the truth...and they spent time on their knees and
poring over the books in their studies. Their entire
lives were a benediction because they saw themselves as trustees of the divine revelation. But that

was then, and this is now. Today the ranks of true and reliable expositors are embarrassingly thin.

What can the church do to stop the famine that is occurring?

Let's Respect the Words of Three Bold Prophets

Rather than examine several contemporary spokesmen for God, let's go back more than twenty-five centuries and interview three individuals from the Old Testament. They may seem an unlikely sort to pick, especially in this book about the church, but they are models of preachers who stood for the truth in cultures that were spiritually adrift. Not only that, but their lives were a benediction to their words. And their words? They are inspired.

Ezekiel Speaks to a Fickle Congregation

The prophet Ezekiel had his work cut out for him. The Babylonian army had invaded Jerusalem, sacked the city, destroyed the walls, and reduced the temple to ashes. Around ten thousand Jews were hauled off to exile in Babylon, where they found themselves living in a concentration camp of sorts. As the psalmist wrote,

By the rivers of Babylon,
There we sat down and wept,
When we remembered Zion.
Upon the willows in the midst of it
We hung our harps.
For there our captors demanded of us songs,
And our tormentors mirth, saying,
"Sing us one of the songs of Zion."
How can we sing the LORD's song in a foreign
*   land?* (Psalm 137:1–4)

God's people are now aliens, exiles, and foreigners in a strange land. What's worse, they have become cynical. Rather than this experience humbling them, they have become a sneering, songless, rebellious lot. It is to this defiant people God sends Ezekiel. Ponder how the prophet describes his calling from God:

"Son of man, stand on your feet that I may speak with you!" As He spoke to me the Spirit entered me and set me on my feet; and I heard Him speaking to me. Then He said to me,

"Son of man, I am sending you to the sons of Israel, to a rebellious people who have rebelled against Me; they and their fathers have transgressed against Me to this very day....And you, son of man, neither fear them nor fear their words, though thistles and thorns are with you and you sit on scorpions; neither fear their words nor be dismayed at their presence, for they are a rebellious house. But you shall speak My words to them whether they listen or not, for they are rebellious." (Ezekiel 2:1–3, 6–7)

Now that's what I call a tough ministry! Ezekiel is to preach to people who respond to him like thorns and thistles and stings on his backside. They have no interest in what he has to say. God tells him, "They are rebellious." Please observe three significant facts:

1. His calling required that he listen to God, not to those around him (2:1–3).
2. His message was to sound forth whether or not those who heard it heeded it (3:7–11).
3. His determination must remain resolute, regardless of how he was treated (33:30–33).

A tough assignment!

Years ago one of my mentors told me that the last four verses of Ezekiel 33 would be a good description of my future in ministry. After hearing this, I made a beeline to my Bible, thumbed my way to Ezekiel's thirty-third chapter, and read these verses for the first time:

> But as for you, son of man, your fellow citizens who talk about you by the walls and in the doorways of the houses, speak to one another, each to his brother, saying, "Come now and hear what the message is which comes forth from the LORD." They come to you as people come, and sit before you as My people and hear your words, but they do not do them, for they do the lustful desires expressed by their mouth, and their heart goes after their gain. (Ezekiel 33:30–31)

It wasn't long before I had committed those verses to memory (as well as the two that follow). A wise minister of the gospel would memorize those four verses. Why? They represent one of the most eloquent sections in all the Old Testament on the preacher's role. This passage is painfully relevant to our times, and it offers splendid counsel to every preacher who is treated with contempt. It will also put a check on your expectations! It exposes how a congregation can work against the one who is called to speak for God in their midst. Sometimes the Bible writes of faithless spokesmen who fail to stand and deliver the truth. Other times—as in this case—it reveals how those roles can reverse, and the fault lies with those who *hear*—not with the one who *stands and delivers.*

This is twenty-first-century stuff! The people gather from all around in order to be entertained. "Tell me what I want to hear. Tell me how great I am. Tell me a few self-help principles so I can feel better about myself. But *please*, don't talk about my sin." Sadly, after hearing enough of this, some preachers have capitulated to the crowds. I saw an interview of a "pastor" (whose name you would know) who thinks of himself as a spokesman for God. I was stunned when he admitted, "Oh, I never use the word *sin*. People already know about that." Oh, really? That type of compromise doesn't square with God's command to Ezekiel: "You shall speak My words to them whether they listen or not." Notice the Lord said, "speak My words." That includes the *S* word.

Ezekiel refuses to pander to the people. Obedient to his Lord, he proclaims the truth. He does it so eloquently, in fact, that word gets out: "If you want to hear somebody speak well in public, you need to hear Ezekiel. The man is the best preacher I've ever heard! Let's go listen!" And so the people come... and sit... and listen—but they neglect to *apply* what they hear. Why? They'd rather do what *they* want to do—chasing the "lustful desires" of their greedy hearts. In short, it's all about them. So why do they even come to Ezekiel? God exposes the reason:

Behold, you are to them like a sensual song by one who has a beautiful voice and plays well on an instrument; for they hear your words but they do not practice them. (Ezekiel 33:32)

One paraphrase says it this way: "You're merely entertainment—a country singer of sad love songs, playing a guitar" (MSG). They see the preacher as an entertainer with a beautiful voice... eloquent words... and an impressive delivery. But after the applause dies down, nothing changes. The message is forgotten. Sin remains.

Hearing the Word of God isn't about being entertained, or feeling good, or leaving impressed

with a speaker's ability, or merely listening to someone talk. It's about life change. The next verse lands
like a gavel on a judge's bench:

So when it comes to pass—as surely it will—
then they will know that a prophet has been
in their midst. (Ezekiel 33:33)

There's a hollow ring to the verse that ends the
chapter. When hard times come...when the voice
of the faithful preacher is no longer heard...when
it's all a distant memory...when the church is
reduced to an empty, hollow shell of what it once
was, the regret is palpable! There will be merely the
memory: "We once had a prophet here."

Cynthia and I recently met with a longtime
friend who serves on the staff of a large church. At
one time, it was a contagious place with powerful
preaching, lifestyle evangelism, mission involvement, meaningful fellowship, inspiring worship,
multiple services, and a far-reaching CD-recorded
ministry. The church enjoyed a magnificent balance of God's work in its midst. So I asked our
friend, "Hey, I'd love to know how your church is
doing." He immediately closed his eyes, shook his
head, and literally groaned.

"You wouldn't believe it," he sighed. "It's dreadful. I don't know how we can keep going like we are. The church doesn't even look like what it once was."

Stunned, I asked hesitantly, "Well, at least... how's the CD ministry?"

"The CD ministry?" he blurted. "There's nothing to record!" On and on he went... and the more he shared, the sadder I became. He could remember a time there was a prophet in their midst. But the church's great days of passion for the Word of God have chilled into cold mashed potatoes. I'll never forget the hollow ring in his voice as he grieved what had been lost.

One man puts it this way:

For some, a major life crisis may cause them to attend church, but only as superficial hearers. Like Ezekiel's audience, they may find the form of the message interesting and stimulating, but they never feel its power in their hearts as a life-changing reality. Those of us who are preachers need to be careful that we do not foster such shallow attention. In our day, there is a focus on "seeker-sensitive" services that will present the gospel in a way that will be attractive to such people. The task of the church, however, is not to assemble seekers but to make disciples.... The seriousness of the message must never be obscured by the desire to make the medium more attractive. The preacher's task is not to entertain or inform but to plead passionately with men and women to flee the wrath that is to come on account of sin.[3]

If our interview with Ezekiel teaches us anything for the church, it says to God's people: don't just come on Sundays to sit and listen, but come to do business with God deep within your heart; allow the Word of God to invade your mind and change your life (see James 1:22–27). It says to God's spokesman: be faithful to your calling... refuse to be discouraged by others' responses... don't be deceived by flattering words (they're often a cover-up). May we never forget that a strong church today doesn't guarantee a strong church tomorrow (see 2 Tim. 4:2; Rev. 2:4).

Amos Warns of a Coming Famine

Let's move our interview microphone from a preacher named Ezekiel to a prophet named Amos.

I've always liked Amos. He is a country boy from a backwoods town in Judah called Tekoa. As far as his vocation, Amos is a sheepherder who also picks sycamore figs. All of that makes Amos sound like a redneck: the man's a fig-picker from Tekoa!

The Lord tells this rawboned prophet to scuttle up north and speak in the face of a king who is cruel, immoral, unfaithful, and unfair. Israel has failed to square with God's plumb line. So Amos shows up (maybe in his bib overalls?) at the king's palace and gives the treacherous king God's message:

> Therefore, thus says the LORD, "Your wife will become a harlot in the city, your sons and your daughters will fall by the sword, your land will be parceled up by a measuring line and you yourself will die upon unclean soil. Moreover, Israel will certainly go from its land into exile." (Amos 7:17)

There is *nothing* easy to hear in a message like that. And what an opening line! "You need to tell the king that his wife will be a prostitute before long, and all his children will be stabbed with the sword" (that's a Swindoll paraphrase). Hardly a message that wins friends and influences people!

387

But winning friends isn't a faithful prophet's goal. It isn't the job of God's spokesman to shape his words so that they're easy to hear. Yes, they need to be accurate. Absolutely, they need to be relevant. *But they must never be compromised.* Amos didn't garble the message at all. Later he says,

> *"Behold, days are coming," declares the* LORD *God,*
> *"When I will send a famine on the land,*
> *Not a famine for bread or a thirst for water,*
> *But rather for hearing the words of the* LORD.
> *People will stagger from sea to sea*
> *And from the north even to the east;*
> *They will go to and fro to seek the word of the*
> LORD,
> *But they will not find it."* (Amos 8:11–12)

Talk about a passage appropriate to the twenty-first century! I understand the historical context of this passage—fulfilled in Israel's exile of 722 BC—but the principle of this text is as timeless as it is true. Amos predicts that there will come a day when the land once filled with stronghearted prophets will languish, longing for a powerful voice from

God—anyone who will stand courageously, and politically incorrectly, for what is right.

I don't know of a more apt statement to define our times than Amos 8:11–12. As in the day of Amos, our day is also experiencing a famine for the Word of God.

In an outstanding book entitled *Revive Us Again,* Walt Kaiser writes,

Too often the Bible is little more than a book of epigrammatic sayings or springboards that give us a rallying point around which to base our editorials. But where did we get the audacious idea that God would bless our opinions or judgments? Who wants to hear another point of view as an excuse for a Bible Study or a message from the Word of God? Who said God would bless our...ramblings...? Surely this is a major reason why the famine of the Word continues in massive proportions in most places in North America. Surely this is why the hunger for the teaching and proclamation of God's Word continues to grow year after year. Men and women cannot live by ideas alone, no matter how eloquently they are stated or argued, but solely by a patient reading and explanation of all the Scripture, line after line, paragraph after paragraph, chapter after chapter, book after book. Where are such interpreters to be found, and where are their teachers?[4]

Kaiser speaks like a prophet of old, even though he lives as one of our contemporaries (and practices what he preaches). People *long* to have their souls fed and their lives nourished by the Word of God, but they are not finding it. I repeat: there is a terrible famine in our land. The starving congregation I saw confirms it.

Amos's experience reveals another reason for the famine. In his day, the leadership of Israel had gone to seed. The guidance of the nation had become corrupt, and it needed direct confrontation from a preacher who refused to compromise the truth. In his outstanding book *Spiritual Leadership*, J. Oswald Sanders says,

No one need aspire to leadership in the work of God who is not prepared to pay a price greater than his contemporaries and colleagues are willing to pay. True leadership always exacts a heavy toll on the whole man, and the more effective the leadership is, the higher the price to be paid.[5]

Many years ago I pastored a small church. While serving there, I encountered an extremely difficult person in a position of leadership. He had been very influential in my coming to the church, and I discovered that he intended to remain influential after I arrived. I noticed the longer I was there, the greater the sense of strain grew between us. When I would attempt to resolve the tension, he verbally stiff-armed me. He didn't want to work it out. In fact, he even denied that we had a conflict. I began to feel increasingly more alone and intimidated. I had no advocate. I had no one to whom I could turn, because the elders felt that everything was fine and dandy.

Finally, after several more incidents that only intensified the pressure, he showed up at my study one cold winter day. We were all alone at the small church when he marched in, leaned over my desk, and uttered, "I want to show you something you don't know." He opened his coat and said, "I carry a gun." To my surprise, he pulled it out of its holster and popped the butt of the weapon against his hand. Out fell six shells. "I keep it loaded. Just thought you should know that."

(I wanted to say, "Well, thank you.")

He reloaded the pistol in front of me, snapped a bullet in the chamber, and looked me in the eye. "Don't you *ever* cross me," he warned…and walked out.

That, friends and neighbors, is what you call a threat! I don't know that I've *ever* been more scared in my life, including my hitch in the Marine Corps. Believe it or not, this man was in *leadership* at our little church; what's more, everybody liked the guy. Talk about a wolf in sheep's clothing! James Montgomery Boice offers this helpful perspective:

> At the height of the Reformation, when Martin Luther was challenging the corruptions of the medieval church by a rediscovery of sound biblical exegesis and preaching, Pope Leo X issued a papal bull against Luther that complained that "a wild boar is ravishing God's vineyard." Luther was not doing that, of course. He was more like an Old Testament prophet, recalling a wayward church back to its apostolic roots. But wild boars

really have ravished the church from time to time.[6]

Some of you are in leadership in your churches and are paying a tough price for your principles. I respect you for that. I sincerely thank you for being men and women of courage and conviction. I regret that you have to deal with the boars who have invaded God's vineyard. But that is part of our job as leaders. As the apostle Paul reminds the Romans:

Now I urge you, brethren, keep your eye on those who cause dissensions and hindrances contrary to the teaching which you learned, and turn away from them. For such men are slaves, not of our Lord Christ but of their own appetites; and by their smooth and flattering speech they deceive the hearts of the unsuspecting. (Romans 16:17–18)

Trouble in ministry is nothing new. Even in the first century, there were Pharisees with their legalism. There were heretics with their false teaching. There were defectors who became cynical and bitter. There have always been deceivers and impostors with their cunning and duplicitous actions, fighters who took on various apostles and fellow Christians. Paul, by his own admission, was himself ravaging the church when he was lost (see Acts 8:3; 9:1–2; 1 Tim. 1:13). He knew to warn the Ephesian elders at Miletus to "be on guard" against the savage wolves that would rise up from their own congregation (see Acts 20:28–31). There were also legalists who threatened the Christian liberty of the Christians in Galatia (see Gal. 2:4). Paul's implacable enemy was "Alexander the coppersmith" (2 Tim. 4:14). John the aged apostle warns of "Diotrephes, who loves to be first" (3 John 9). I call him the "church boss." (Maybe he, too, packed a weapon.)

Now, obviously, God could stop every single boar in every single vineyard, but He doesn't. He often lets them stay on the loose. (Someday, I hope to find out why.) As men and women in ministry, we need to face the fact that there will *always* be those who will cause dissensions and hindrances. It is inescapable. So we must stand against them. Often I call to mind Paul's words to the Romans, written just after the warning about the boars:

The God of peace will soon crush Satan under your feet. The grace of our Lord Jesus be with you. (Romans 16:20)

Aren't we grateful for that promise? I confess, however, that I am impatient for it. I often think, *Lord, I know You're sovereign . . . I know You're powerful . . . I know You're good . . . so will You please hurry up!* We want God to crush Satan *now*. But He hasn't yet. Why? Because Jesus is still building His church. In the meantime, Satan continues to attack it.

By the way, the adversary would *love* to work through you or me to carry out his diabolical plans. If we aren't careful, we can become boars ourselves. We can change from critical thinkers to cynical naysayers. We need to guard against our impulsiveness in taking control . . . against operating our ministries in the flesh . . . and against a perfunctory spirit in ministry. The longer you're in ministry, the more you will discover you can perform many tasks easier and quicker than at first. Before long, you can begin to exhibit that ho-hum, business-as-usual attitude the Ephesian church fell prey to after several decades. Don't go there. Don't even take the first step in that direction! Guard against it. "Soon," God promises, "I'm going to crush the enemy and he's going to be gone. Until then, may the grace of the Lord Jesus be with you."

We have met with Ezekiel and heard his baleful

words to a congregation that didn't want to listen. We've interviewed Amos and watched him stand toe-to-toe with the political heavyweights of his day. But we're not through with our prophetic interviews until we dialogue with another man. This one has good news for a change.

Joel Promises a Hopeful Future

Years ago, when my family lived in California, we were traveling on our way home from a delightful week at Mount Hermon Conference Center. About dusk the family was asleep, and I pulled into a service station to fill up the tank. As I opened the car door and stepped out, I could feel the crunching of something underneath my feet. No, it wasn't Satan...it was insects! Before long, my whole windshield was covered with bugs. I even felt them crawling on the back of my neck and on my clothing. I quickly opened the gas cap and shoved in the nozzle to keep the bugs out. They were everywhere! They made a constant buzzing noise, like a motor idling. (It felt as if I were in an Alfred Hitchcock movie, or something worse.) As I paid the attendant, I asked him, "What *is* this?"

"Oh, it's those *blankety-blank* locusts," he muttered. "The seven-year plague has come through." He pointed in the distance and said, "Look there."

I turned and saw that what had once been crops now looked like brown, naked stalks sticking out of the ground.

He pointed the other way: "Now, look over there."

I did, and it was green. The locusts were moving, slowly and steadily, across the land.

"We *live* for the day this is over," he told me. "They're eating everything in their path!"

I had never seen anything like it before, nor have I since.

The people in the prophet Joel's day also experienced a famine on the land. In fact, it was the most devastating plague they had ever known. Every kind of locust imaginable ravaged the ground, from the creeping locust to the swarming locust to the stripping locust to the gnawing locust. Joel records a fascinating perspective from God; He refers to the locusts as "My great army which I sent among you" (Joel 2:25). The Creator is able to control the creation, and He says to the locusts, "Sic 'em!" (or whatever He says to locusts to get them moving).

Wave after wave of these destructive pests had swept across their land. Joel identifies that famine as coming from the hand of God.

But there's good news too. That same verse holds out a strong promise from the same God. Here's how the whole verse reads:

> *Then I will make up to you for the years*
> *That the swarming locust has eaten,*
> *The creeping locust, the stripping locust*
> *   and the gnawing locust,*
> *My great army which I sent among you.*
> *   (Joel 2:25)*

Joel writes words of great hope in the midst of great desolation. God promises to restore the years of devastation caused by the locust. How? What will it take to stop the plague and end the famine? Joel reveals how it can occur:

> *"Yet even now," declares the* LORD,
> *"Return to Me with all your heart,*
> *And with fasting, weeping and mourning;*
> *And rend your heart and not your garments."*
> *Now return to the* LORD *your God,*
> *For He is gracious and compassionate,*

Slow to anger, abounding in lovingkindness
And relenting of evil. (Joel 2:12–13)

Our God is so merciful! "Even now—after all the sin you've committed, in spite of all the damage you've caused, regardless of the devastating results of your unfaithfulness—your repentance will bring restoration." What a promise! God tells them, "Return to Me with all your heart," which for them was to be outwardly displayed in fasting, weeping, and mourning. But it's not the outward acts God wants; they only represent the heart: "Rend your heart, and not your garments," the Lord commanded. An ancient Hebrew would "rend" or tear his garments as a sign of mourning or of great pain. A similar command is given elsewhere to "circumcise your heart" (Deut. 10:16). As Christians, we might put it this way: "Baptize your hearts, not your bodies." In other words, don't do the actions without the attitude. Joel says that, if the people and the ministers of God will gather, weep, and pray in sincerity (see 2:16–17), *then* God will respond. Don't miss what God promises:

Then the LORD will be zealous for His land and will have pity on His people.... *Then* I will make up to you for the years that the swarming locust has eaten. (Joel 2:18, 25, emphasis added)

This is one of my favorite sections in the Old Testament. Why? Because God's grace promises to shower God's people when they return to Him in genuine repentance. That is what I want for the church of Jesus Christ today! That describes the church awakening!

Now how do we get there?

Let's Acknowledge the Changes That Must Occur

We must acknowledge three changes in order to bring about the end of the famine and the beginning of God's favor upon the church.

The People of God Must Return to a Hunger and Thirst for Righteousness

It is high time that believers protest against those who have taken the church in the wrong direction. As Christians, we must demand a halt to superficial religion that substitutes for personal faithfulness. We should refuse to be entertained any longer. We must stop calling it "worship." It's time we openly state that we expect deep teaching from the Word of God from our pastor, not a twelve-minute sermonette. We must begin looking to our pastor to equip *us* to do the work of ministry and not expect him to do ministry *for us*.

In addition, the people of God need to stop watching and financially supporting media ministries that water down the truth. These "ministries" dish out shallow, self-serving junk food that cannot nourish the soul. Not until enough of God's people rise up against such trendy nonsense will it stop flourishing. Put positively, we need to hunger and thirst for righteousness...a righteousness that is taught and found only in the Word of God.

The Ministers of God Must Repent of Their Failure to Fulfill Their Calling

When people in the medical profession fail to do their jobs, it's called *malpractice*. Without exception, we refuse to stand for it because malpractice is inexcusable. When investors take advantage of those who trust them to handle their finances with integrity, it is called *fraud*. Fraud is a criminal act, and we won't tolerate it. But for some reason, when ministers fail to fulfill their calling, the public shrugs it off and quietly leaves. This cannot continue!

One pastor who downplays the importance of preaching in church suggests "a much more multisensory approach" to worship. By that, he means:

> We now see art being brought into worship, the use of visuals, the practice of ancient disciplines, the design of the gathering being more participatory than passive-spectator. Instead of the pulpit and sermon being the central focus of worship gatherings (at least in most evangelical churches), we now see Jesus as the central focus through a variety of creative worship expressions. True, every preacher says that Jesus is the center of their preaching! What I mean here is that teaching and learning in the emerging church happen in various ways; it's no longer only one person standing on a stage preaching to everyone else.[7]

God has called the pastor to be a teacher and a shepherd, one who equips "the saints for the work of service, to the building up of the body of Christ" (Eph. 4:12). In fact, the role of a pastor is so integrated with his teaching role that in a list of spiritual gifts, the apostle Paul links the two together: "pastors and teachers" (Eph. 4:11)—or literally, "pastor-teachers." And what is the pastor to teach? Paul leaves no room for guesswork:

Preach the word; be ready in season and out of season; reprove, rebuke, exhort, with great patience and instruction. (2 Timothy 4:2)

Be diligent to present yourself approved to God as a workman who does not need to be ashamed, accurately handling the word of truth. (2 Timothy 2:15)

Give attention to the public reading of Scripture, to exhortation and teaching. Do not neglect the spiritual gift within you....Take pains with these things; be absorbed in them. (1 Timothy 4:13–15)

Those words mean exactly what they say. Believe me, there are days when it is downright painful for the pastor to stay in the study and work...it is challenging to remain diligent...it is agonizing to keep seated for the extended periods of time it takes to "accurately handle the word of truth." If I may be brutally frank here, many pastors need to admit that they're just plain lazy—that they'd rather play golf than fulfill their calling in their study. In spite of Timothy's giftedness as a pastor-teacher, Paul commanded that he "take pains with these things." That applies to every pastor, no matter how gifted he may be. It is hard work.

Just as the first-century believers continually devoted themselves to the apostles' teaching, so the twenty-first-century church has as its priority in worship the preaching of the Word of God. Stephen Olford tells pastors, "The reading of Scriptures is the only part of your message that is infallible."[8] Wise words. Everything else is fallible. When we read the Scriptures in public, we are exposing people to the infallible, inerrant message of God. David Wells puts it this way:

This apostolic framework of belief is not something that many in the contemporary church want out in the open. So they hide it. The first Christians guarded it. We venture far beyond it. They treasured it and lived within it. We think it will get in the way of our church's success. They thought that without it, front and center, there could be no church. They were right and we are wrong.[9]

My plea is that we return to the exposition of the Scriptures. For decades, expository preaching could be found in most evangelical churches and many of the mainline denominational Protestant churches.

If you are a pastor, you know better than most how *tough* it is to state in succinct and precise terms what we mean by "expository preaching." I was recently asked to provide a definition. Not an easy assignment! I checked about five fairly reliable sources and found that their definitions were too long, too convoluted, or just plain confusing! So, I decided to start from scratch and hammer out one on my own. Two hours later, I came up with this:

- Expository preaching is the proclamation of Holy Scripture delivered for the purpose of enabling others to understand what God has written, why that is important, and how it relates to one's personal life.
- Understanding what God has written requires the expositor to be accurate in both

preparation and delivery of the Scriptures, so that the Bible is allowed to speak for itself.

- Understanding why God's Word is important calls for the expositor to be passionate in communicating the truth, so that the one receiving the message is compelled to listen and eager to respond.

- Understanding how that message relates to life means that the expositor uses terms that are clear, delivers the message in ways that connect with needs, and applies it so specifically the hearer realizes the relevance of God's Word and the necessity of aligning his or her life to it.

There's nothing inspired about this definition, but I must admit that the process of thinking it through reignited my passion for expository preaching. Let me urge you to do some original work in the Scriptures, to mull through the biblical mandates of a pastor, and to craft your own working definition. If you are a pastor, the process will help you as a preacher...and also provide a standard to evaluate your messages. Let me urge you to buck the tide and to put the preaching of the Word of God back in its central place of the church's worship. But I warn you, you'll probably have some people think you've been reading their mail.

What is needed in the ranks of ministry? A massive repentance—a rending of the pastoral heart and not the pastoral robes! Once again, Eugene Peterson writes,

> I don't know of any other profession in which it is quite as easy to fake it as in ours. By adopting a reverential demeanor, cultivating a stained-glass voice, slipping occasional words in like "eschatology" and *heilsgeschichte* into our discourse—we are trusted, without any questions asked, as stewards of the mysteries.... Even when in occasional fits of humility or honesty we disclaim sanctity, we are not believed.... If we provide a bare-bones outline of pretense, they take it as the real thing and run with it, imputing to us clean hands and pure hearts.[10]

We ministers need to stop the phoniness! How many of us really do spend time with God? How many pour out our hearts in prayer before the Lord? How many really do plead for the souls of the lost? It's time we repent from the fakery, from the greed, from the perfunctory spirit, and from the lack of diligent and devoted prayer. We in ministry need to return to the study; to serious, protracted meditation; to seeking God's mind; to courageous and contagious preaching; to a zealous and passionate commitment to God. Our counseling needs to be honest and practical. We need to confront wrong. We need to stop giving preferential treatment to the wealthy. We need to stop worrying about pleasing people. We need to stop trying to impress others.

While I'm at it, we must also stop ignoring our wives and children in the process. Who knows how many pastors could claim their ministry as their first wife? Many wives wait and wait, longing for the love and affection of husbands who are married to the church. That calls for repentance. Every one of my mentors who marred me for life had a strong home and family, because every one was devoted to his wife and children. I don't mean they all turned out perfectly; they were all flawed individuals. But there was no question about it: ministry was *second* to the responsibility of the home and family and—most of all—to their genuine relationship with the living God.

Fellow pastors, we have a calling. Don't you dare let some "boar" drive you away! Don't allow some stubborn, twisted individual to convince you that you're a failure and you should resign. However, if God leads you somewhere else, then you must follow. (Just be sure it's God and not somebody who packs a gun.) While it becomes harder the longer you're in ministry, I promise you, it also becomes more rewarding. God has called you into His work. You have the inestimable privilege of preaching the Bible in God's matchless name and speaking it openly and boldly before a world that's lost its way. Fellow pastor, I plead with you: fulfill your calling.

The House of God Needs to Represent Its Biblical Purpose for Existence

It is a house of prayer, not a house of business. It is a place of worship, not a place of entertainment. Jesus is our Savior whom we worship, not a brand to market. The body of Christ is a sanctuary of protection for the vulnerable—for children, single women, the abused, and the bruised and broken in life. The house of God is a refuge for those who have special needs and can't keep up. It's a harbor of hope for those who are addicted and struggling. For those trying to find a reason to go on after a death or divorce, the church has a powerful opportunity to offer the hope that God gives.

*   *   *

The marvelous opportunity of ministry that lies before the church awaits only one thing: the church's awakening. Stated simply, *the people of God* must return to a hunger and thirst for righteousness... *the ministers of God* must repent of their failure to fulfill their calling...and *the house of God* needs to represent its biblical purpose for existence. In spite of all the spiritual devastation and famine in our land, it is not too late to turn it around—by God's grace.

Conclusion

The church is scarred by wars,
buffeted by storms and eroded
by pollution, and God is at work
restoring His own—repairing,
cleaning, purifying.

—Ruth Bell Graham

Conclusion

We have examined the church's biblical purpose for existence for the past eight chapters, beginning with the words of Jesus: "I will build My church; and the gates of Hades will not overpower it" (Matt. 16:18). May we never forget both His prediction and His promise! Jesus *will* keep building His church... *even against great odds*. I recently enjoyed reading an insightful excerpt by the late Ruth Graham, wife of evangelist Billy Graham. The piece is entitled simply, "Scaffolding."

Scaffolding

The famous Tienanmen (Gate of Heavenly Peace) in Beijing, China, was shrouded in bamboo scaffolding. The impressive structure, originally erected during the reign of Emperor Yung Lo in 1417, was restored in 1651. But the old gate was showing the wear of time, the brutalizing of wars and revolts, and the ravages of pollution, so more necessary restoration was now under way.

I was in China in 1980 with my two sisters and brother as part of a two-week pilgrimage to our old home. The pilgrimage completed, we parted company in Hong Kong. My older sister, Rosa, had never traveled through Europe, and it was now or never, so we boarded the plane together for Athens.

In Athens, we could see the Parthenon from our hotel room. It was covered with scaffolding. What weather and wars had failed to do in 2,500 years, pollution had accomplished in just a few.

Our next stop was Paris. Jeanette Evans, whom we've known since college days, met us, gave us a swift and amazingly comprehensive tour of Paris, and then took us to her and her husband Bob's home near Versailles. After a night's sleep, we toured Versailles— that is, we walked through a small part of it.

Versailles, which was completed in 1689

after around thirty years of construction, has to be seen to be believed! In the 1700s the Royal Chapel was added, completed in time for the marriage of Louis XVI to Marie Antoinette. And wouldn't you know—the chapel was covered with scaffolding.

We drove the forty miles to Chartres to see its great cathedral, which is one of the finest examples of the French Gothic cathedrals. Once more we found scaffolding.

From Paris we flew to London where even a whirlwind tour is better than no tour at all—especially if it includes Westminster Abbey. As we approached the exquisite abbey, so alive with history, what did we see? You've already guessed: scaffolding.

Is that the way the world sees the church?

The church is scarred by wars, buffeted by storms, and eroded by pollution, and God is at work restoring His own, repairing, cleaning, purifying. He sees the end from the beginning. He sees us *complete in Christ.* The day will come when *we shall be like Him.*

But in the meantime, the world sees mainly the scaffolding.[1]

Jesus is building the church—authentic believers in Him—to share His Word and to engage in good works, which God has prepared ahead of time for us to walk in (see Eph. 2:10). But even in healthy churches, we learned, the devil is alive and well, doing all he can—through worship wars, moral pollution, and doctrinal erosion—to dismantle what Jesus is building. In addition, human depravity is always present—even among Christians. We can prevent the slow, silent, and subtle erosion—the drift from Christ's master plan—only by allowing clear, biblical thinking to override a secular, corporate mentality based on human opinion. By examining both the challenges and priorities of the struggling, early church, we learned that the Lord will honor and bless any plan that upholds His inspired design and promotes prevailing prayer.

Even in a culture marked by postmodernism and addicted to consumerism, the church doesn't need gimmicks to attract people. Instead it needs biblical truth taught in an interesting manner and lived out in unguarded authenticity—in our relationship with our Lord and with one another. The Bible affirms that a ministry is contagious when it remains strong in grace, when the older mentor the young, when it pulls together in tough and desperate times, and when it endures regardless of the challenges. Welcome to life on the scaffold!

Amazingly, one of the greatest challenges the church has faced in recent years centers on the one element that makes the church unique in a secularized society: meaningful worship. It is *how* we worship that has become a lingering battle, what I mentioned earlier as "worship wars." We must remember the difference between the *essence* of worship—what it represents—and the *expression* of worship—how we connect to God and one another. The first is essential, but the second is not...and hardly worth the war.

The church must awaken and face the reality that we live in difficult times. Savage times! These treacherous days will ravage our homes and hearts if we do not awaken and stay alert. In light of such perilous times, we must remain convinced of the long-standing truths of the Bible, without which we would never find our way. Furthermore, we must allow those truths to fulfill their purpose in our everyday lives through personal application, so that we will never lose our way.

When the church fails to realize the times and react appropriately, erosion will take its toll. Please don't forget the church of Ephesus, a ministry that began with a burning passion but whose love for the Lord cooled and eroded over the years. Each believer must regularly evaluate his or her own level of spiritual erosion and return to a vibrant relationship with Jesus Christ. The spiritual disciplines play a major role in an awakened church. A clear mind must blend with a warm heart. Doctrine must always be balanced with devotion.

We learned that in most churches there are "wild boars" who ravage the ministry by resisting authority and stirring up trouble. If they are, in fact, Christians, they are carnal Christians who have selfish agendas. God's Word says that these boars must be watched, confronted, and ultimately removed, if they refuse to repent. Candidly, the problem is not limited to those in the pews—sometimes boars are found in the pulpits. The great hope of the church awakening begins when the ministers of God become aware of what it means to fulfill God's calling and when the people of God genuinely hunger and thirst for God's righteousness. Ultimately, I'm convinced, many will come to realize what they are missing. Some who seem so entrenched in themselves and blind to the truth will be rescued from the misinformation they have believed.

As I come to the end of my book, I want to

tell you a story, perhaps apocryphal, that illustrates how the truth has a way of breaking through.

A number of years ago, a young man who excelled at the sport of high diving was training to compete in the upcoming summer Olympics. He chose a university where his skill could be perfected through a fine coach and excellent facilities. What he didn't plan on, though, was that his roommate would be a strong, outspoken Christian.

As the weeks passed, the roommate faithfully shared with him about his need for the Savior, who died on the cross to pay the penalty for his sins. The diver, however, showed no interest in spiritual things. His only passion? Winning a gold medal. Yet inwardly, on occasion, he did feel disturbed by what he heard. He came to realize he had never considered life beyond death. And while he never shared the growing struggle with anyone, the consciousness of his sin became more and more of a burden.

Unable to sleep one night, he arose and took a walk across campus to the indoor pool where he trained. To clear his mind, he decided to practice some dives. A large roof of glass panes covered the university pool, and the full moon that night provided enough dim light for him to make his way to the ten-meter diving platform. While struggling with his burden, he stripped down to his swimsuit and climbed to the top. He walked to the edge, turned around, and stretched out his arms, preparing to dive. Before he jumped, his eye caught a glimpse of his own shadow—cast on the wall by the moonlight. He paused and stared at the silhouette...it was his own human shadow forming the shape of a cross.

Just then a custodian flipped on the lights to the pool and yelled to the diver not to jump! The diver looked down in horror to see that the pool had been drained that evening. As he stood there, he realized that he had missed death by a split second...and that the cross he had seen had saved him. He knelt on that platform and released his burden to God, believing in the One who had died on the cross for him.

We live in treacherous, savage times—dark times. It's no wonder the world has lost its way. Poised on the edge of destruction, only the cross of Christ stands between billions of people and their plummet to destruction. And the appointed messenger of that cross?

The church.

In the midst of all the locusts and all the desolation and all the barrenness that has ravished the times in which we live, the Lord is calling His church to stand in the gap...to stay on the scaffold. He wants His people to press on and remain engaged in this rebuilding project. We must personify the passion that marked Ezekiel and Amos and Joel as well as Paul and the early church. And, of course, Jesus Himself.

My hope is that as a result of the time we have spent together in this book, you will begin to put your mind back in gear where you have allowed it to go into neutral. I urge you to become engaged in the solutions for our times—which are rooted in the Scriptures, rather than be swept along with the unending problems of our day.

It will not be easy. It is *never* simple to think for yourself. It is *never* comfortable to act among the minority. But such is life on the scaffold! When Jesus stood strong, He was crucified. When the apostles spoke the truth, they were martyred. When the early church modeled the message, they were persecuted. But they turned the world upside down. Many were rescued from emptiness and despair by their message of the Cross! Is our calling any different?

* * *

There is no Rip van Winkle to awaken. *We* are to awaken! May we become people of discernment in a culture of apathy. We must have the courage to acknowledge the erosion that is occurring in our churches. We must define our lives based on what we know the church ought to do. As we experience the church awakening to its high and holy purpose, I am convinced God will "restore the years" the locusts have eaten.

It is time for the church to climb onto the scaffolds and awaken... to renew our passion for what Jesus is building.

Paul's great doxology in Ephesians 3:20–21 reminds us that we are not alone:

> *Now to Him who is able to do far more*
> *abundantly beyond all that we ask or think,*
> *according to the power that works within us,*
> *to Him be the glory in the church and*
> *in Christ Jesus to all generations*
> *forever and ever.*
> *Amen.*

Notes

Introduction

1. Woodrow Kroll, *Back to the Bible: Turning Your Life Around with God's Word* (Sisters, OR: Multnomah, 2000), 134.
2. Francis A. Schaeffer, *The Great Evangelical Disaster* (Wheaton, ILL: Crossway Books, 1984), 37.

1. The Church: Let's Start Here

1. *Merriam-Webster's Collegiate Dictionary*, 11th ed., s.v. "erode."
2. C. S. Lewis, *The Screwtape Letters* (New York: HarperCollins, 2001), 61.
3. Johannes P. Louw and Eugene A. Nida, eds., *Greek-English Lexicon of the New Testament Based on Semantic Domains*, 2nd ed. (New York: United Bible Societies, 1988, 1989). Electronic text

hypertexted and prepared by OakTree Software, Inc. Version 3.2.

4. John R. W. Stott, *The Spirit, the Church and the World: The Message of Acts* (Downers Grove, ILL: InterVarsity Press, 1990), 79.

5. F. F. Bruce, *The Spreading Flame: The Rise and Progress of Christianity from Its First Beginnings to the Conversion of the English* (Eugene, OR: Wipf & Stock, 2004).

6. A. W. Tozer, *Rut, Rot or Revival: The Condition of the Church* (Camp Hill, PA: Christian Publications, 1992), 178.

7. E. E. Cummings, as quoted by Ted Goodman in *The Forbes Book of Business Quotations: 10,000 Thoughts on the Business of Life* (New York: Black Dog & Leventhal, 2007), 553.

8. Louw and Nida, *Greek-English Lexicon.*

2. Challenges, Struggles, Solutions, Priorities

1. Story published November 13, 2008, in the *Seattle Times.* Accessed from: http://www. seattletimes. nwsource.com/html/nationworld/2008386420_ apeurussiastolenchurch.html.

2. Quoted from Mark Hatfield, *Between a Rock and a Hard Place* (Waco, TX: Word Books, 1977), 187.

3. Quoted by Skye Jethani in *The Divine Commodity: Discovering a Faith Beyond Consumer Christi-*

anity (Grand Rapids: Zondervan, 2009), 11. Used by permission (www.zondervan.com).

4. John Piper, *Brothers, We Are Not Professionals: A Plea to Pastors for Radical Ministry* (Nashville: B&H Publishing, 2002), 1–2.

5. Johannes P. Louw and Eugene A. Nida, eds., *Greek-English Lexicon of the New Testament Based on Semantic Domains*, 2nd ed. (New York: United Bible Societies, 1988, 1989). Electronic text hypertexted and prepared by OakTree Software, Inc. Version 3.2.

6. Ibid.

7. This humorous story is most probably false. See http://www.snopes.com/horrors/techno/radar. asp, accessed December 7, 2009.

8. Vance Havner, as quoted in Charles R. Swindoll, *The Quest for Character: Inspirational Thoughts for Becoming More Like Christ* (Grand Rapids: Zondervan, 1982), 39.

9. Alexander Whyte, source unknown.

10. John Chrysostom, *Six Books on the Priesthood,* trans. Graham Neville (Yonkers, NY: St. Vladimir's Seminary Press, 1996), 65.

11. Kevin A. Miller, "God Turns Persecution into Opportunity," PreachingToday.com, accessed May 13, 2009.

12. Marvin R. Vincent, *Vincent's Word Studies in the New Testament* (New York: Scribner's, 1905), 472.

13. Quoted from "A Declaration of Unity in the Gospel" adopted by the National Religious Broadcasters, February 6, 2009.

14. I remember my Greek professor, Dr. Stan Toussaint, teaching me about the onomatopoeia, *goggusmos*, during my seminary days.

15. David Wells, *The Courage to Be Protestant: Truthlovers, Marketers, and Emergents in the Postmodern World* (Grand Rapids: Eerdmans, 2008), 4.

16. A. W. Tozer, *The Knowledge of the Holy* (San Francisco: Harper&Row, 1961), 27.

17. Piper, *Brothers*, 4.

18. E. M. Bounds, *Power Through Prayer* (New Kensington, PA: Whitaker House, 1982), 9–11.

19. Quoted by Allan Dobras in "Denominational Drift: The Bible Doesn't Need 'Rescuing,'" published by *BreakPoint* on April 11, 2006.

20. Ibid.

21. Statistics from the Barna Group of Ventura, California, http://www.barna.org/barna-update/article/12-faithspirituality/260-most-american-christians-do-not-believe-that-satan-or-the-holy-spirit-exits, accessed May 13, 2009.

22. Eugene H. Peterson, *The Message: The New Testament in Contemporary English* (Colorado Springs: NavPress, 1993), 478.

23. *1001 Quotations that Connect* (Grand Rapids: Zondervan, 2009), 10.

3. Distinctives of a Contagious Church

1. Story taken from Gene Weingarten, "Pearls Before Breakfast," *Washington Post*, April 8, 2007, http://www.washingtonpost.com/wp-dyn/content/article/2007/04/04/AR2007040401721.html, accessed December 7, 2009.
2. *Merriam-Webster's Collegiate Dictionary*, 11th ed., s.v. "contagion."
3. Marty Neumeier, *The Brand Gap: How to Bridge the Distance Between Business Strategy and Design* (Berkeley, CA: New Riders, 2006), 41.
4. Tyler Wigg-Stevenson, "Jesus Is Not a Brand: Why It Is Dangerous to Make Evangelism Another Form of Marketing," *Christianity Today*, January 2009, vol. 53, no. 1.
5. Cynthia and I first met Ford and Barbara Madison in the summer of 1960 when we attended a Navigators conference at Glen Eyrie in Colorado Springs. We quickly discovered a shared passion for God's Word and a desire to commit it to memory. Thirty-four years later, we became reacquainted with Ford and Barbara when I served as president of Dallas Theological Seminary and

Ford was a member of the school's Board of Incorporate Members. Cynthia and I were shocked to learn that Barb had been diagnosed with cancer and that she had only a short time left to live. She passed into the Lord's presence on April 23, 2009, just seventy-nine days after her initial diagnosis. But the legacy this remarkable woman left her family will never be forgotten. (Note: Letter produced as written without correction.)

6. John Pollock, *The Apostle: A Life of Paul* (Wheaton, ILL: Victor Books, 1985), 304.

7. James Stalker, *The Life of St. Paul* (Grand Rapids: Zondervan, 1983), 141. Used by permission of Zondervan (www.zondervan.com).

8. Molly Worthen, "Who Would Jesus Smack Down?" *New York Times* magazine (January 11, 2009), 20.

9. Phyllis Tickle, *The Great Emergence: How Christianity Is Changing and Why* (Grand Rapids: Baker Books, 2008), 162.

10. David Wells, *The Courage to Be Protestant: Truthlovers, Marketers, and Emergents in the Postmodern World* (Grand Rapids: Eerdmans, 2008), 77–78.

11. Ibid., 11, 37.

12. Quote taken from videos at: http://revealnow.com/story.asp?storyid=49, accessed June 3, 2009.

13. Walter Bauer et al., eds., *A Greek-English Lexicon of the New Testament and Other Early Christian Literature*, 2nd rev. ed. (Chicago: University of Chicago Press, 1979), 623.

14. Howard G. Hendricks, *Standing Together: Impacting Your Generation* (Gresham, OR: Vision House Publishing, 1995), 98.

15. Collin Hansen, "The X Factor: What Have We Learned from the Rise, Decline, and Renewal of 'Gen-X' Ministries?" (LeadershipJournal.net), http://www.christianitytoday.com/le/communitylife/evangelism/thexfactor.html?start=1, accessed September 2, 2009.

16. *Merriam-Webster's Collegiate Dictionary*, 11th ed., s.v. "mentor."

17. Dietrich Bonhoeffer, *Life Together*, trans. John W. Doberstein (San Francisco: Harper&Row, 1954), 110–11.

18. Johannes P. Louw and Eugene A. Nida, eds., *Greek-English Lexicon of the New Testament Based on Semantic Domains*, 2nd ed. (New York: United Bible Societies, 1988, 1989). Electronic text hypertexted and prepared by OakTree Software, Inc. Version 3.2.

19. Dietrich Bonhoeffer, *The Cost of Discipleship*, rev. ed. (New York: Collier Books, MacMillan, 1959), 99.

20. Warren W. Wiersbe, *On Being a Servant of God,* rev. ed. (Grand Rapids: Baker Books, 2007), 46.

21. John R. W. Stott, *Guard the Gospel: The Message of 2 Timothy* (Downers Grove, ILL: InterVarsity Press, 1974), 57–58.

22. Louw and Nida, *Greek-English Lexicon.*

23. Charles Paul Conn, *Making It Happen: A Christian Looks at Money, Competition, and Success* (Grand Rapids: Revell, 1981), 95.

4. Worship: A Commitment . . . Not a War

1. Charles E. Hummel, *Tyranny of the Urgent* (Downers Grove, ILL: InterVarsity Christian Fellowship, 1967, rev. ed. 1994), 4–5.

2. Gordon Dahl, *Work, Play, and Worship in a Leisure-Oriented Society* (Minneapolis: Augsburg, 1972), 12.

3. *A Hebrew and English Lexicon of the Old Testament* (abridged). Based on F. Brown, S. R. Driver, and C. A. Briggs, *A Hebrew and English Lexicon of the Old Testament* (Oxford: Clarendon Press, 1907). Digitized and abridged as a part of the Princeton Theological Seminary Hebrew Lexicon Project under the direction of Dr. J. M. Roberts. Used by permission. Electronic text corrected, formatted, and hypertexted by OakTree Software, Inc. This

electronic adaptation © 2001 OakTree Software, Inc. Version 3.4

4. Walter Bauer et al., eds., *A Greek-English Lexicon of the New Testament and Other Early Christian Literature*, 2nd rev. ed. (Chicago: University of Chicago Press, 1979), 716.

5. *Webster's New World Dictionary of the American Language* (New York: WorldPublishing, 1966), 1686.

6. Charles Wesley, "Love Divine, All Love Excelling." Public domain.

7. David Wells, *The Courage to Be Protestant: Truthlovers, Marketers, and Emergents in the Postmodern World* (Grand Rapids: Eerdmans, 2008), 7.

8. *Merriam-Webster's Collegiate Dictionary*, 11th ed., s.v. "doxology."

9. As quoted in Kenneth W. Osbeck, *101 Hymn Stories* (Grand Rapids: Kregel, 1982), xi.

10. Ibid.

11. Frank E. Gaebelein, ed., *The Expositor's Bible Commentary* (Grand Rapids: Zondervan, 1990). Used by permission of Zondervan (www.zondervan. com). Electronic text hypertexted and prepared by OakTree Software, Inc.

12. Traditional African-American lyrics. Public domain.

5. *What Must the Church Realize?*

1. Information taken from http://www.wackywarn-ings.com, accessed August 17, 2009.
2. Adapted from Scott Bowles, "Hesitation Is a Fatal Mistake as California Firestorm Closes In," *USA Today*, October 30, 2003.
3. Information taken from http://www.berro.com/joke/court_disorder_lawyer_witness_funny_exchanges.htm, accessed December 8, 2009.
4. John R. W. Stott, *Guard the Gospel: The Message of 2 Timothy* (Downers Grove, ILL: InterVarsity Press, 1974), 83.
5. Johannes P. Louw and Eugene A. Nida, eds., *Greek-English Lexicon of the New Testament Based on Semantic Domains*, 2nd ed. (New York: United Bible Societies, 1988, 1989). Electronic text hyper-texted and prepared by OakTree Software, Inc. Version 3.2.
6. Quoted in *Mothers of Influence: Inspiring Stories of Women Who Made a Difference in Their Children and in Their World* (Colorado Springs: Bordon Books, 2005), 121.
7. Louw and Nida, *Greek-English Lexicon*.
8. William Barclay, *The Letters to Timothy, Titus, and Philemon* (Philadelphia: Westminster Press, 1975), 189.

9. Frank E. Gaebelein, ed., *The Expositor's Bible Commentary* (Grand Rapids: Zondervan, 1990). Used by permission of Zondervan (www.zondervan.com). Electronic text hypertexted and prepared by OakTree Software, Inc.

10. Louw and Nida, *Greek-English Lexicon.*

11. Paul Babiak and Robert D. Hare, *Snakes in Suits: When Psychopaths Go to Work* (New York: Harper, 2007).

12. Louw and Nida, *Greek-English Lexicon.*

13. Ibid.

14. Ibid.

15. Ibid.

16. Thomas C. Oden, *First and Second Timothy and Titus—Interpretation: A Bible Commentary for Teaching and Preaching* (Louisville, KY: John Knox Press, 1989), 74–77.

17. David Wells, *The Courage to Be Protestant: Truthlovers, Marketers, and Emergents in the Postmodern World* (Grand Rapids: Eerdmans, 2008), 109, 133.

18. Mark Water, comp., *The New Encyclopedia of Christian Quotations* (Grand Rapids: Baker Books, 2000), 1061.

19. John R. W. Stott, *Guard the Gospel: The Message of 2 Timothy* (Downers Grove, ILL: InterVarsity Press, 1974), 88.

6. How Should the Church React?

1. Winston S. Churchill, *The Gathering Storm: The Second World War*, vol. 1 (New York: Houghton Mifflin, 1948, 1976), x.
2. Eugene H. Peterson, *Christ Plays in Ten Thousand Places* (Grand Rapids: Eerdmans, 2005), 288.
3. Walter Bauer et al., eds., *A Greek-English Lexicon of the New Testament and Other Early Christian Literature*, 2nd rev. ed. (Chicago: University of Chicago Press, 1979), 690.
4. Ibid.
5. Thomas C. Oden, *First and Second Timothy and Titus—Interpretation: A Bible Commentary for Teaching and Preaching* (Louisville, KY: John Knox Press, 1989), 167.
6. David Wells, *The Courage to Be Protestant: Truthlovers, Marketers, and Emergents in the Postmodern World* (Grand Rapids: Eerdmans, 2008), 212–13.
7. John Calvin, *Commentaries on the Epistles to Timothy, Titus, and Philemon*, trans. William Pringle (Grand Rapids: Christian Classics Ethereal Library), public domain.
8. John R. W. Stott, *Guard the Gospel: The Message of 2 Timothy* (Downers Grove, ILL: InterVarsity Press, 1974), 98.

9. Stephen Carter, "When 7 × 5 = 75," *Christianity Today*, December 2006, vol. 50, no. 12.

10. Billy Graham, *Just as I Am: The Autobiography of Billy Graham* (San Francisco: HarperSanFransisco, 1997), 139. Used by permission of Zondervan (www.zondervan.com).

11. Wells, *Courage to Be Protestant*, 45.

12. Johannes P. Louw and Eugene A. Nida, eds., *Greek-English Lexicon of the New Testament Based on Semantic Domains*, 2nd ed. (New York: United Bible Societies, 1988, 1989). Electronic text hypertexted and prepared by OakTree Software, Inc. Version 3.2.

13. Bauer, *Greek-English Lexicon*.

14. Louw and Nida, *Greek-English Lexicon*.

15. Bruce M. Metzger, *Lexical Aids for Students of the New Testament* (New Jersey: Theological Book Agency, 1983), 34.

16. Larry Fowler, *Raising a Modern-Day Joseph: A Timeless Strategy for Growing Great Kids* (Colorado Springs: David C. Cook, 2009), 28–30. Used with permission. Permission required to reproduce. All rights reserved.

17. R. Kent Hughes and Bryan Chapell, *1 and 2 Timothy and Titus: To Guard the Deposit* (Wheaton, ILL: Crossway Books, 2000), 235–36.

7. The Church on a Long Drift

1. Johannes P. Louw and Eugene A. Nida, eds., *Greek-English Lexicon of the New Testament Based on Semantic Domains,* 2nd ed. (New York: United Bible Societies, 1988, 1989). Electronic text hypertexted and prepared by OakTree Software, Inc. Version 3.2.

2. John F. Walvoord, "Revelation" in *Bible Knowledge Commentary: New Testament,* ed. John F. Walvoord and Roy B. Zuck (Wheaton, ILL: Victor Books, 1986), 933–34.

3. Wayne Stiles, *Walking in the Footsteps of Jesus: A Journey Through the Lands and Lessons of Christ* (Ventura, CA: Regal Books, 2008), 166–67, 174–75.

4. C. S. Lewis, *Letters to Malcolm: Chiefly on Prayer* (New York: Harcourt, Brace, and World, 1964), 98.

5. F. B. Meyer, as quoted by Charles R. Swindoll in *The Finishing Touch: Becoming God's Masterpiece* (Dallas: Word, 1994), 543.

6. Lewis Sperry Chafer, no source available, based on the recollections of Charles R. Swindoll and John F. Walvoord.

7. A. W. Tozer, *God Tells the Man Who Cares* (Camp Hill, PA: Christian Publications, 1992), 92.

8. Jack Hayford, "Majesty!" © 1981 Rocksmith Music (admin. by Trust Music Management)/ ASCAP.

8. It's Time to "Restore the Years"

1. Steven J. Lawson, "The Priority of Biblical Preaching: An Expository Study of Acts 2:42–47," *Bibliotheca Sacra* 158 (April–June 2001), 198–99.

2. Eugene H. Peterson, *Working the Angles: The Shape of Pastoral Ministry* (Grand Rapids: Eerdmans, 1987), 1–2.

3. Iain M. Duguid, *The NIV Application Commentary: Ezekiel* (Grand Rapids: Zondervan, 1999), 389. Used by permission of Zondervan (www.zondervan.com).

4. Walter C. Kaiser Jr., *Revive Us Again* (Nashville: Broadman & Holman, 1999), 166–67. Used by permission.

5. J. Oswald Sanders, *Spiritual Leadership* (Chicago: Moody Press, 1989), 141.

6. James Montgomery Boice, *Romans, Volume 4: The New Humanity, Romans 12–16* (Grand Rapids: Baker Books, 1995), 1928.

7. Dan Kimball, *Emerging Worship: Creating Worship Gatherings for New Generations* (Grand Rapids: Zondervan, 2004), 5. Used by permission of Zondervan (www.zondervan.com).

8. Stephen Olford, "Why I Believe in Expository Preaching," audiotape of pastors' luncheon message at Dauphin Way Baptist Church, Mobile, Alabama, March 22, 1999.
9. David Wells, *The Courage to Be Protestant: Truthlovers, Marketers, and Emergents in the Postmodern World* (Grand Rapids: Eerdmans, 2008), 94–95.
10. Peterson, *Working the Angles.*

Conclusion

1. Ruth Bell Graham, *Legacy of a Pack Rat* (Nashville: Thomas Nelson, 1989). All rights reserved. Reprinted by permission.

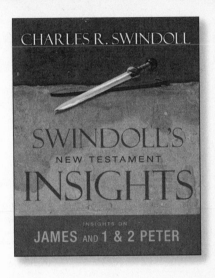